Thank God for
Angels

BOOK ONE

TWINS AND THEIR
GUARDIAN ANGELS

RALPH D. CARACOZA, JR.

PAGE PUBLISHING, INC.
Conneaut Lake, PA

First originally published by Page Publishing 2020

ISBN 978-1-64462-467-8 (pbk)
ISBN 978-1-64628-401-6 (hc)
ISBN 978-1-64462-468-5 (digital)

Printed in the United States of America

DEDICATIONS

*T*his book is dedicated to my grandsons, Ryan, Logan, and Austin, who have always brought me such a great deal of joy in my life and are my inspiration to complete this book. It is Ryan's request that I should complete it as quickly as possible before I become senile.

*T*o my son, Shawn, who has always inspired me and in whom I have such pride for his accomplishments as a father and husband, and in his professional career and who has always tried to keep me focused and grounded.

*T*o my daughter-in-law, Trina, who always placed family first, who is intelligent, beautiful, and is such an inspiration for the entire family and who has always had my best interests at heart.

*T*o the sisters of the Carmelite Sisters of the Most Sacred Heart, who have always worked faithfully in providing me and every child who have been entrusted into their care with a solid education. With special acknowledgments to the sisters whom I was fortunate to have as my teachers: Mother General Sister Mary Josephine, Sister Mary Christina, Sister Mary Gonzaga, Sister Mary Grace, and Sister Mary Theresa.

SPECIAL ACKNOWLEDGMENTS

My undying gratitude goes to Susan Dickson, who assisted me immensely in writing my manuscript. Susan and her husband, Ken, have been loyal friends over many years and supporters of me in completing my work. It was Susan who was always available in not only giving me great advice but who also worked tirelessly as technical editor and proofreader of my text. She also fact-checked every detail and by asking questions kept me focused. I cannot thank her enough.

My appreciation also goes to Letty Raquel Lopez for being a loyal friend who provided invaluable help daily with computer needs. God only knows how a sophisticated computer can be a writer's nightmare. I'm sure that I would have been more successful completing a correspondence course in neurosurgery than knowing all the bells and whistles of my computer that insist on telling me what to write. Thank you, Letty, for always being there when I drastically needed you in helping me in keeping my computer in check. I value your friendship and unwavering support.

Thank God for

CHAPTER 1

*A*s they were walking their bikes uphill, Andrew, always looking for excitement, yelled out loud to his twin sister Mia and to Noah, "Last one to the top of the hill has to eat three tablespoons of dog food and two dog biscuits for dinner!"

Jubilation immediately shot through Mia's veins like an adrenaline kick. She always had an incomprehensible and insatiable appetite for irresistible challenges—and any opportunity for embarrassing her big brother. Immediately, the twins simultaneously turned to face each other, their eyes flickered and hardened at one another, and then simultaneously each displayed a huge grin, running uphill as quickly as they could. Holding onto the handlebars of their bicycles, each gave a Herculean last push as they jumped, straddled their bikes, and accurately landed on the center of their bicycle seats.

Noah, obviously intrigued with whatever was going on and, although on foot, without any effort, was able to breeze right by them, as if both twins were standing still. Not that he would mind coming in last place. As a matter of fact, he would prefer it! Dog food, next to pizza, you see, was almost his favorite thing, being that he was Andrew's and Mia's prize-winning Saint Bernard.

Not that Noah understood exactly what all the commotion was about, but intuitively he was able to sense that there was some sort of game or challenge at hand. And with his competitive spirit, he was not about to be beaten by anyone, not even by the two he loved most in the world. Besides, beating them would only help them develop character, and who was he to stand in the way of their education and personal growth?

Halfway up the hill, as both were gasping for air, with their hearts beating as fast as a thoroughbred horse running in the final stretch of the Kentucky Derby, Andrew looked over to his right side. He saw that Mia was in a dead heat with him, matching pedal stroke for pedal stroke, as if they were synchronized swimmers at the summer Olympics.

Andrew was thinking to himself, *How can she be keeping up with me? She's only a girl, and besides, I'm older, even if it's only by three minutes and fifteen seconds.*

Andrew looked forward toward his goal, focusing on standing solo at the top of the hill, and again with concentrated determination that he was not going to be beaten by his younger sister, not this time, not ever again. Gritting his teeth, digging deep within himself for all the inner strength that he possessed, and with his heart pounding in his neck, he pushed forward and downward on the pedals. He suddenly began to feel a fresh surge of adrenaline flowing freely throughout his body. He was getting his second wind—there was no way that his little sister could physically keep up with him now. He was convinced that he was going to win.

Noah was already at the top of the hill, eagerly waiting for the second-place winner, his long tail whipping back and forth in a frenzy. He was ready to be crowned and presented with the prize.

Almost completely out of breath, knowing that he gave his all as he reached the top of the hill, Andrew quickly looked over to the front tire of his sister's bike. He acknowledged that her movements were both graceful and efficient. She was slim, athletically built, with eyes of deep blue, her blond hair under her baseball cap swinging past her shoulders and parting to reveal her lovely eyes.

It was a photo finish. *This is extremely infuriating, and this is not acceptable* were Andrew's initial thoughts. It was like both bikes were welded together side by side. Looking down, Andrew started to mumble. He then became infuriated with himself as he pounded furiously on his handlebars with the palm of his right hand, ignoring everything else around him. *What in the world do I have to do to be victorious over my sister?* Then after impatient silence, he started mumbling and thinking to himself, *Why do I always put myself though such torture?* as he viewed himself in the most painful and humiliating way possible. *I guess it's just another minor disappointment in life that needs to be repressed. I can see now that I'm going to need therapy, years and years of psychological therapy.*

Exhausted, huffing and puffing, gasping for air, as their legs were throbbing for oxygen, and without saying a word, the twins dismounted their bikes and slowly walked them to the side of the road. As they reached its grassy shoulder and with total disregard for the care of their bicycles, they let them fall over on their sides. Then both twins fell to the ground, sitting side by side at the shoulder of the road, with their heads leaning toward each other and awkwardly resting against each other.

Finally finding the ability to talk and simultaneously raising their heads, they cried out, "It's a tie!" Both started to laugh uncontrollably while giving each other a high five. "Don't you find it fascinating and intriguing that we can almost always instinctively think and say the same thing at the same time?" Mia queried. Her heart was beating as fast as a sprint car at Daytona, and her leg muscles pulsated with exhaustion, as her eyes danced with amusement. Wearing a smile of triumph on her face, she flashed her brother a smile of perfect white teeth. She may not have won, but she didn't lose either. *Where is my cell phone for a selfie so that I can document this Kodak moment?* she thought.

"I don't know. I suppose it's because we're twins," replied Andrew, with his head down and his chin almost resting on his chest. "I think almost everyone has heard stories about how certain twins unknowingly and inexplicably have the ability to feel and communicate with each other, even when they're miles apart. I guess they can include us in those statistics. And I guess even though you're a real pain in the neck most of the time, you're still my best friend."

"I think maybe you found the answer. You not only have to be twins, you have to be best friends too," Mia agreed with a girlie giggle. "Go ahead. I think you can now write that theory in stone."

"Maybe! All I know for sure is that this is my favorite place in the entire world," responded Andrew as he sat on the hilltop with the most beautiful panoramic view of the entire valley. Mia looked up with cool blue eyes that seemed to be able to see everything, scanned the scene, and agreed. The landscape was as beautiful and majestic as Mother Nature meant it to be. This area of the country remained unspoiled and probably was the same since the beginning of time. As they both watched a picturesque sunrise in the east, they just sat there resting speechless as they regained their energy and breath. Just to be able to see the vastness of it, the trees shimmering with the last remnants of winter, was such a reward. It was still early morning, and even though clouds were piled halfway up the sky in a thick, frothy layer, along the horizon they could see the first touch of rain. The sun was still rising with its light filtering through the tall oak trees; birds were chattering from the branches of budding trees. It was a week before spring, and there was still a slight chill in the fresh air, just the way Andrew preferred it best.

If he faced north from this hilltop and completely ignored everything behind him, Andrew could see for miles and absorb the beauty and serenity of nature, as its Creator must have originally designed it. In the distance, on both sides of the road, he observed other hilltops covered with majestic trees spearing up into the darkening sky and up to the heavens. Beneath were beautiful green valleys covered with tall grass and collections of shrubs just beginning to bloom. These areas were uninhabited and managed by the US Forestry Service.

I can't think why anyone would want to live anyplace else, Andrew was thinking to himself, *but thank God we do.*

Turning around 180 degrees to the south, they could see the road as it traversed back and forth over to the base of the mountains. Twenty-five minutes away was the closest urban center, more commonly known to the locals as the Flatlands.

"Andrew!" Mia interrupted as movement caught her eyes. "Look, it's Whiskey!" Mia pointed. "What's he up to now?" exclaimed Mia, watching with pessimistic eyes.

Breaking his train of thought, Andrew again pivoted around to find Whiskey at the base of a dry ravine, chasing something in the knee-high grass, which was obscured occasionally by shrubbery.

"Noah! Stop Whiskey...Stop Whiskey!" Mia repeated as she pointed in Whiskey's direction, drawing a deep breath as she continued to focus on what Whiskey was chasing. *Why do they always think that they don't have any boundaries?* Mia was thinking to herself.

Without any further instructions, Noah excitedly darted down the hill and into the tall grass in hot pursuit of Whiskey, not that Noah needed a second command. Noah always felt that one of his main responsibilities, after protecting the safety of Mia and Andrew, was to prevent incorrigibles like Whiskey from access to the Brooks family's property.

Whiskey, a well-trained English pointer, used by his owner Mr. O'Connor for hunting expeditions, never lost any opportunity to show off the behavior that gave his breed its name. For hundreds of years, people have raised pointers to chase small game and to use their bodies to signal the location of birds or other animals of interest. You must admit, no dog can run with the gracefulness, energy, and strength of Whiskey—no one, that is, except Noah.

It was readily noticeable that Noah was making great progress in closing the distance on Whiskey, being three times the size and with twice the stride of Whiskey.

Andrew and Mia on foot were now also in hot pursuit, and even though they were unable to identify what Whiskey was chasing, they did know one thing for sure—Whiskey was on the wrong side of the road. This was their property, property that had been in the Brooks family for almost four hundred years, property inherited from ancestors dating back to the Pilgrims of 1620, property that had been passed down from generation to generation.

All that they were able to see for sure was that Whiskey definitely was chasing something. Neither Andrew nor Mia could make out what he was in pursuit of—all they could see was the top of the head of some kind of small animal, maybe that of a raccoon or possum bobbing up and down in the tall grass as it ran.

As quickly as he started, suddenly Whiskey stopped and stood absolutely motionless in the tall grass. With his whole body tense and still, Whiskey bent his right front leg, stretched his neck forward, stiffened his tail, and stared straight ahead with hard and defiant eyes and every sense alerted.

No sooner had Whiskey gone into his well-trained pointing form, staring at his prey to show its location, than Noah reached both Whiskey and the object of his attention.

Noah stopped just short of Whiskey's location and positioned himself between Whiskey and the object of his attention, no more than eight or nine feet away from Whiskey. While staring right into Whiskey's eyes, Noah began to bark ferociously with an occasional growl, hopping forward and from side to side, each time pushing off his massive hind legs with each bark.

Whiskey refused to move, acknowledging that if he did—or even worse, if he made any aggressive move—he would surely taunt Noah into a ferocious fight.

Although Whiskey wasn't one to abandon a good fight and go toe to toe with any canine his size, he was no dummy either. Noah was a massive Saint Bernard, huge even for male breed standards.

No, Whiskey decided, as his best instincts dictated, his best tactic at this time was to remain in his pointing stance, and hope for the opportunity to retreat without encouraging Noah to attack.

From the distance, Noah could hear Mia's commands. "Don't hurt him, Noah! Don't hurt him! Just chase him away…Chase Whiskey away, Noah!"

Don't hurt him, Noah thought. *What are you talking about? If you can't run with the big dogs, you should just stay home and sit on the porch.*

With his sister completely out of breath, Andrew and Mia finally reached Whiskey's and Noah's location. Even though Mia was quite an athlete in her own right, she didn't have the size and bulk of a male athlete like her brother. Therefore, it was much easier and quicker for Andrew to recover from any physical activity. Because Mia hadn't recovered fully from the bicycle race, she was still short of breath, so carefully and firmly she ordered herself to inhale, exhale, inhale, exhale. Her heart still pounding and her knees shaking, she thought to herself, *I've got to get myself in better shape if I want to keep up with Andrew, and maybe my stomach wouldn't be jumping like a pond full of frogs next time.*

Noah, feeling very confident, started barking even harder with his tail wagging furiously back and forth, trying to show the twins that he was now in total control of the situation. As both Andrew and Mia slid to a stop in the dew-covered grass, Noah for a moment veered his eyes away as he turned and looked over his shoulder anticipating praise for a job well done. Whiskey, noticing that Noah's attention momentarily was now focused on the twins, saw the opportunity that he was waiting for. He darted across the open field trying to reach the road and beyond to the property of his master, knowing that it would mean sanctuary for him and evading another encounter with that do-gooder Noah who always seemed around to disrupt his fun.

As both Andrew and Mia stopped and drew an extra breath, leaning forward and placing their hands on their knees, they were finally able to identify exactly what Whiskey was chasing.

"It's a little fox!" exclaimed Mia as she leaned forward and knelt to the ground. And with a great deal of exuberance in her voice, her adrenaline surged, which she masked with a bright smile as she angled her face up toward Andrew.

In bewilderment, with a deer-in-the-headlight expression, Andrew looked with the corner of his eyes at Mia and asked, "What's wrong with him? It looks like he can't stand up," as his expression turned from puzzlement to concern. As Mia was trying to read Andrew's face, she easily detected the concern that he had.

It was always obvious to everyone who knew the twins that because they had such a deep love for animals in every chamber of their hearts, they would eventually go into some type of field concerning animal science.

Observing the small, fragile fox lying on his side—traumatized and struggling to stand, following ingrained habits for survival—Mia was able to see little lights of panic flickering in his eyes. "I think that he's just terrified," muttered Mia, not really sure of her diagnosis.

As both twins slowly stooped down to conduct a better and closer assessment, the little fox now in total fear for his safety and watching both Mia and Andrew with fearful and turbulent eyes, attempted to stand on three legs, trying to escape.

Realizing now that he was unable to stand upright and obviously in a great deal of pain, the little fox kept striving vigorously to gain his balance without any success. He kept falling to the ground on his side.

Knowing that the little fox was scared to death, Mia, as tears started to form in the corners of her bold and brilliant blue eyes, attempted to reassure the fox that she was there only to help him while trying to convince him that she would never cause any harm to any animal.

"Please! Please don't struggle!" Mia cried out anxiously, smiling as sweetly as she could to calm the fox. "I won't hurt you." But as desperately as she continued to try to help, she knew it was to no avail because she continued to see those little lights of terror still flickering in his eyes.

Without any calming effect on the fox, Mia pleaded with her brother, "Andrew, please help me. He doesn't understand that I'm trying to help him."

Andrew, as he tried to rubberneck around her to get a better view and without any answers, could only reply quickly with a sarcastic tone, "If he doesn't understand you, what makes you think that he's going to understand me?"

Mia, with silent tears trickling down her face, sharing anxiety with the fox, attempted over and over to reassure the fox that her intentions were pure and honorable but could only sense the fear that simmered in his eyes. She saw him looking so desperate.

With tears now flowing freely, Mia again pleaded to the little fox, "Please, please, don't struggle. You're going to hurt yourself even more."

Unable to control her emotions and tears and looking to her brother for reassurance, Mia asked again in exasperation, "What should I do, Andrew? He doesn't understand me," as she rubbed her cheeks dry with the heels of her hands.

While Andrew struggled for a reply, in a very soft and almost musical tone came an unfamiliar voice, "Just lower your tone and speak softly to him again, he'll understand you now."

Immediately Andrew and Mia turned around and looked up. There was the most beautiful couple, impeccably dressed all in white, as if they had just stepped off a cover of *Vogue* magazine as members of the most elegant wedding party.

Almost in unison and with astonished expressions, both Andrew and Mia, stumbling from their hunched position and now fully sitting on the ground, responded in total bewilderment, "Where did you come from? And who are you?"

"I'll be happy to answer those questions," responded the male, with the gentlest and most reassuring voice.

"My name is Simon." He appeared to be about 180 pounds, six feet tall, muscular, with a chiseled face—and with his right arm reached out with his palm up toward his most beautiful and immaculate companion. "And this is Star." She possessed such a beautiful face with an amazingly smooth complexion, was of medium height, slim, with deep-green eyes and lustrous red hair. "We are two of your closest friends. Actually, we are not only two of your closest but also your intimate friends. Even as close to you as you are to each other."

Completely forgetting that they were hovering over an injured fox, again in perfect harmony, both Andrew and Mia's first response was "Friends! How can that be? We don't even know you. We've never even seen you before in our lives!"

Again, speaking with such a gentle voice and with a beautiful smile, the person now identified as Star responded first, "Sure you do. You know us as well as you know yourselves. Actually, whenever you talk to yourselves or whenever you're in a sticky situation and you ask yourself a question on what you should do next, you're actually talking to us."

Mia, rubbing her eyes and thinking everything through, and with a complete expression of puzzlement on her face, using just her head, turned to Andrew. Mia cleared her throat, and while Andrew inched forward, she asked, "You're the older brother. Do you understand what they're talking about?"

Almost speechless and after what seemed to be several moments of contemplation, Andrew slowly rolled his eyes toward Mia and whispered softly, responding as if they were in church, "I think so. I think they're trying to tell us that they are our guardian angels."

"What!" responded Mia. She frowned at Andrew, raising her voice and sounding almost sarcastic, looking directly into Andrew's eyes. She was able to hear the lack of conviction in his tone. Mia thought for a moment and finally blurted, "You can't be serious!"

After a long pause of silence, while both Andrew and Mia were thinking to themselves, they slowly pivoted so that they were now directly facing the two they believed to be complete and total strangers.

And again together, trying to be courageous and with total respect in their voices, they asked, "Are you our guardian angels?"

"I love it when you do that!" responded Simon.

"Do what?" answered Andrew with an attentive expression on his face.

"You know, be able to think and say the same thing at the same time," responded Simon with a jolly voice. "I wish Star and I could do that."

"I think we're able to do it because we're twins," replied Mia, still in total confusion.

"You still haven't answered our question," Andrew asked for a second time, still trying not to offend anyone. "Are you trying to tell us that you are our guardian angels?"

"Would that be so hard to believe?" asked Star.

Andrew cocked his head and needed a moment to analyze the probabilities.

As doubts crowded Mia's thoughts, "Well, yes," she responded, "so let's cut through the amenities. No one is supposed to be able to see or hear their guardian angels. Everyone knows that! If you're really our guardian angels, you would know that both Andrew and I are students at Holy Family, and when we were in first grade, Sister Mary Josephine covered everything about the creation of angels at length. She made it clearly understood when she told us that even though we would never be able to see or hear our guardian angels, we need to have blind faith and believe in their existence. So explain to us why are we supposed to believe now that we are able to see and hear you? Why are you trying to contradict what Sister Josephine told us? Wait, I'll tell you why. Could it be because you're not our guardian angels?"

"Actually, you were in the second grade, and it was Sister Mary Grace who talked about guardian angels," answered Star in a non-confrontational tone. "But that's why Simon and I were sent to you, so that we could introduce ourselves and to deliver a message to both of you, a message of two of the most beautiful and well-deserved gifts from God."

"Two gifts from God?" replied Andrew, still not sure if he was hallucinating.

"Yes! Two precious gifts," answered Star. "The first gift is… because both of you have worked so arduously in finding and helping so many sick and injured loving creatures of God, and for nursing them back to health then returning them to the care of nature, you are now permitted to see and hear your guardian angels. Simon and I have always been able to see and hear you. Now you will be able to see and hear Simon and me."

"You said that there were two gifts?" Mia respectfully reminded Star.

"Yes!" Star continued. "Your second precious gift is that you will also have the ability to communicate freely with all the wildlife in the world. And to make it even more interesting, you will be able to hear and understand the animals via a form of mental communication."

"That's it! This is ridiculous!" Mia said sarcastically, seething with frustration and not trying to be polite any longer. "I don't know who these two people are, but one thing I know for sure is that they're both nutcases and should be replying 'Present' or 'Yo' or something like that when taking attendance at the funny farm."

"Mia, please!" cried Andrew exasperatedly with his heart thundering, trying to get Mia to compose herself. "Let's stop and think for a minute."

"What's there to think about?" with her voice a little frosty. "You really don't think that these two crazy people, who must have escaped from a mental institution, are our guardian angels? Well, do you? You think that we can now not only see and talk to them but also now be able to communicate with the animals. Does it look like most of my brain has been surgically removed recently? Andrew, I never had to question your sanity before, but stop and think! Do you actually think what they're saying is for real? If so, you must be out of your mind too!"

"So you don't believe in any of this?" questioned Andrew as his breath caught in the back of his throat.

"Get serious here! Of course not…not if I live to be a zillion and five years old! Would you believe in talking two-headed monkeys? Not me, not even if we lived in a world where there were pink fairies singing and dancing while riding green horses."

"Ouch! You have a real talent with the English language, Mia."

"Yeah, it's a gift," replied Mia sarcastically.

"So just indulge me for a minute. You always pride yourself on always thinking things out very carefully and thoroughly, and you like to weigh the odds, the options. You always say that you're not a creature of impulse. Okay, so answer this question, with your oh-so realistic intellect," replied Andrew as his voice rose and fell. "Here we are. Had to leave the road to get here…right in the middle of a meadow, surrounded by wet and dirty grass, not to mention passing through quite a few puddles. So why isn't there one speck of grass stains or mud on their perfectly clean and dry white clothes and shoes?"

After observing personally how filthy their clothes and shoes were from running through the meadow with its tall grass covered with the morning dew and crossing through several puddles, Mia, using her powers of observation and deductive talents, with great attention to detail, carefully and critically started to observe and evaluate the couple, starting from the top of their heads to the bottom of their shoes.

Mia let out a long, quiet breath, and swallowing very hard, she gawked at Andrew. Her thoughts raced to connect the possibilities, as her blood rushed to and from her heart. "This can't be happening." She could easily feel her heart race, which made her adrenaline level rise dramatically. Her color started to return somewhat to her cheeks, but Mia felt her heart lurch again, with her eyes steady on Andrew, she stopped, sucked in a hard, deep breath and, with an obvious change in the tone in her voice, hesitated, then continued with difficulty as she replied slowly, with a squeaky voice while simultaneously trying to clear her throat. "Could it be because they're standing about six inches off the ground?"

Both Andrew and Mia pivoted to face each other. Their eyes started to grow to the size of silver dollars, each not wanting to speak first. Andrew could read Mia's face clearly enough to see it flushed with embarrassment. Her stomach rolled a bit, as if she'd eaten something past its expiration date, and she had a queasy feeling that her heart was seeping down into her gut.

As Andrew waited, various expressions raced over Mia's face, and Andrew could read them perfectly, as she finally put on her serious look. Anticipation lit wickedly in both their eyes.

Simon decided to break the silence. "Well, so you don't believe us! Should we put it to a test? Now that you saved the injured fox from Whiskey, what are you planning to do?"

"Holy Mother of God!" exclaimed Mia. "I completely forgot about the fox!"

"Mia..." Andrew looked down and whispered in his church voice from the corner of his mouth. "I can't say strongly enough, you better take much, much better control of your language, being that I think we have Heaven's representatives here."

As both Andrew and Mia again focused their attention on the fox, with kind eyes, they both noticed that he wasn't struggling any longer. He was just lying there in complete submission. It was as though he had been totally tranquilized.

As she brushed back a wave of hair from her face, a breeze blew across her cheek; and with a soft feminine voice, Star repeated, "Go ahead and talk to him. Reassure him, but keep your voice slow and calm."

Very slowly, as she had to swallow once again, hard, Mia drew in a shaky breath. She lowered her right hand, attempting to touch the fox's shoulder, with every gesture trying to express dignity and love. With a softer tone in her voice and anticipating the fox to flinch at any moment, Mia cautiously continued her attempt to console the fox.

Mia was totally shocked when the fox actually permitted her to not only touch him but also pet his back in trying to comfort him. It was like he almost now understood her intentions and was no longer concerned about his safety with the twins.

Over and over again, Mia kept repeating in her softest voice, "Everything is going to be okay. We're not going to hurt you. We're only trying to help."

I know that now. I'm not scared anymore. I voluntarily now place myself into your hands, so please help me, the fox was clearly heard.

In total bewilderment and with a fluttering in both their stomachs, both Andrew and Mia couldn't believe what they had just heard.

Each not willing to commit themselves first that they actually heard and understood the small injured fox, both twins just remained with their mouths open in absolute astonishment and silence. Each praying that the other would speak first, confirming what they thought they had just heard, and weren't experiencing delusions of grandeur. The twins allowed themselves a sense of adventure, which ignited a feeling of excitement within.

Observing that nothing was going to be accomplished, Simon again spoke first, directing his comments to Andrew and Mia. "So do you have a plan in mind? Even though he's trying to be as patient and cooperative as possible, the poor little guy is still in a great deal of pain."

"Oh, oh! Of course, we have a plan!" Mia proclaimed with a crack in her voice. "Our father is a veterinarian."

"Yes, we know," Simon responded with a large smile on his face, whispering while bending at the waist. "Remember, we're your guardian angels. We know everything about you."

"Of course, I remember," Mia muttered, looking at Andrew from the corner of her eyes. "I'm just not sure what the best way is for getting him home."

"I have an idea," Andrew replied while removing his jacket. "Let's wrap him in this to keep him warm. He can ride in the basket on the front of your bike. We'll have him home in no time. Dad will know exactly what to do."

Without any hesitation, the twins cautiously wrapped the fox in Andrew's jacket while trying not to aggravate his injuries. Returning to the roadside, they recovered their bicycles, placing the small fox gently in Mia's front basket, after making a soft mattress of leaves at its base.

The weather had changed, and a killer wind volleyed a bitter April air, with toothy little knives to cut at the bones; and as usual, Mia had forgotten her gloves, although she had remembered her baseball cap.

"The wind is coming up," Andrew observed. "Rain's coming in, and we might get some snow flurries by this afternoon. We better hurry!" Andrew took a long breath, expelling it in a chilly fog. He had closed his eyes against the rush of the wind, clamping one hand on the front of his cowboy hat and holding it in place.

"Well, thank you for the forecast!" Mia responded sarcastically. "Maybe you should call it in to the Weather Channel or, even better, to the National Weather Service." Mia's blond hair fluttered in the wind.

"Why must you always be so cynical, Mia? Can't you ever be just a little gentler and ladylike?"

"And lose my reputation? No way! Do you want people to mistake me for being kind, generous, polite, thoughtful, and considerate? Absolutely no way, big brother, no way! Don't you enjoy a little spice in your life? Doesn't it keep your blood circulating? Why would I want to change and spoil our special relationship?"

Looking over their shoulders to confirm if the self-acknowledged angels were still behind them, the twins realized that they had disappeared as quickly as they had materialized. Was it true what they witnessed? Or was it a figment of their imagination? It must have been true. No one's imagination can be that creative!

Mia, with her eyes now clear and focused, her voice becoming steady once again, was unaware that her knuckles were turning white from squeezing her handlebar grips so tightly. She wanted to pause and reflect on what had just taken place. She had what only could be interpreted as a smug smile on her face as pleasure and excitement rushed through her, replacing confusion and uncertainty.

Mia took the lead, heading homeward. Finally, turning slightly so that she would be able to see Andrew from the corner of her eye, she studied his face and spoke with a burning bright smile. "Andrew, do you realize that we spoke to angels and that we now have a mission from God? What could be more electrifying? It's so beautiful, so thrilling!" Yes, the excitement was there, and the intensity of it nearly burned a hole in her heart.

Searching for the whereabouts of Noah, Andrew finally noticed that this time it was Noah who was on the wrong side of the road, the side of O'Connor's property and in hot pursuit of Whiskey again.

"Come on back, Noah! Get back here!" Andrew shouted. "We must get home. So get back here."

Noah, disobedient as always on just the first command when it applied to stopping a pursuit of either of the two O'Connor's dogs, considered them as just requests and not an order to stop. He didn't appreciate such requests and would respond reluctantly, and only after the third or fourth demand. There was nothing more disturbing to him than to terminate a legitimate pursuit, especially when he was so close to accomplishing the job. Didn't they realize that this was one of his mandates in life?

As all weather, it started to change to be less assaultive in nature and turned to a gentle rain that was driven softly into their faces by a sympathetic breeze. Andrew and Mia found it refreshing. As the twins continued to pedal as quickly as they could, Mia was very conscious to avoid every rock and pothole in the road for a safe and smooth ride for their newly found little friend. Due to the wavelike construction of the road, the twins, to save energy, would occasionally need to alternate their pedaling uphill and coasting downhill on their bikes to maintain a constant speed while looking for any possible traffic and road hazards. They were also concerned to avoid any possibility of scaring their passenger or causing further injury. Andrew was now able to see Whiskey reuniting with Brewski, Mr. O'Connor's other English pointer, racing each other to the main house on their estate.

CHAPTER 2

*M*ia had a challenging time thinking of anything other than being able to see and communicate with their guardian angels. And what about being able to talk to and understand the animals in return? This is beyond belief. This is beyond the imagination. This is insane. What was she going to say? How could she explain to her parents what had just occurred? Would they even believe her when she told them? She was excited with the prospect of telling her best friend White Dove, the Carmelite Sisters at school, and Father Pacarsic, their pastor at Holy Family Church, and of course, seeing the astonishment on their faces when sharing her unbelievable and awesome story to them. Her blood was building to the boiling point with anticipation, and her energy level was similar to what must have accumulated before Pompeii's volcano exploded over the city with ash and molten lava. Uncontrollably, Mia's mind was running away from her like an engineer-less freight train, knowing very well that their lives were irrevocably changed.

As her mind and eyes now turned and were focused on the basket of her bike, Mia could see the little fox still wrapped warmly in Andrew's jacket with his mouth closed as if he were grinding his teeth, now more anxious about being balanced on top of two wheels at a high rate of speed then his possible broken leg.

"Just hold on, little guy. We'll have you home in just a few minutes," Mia comforted the little fox in her best bedside voice. "And I'm going to introduce you to the best veterinarian in the entire world. Our dad, okay? Well, if not in the entire world, he is considered by all the veterinary journals to be, without a doubt, one of the most prominent and respected veterinarians in the country."

"How is he doing?" requested Andrew, talking over his left shoulder, as he was now leading the way home.

I'm okay was heard in a strained, frail voice but still clear enough to be understood.

Andrew started to slow down and moved over to the right so that Mia could catch up. He wanted to ride abreast of her so that he could more easily talk to her. Concerned that he would be considered wacky, Andrew was still hesitant to ask Mia if she also was hearing a voice emanating from the fox. But Andrew's curiosity was killing him. He just had to know whether he was actually hearing the fox's voice or his imagination was just playing tricks on him. But how could he do this without directly asking Mia if she, too, was able to hear the fox?

"Mia, being that you're closer to the fox, have you been able to hear any sounds from him? Is he still okay?" asked Andrew, as he cleared his throat, waiting anxiously for her answer.

"What are you trying to say?" replied Mia. "Why don't you just come out and say it…if I can hear the fox talking to me?"

He hesitated only for an instant. "Okay," Andrew said, frustrated, as his voice cracked. "Did you hear him say anything?"

"Why? Did you hear something?" Mia replied reluctantly in answering the question as she watched Andrew's eyes harden with frustration.

"Stop playing games with me, Mia! Did you hear him say something or not?" Andrew asked almost angrily.

"Okay! What if I did hear him say something, maybe something like 'I know that now, I'm not scared anymore, I voluntarily place myself into your hands' and 'I'm okay'?" replied Mia as she enjoyed taunting her brother while her eyes danced with amusement.

"So you did hear him!" Andrew said in astonishment. "Did you also hear him say things like 'Don't go so fast, I don't want to break another leg' and 'You do know how to ride this thing without falling down'?"

"Oh my god! Andrew, we did hear him talk. We can communicate with animals!" Mia said with wonder in her voice as she grinned with her million-watt smile.

"Stop, Mia! Please stop!" requested Andrew. "I have an idea."

Without hesitation, Mia complied with Andrew's request, slowing down and pulling to the side of the road. Both of them came to a complete stop, and Andrew dismounted from his bike, calling to Noah. Faithfully, Noah briskly trotted over, stopped, and sat directly in front of Andrew.

Feeling his adrenaline level rise dramatically and leaning over and looking directly at Mia with speculation, "I know how to find out for sure if we can talk to all animals or just to the fox." Andrew took Noah's large head in his hands, looked directly into his eyes, and after clearing his throat several times, very slowly and with some reluctance, softly asked him, "Noah, how would you like a big, fresh, delicious dog biscuit?" knowing all along that Noah would never refuse an unsolicited snack.

With his eyes flashing with impatience, Noah very clearly snapped back, *What? Do you think that only foxes can think and talk? And I don't want any stinking dog biscuit. I want one of Mia's oatmeal cookies.*

"Andrew! We really can talk to the animals!" Mia cried out loud with ecstatic delight as her heart rate spiked.

Andrew cleared his throat again, tears in his eyes, his face bright red as he uncontrollably screeched with laughter that was speedily becoming hysterical.

"Mia, do you have any cookies?" he asked, knowing perfectly well that she always carried several of her homemade cookies in her backpack.

While Mia slid a hand inside her backpack searching for the cookies that she had baked the night before, Andrew, with great enthusiasm, began to rub and pat Noah's enormous head, saying over and over again, "Good boy, that's a good boy."

"Did you hear that? Did you hear that beautiful voice?" Andrew repeated over and over again while Noah ate several of Mia's cookies that she had retrieved from her backpack for him. Noah always appreciated the small pleasures of life, and Mia's delicious homemade cookies were one of them.

Well, what about me? asked the fox. *I wouldn't mind a little snack myself. It would be for medicinal purposes, of course. I'm sure that it would lessen the pain in my leg.*

"But of course." Mia laughed. "I have plenty for all of us." She started to pass out cookies to everyone.

Don't forget to scratch behind my ears, Noah requested. *That's my second pleasure in life.*

Both Andrew and Mia started to laugh uncontrollably again as they literally jumped for joy. They were completely flabbergasted. As imaginative as they both considered themselves to be, this was much more than beyond their wildest dreams. They were actually not only going to be able to see and talk to their guardian angels but also to be able to have a conversation with animals. How long was this to last? This had to be their next question that needed an answer. Oh, there were going to be so many more questions that needed to be asked and so many more questions that needed to be answered!

Andrew now felt a light sprinkle just starting to fall again, and as he looked up he could see dark clouds floating their way high above them like gray kites. "Mia, we better start heading home again. It won't be long before it starts to rain," Andrew announced.

The twins reassessed their priorities and, with an unimaginable amount of newly found adrenaline, remounted their bikes. After Mia fed Noah another cookie, she again led the way home, never enjoying anything as much as this excitement. Thinking about their newly acquired abilities, and despite the weather, they felt like they had just broken a piñata and run away with all the candy.

But as they started to pedal their bikes, a nasty and surprisingly chilly rain started to blow in their faces. This certainly had become a most unpredictable day—the encounter with the fox, the meeting of their guardian angels, the ability to communicate with the animals, and now a chilly rain that was not mentioned in last night's weather forecast. Beneath the precipitating clouds came a frosty wind from the northwest through the green pine forest, a wind that whistled down the long road, biting everywhere that flesh was exposed. Now Andrew was concerned whether they would be able to reach their ranch-style home before the weather worsened.

"Andrew! We need to pedal even faster if we can! We need to focus about the fox right now, and how important it is that we get him to Dad," Mia instructed excitedly.

Noah, as always, faithfully followed the twins and was never more than a few feet behind, except when he stopped to sniff a few flowers that caught his attention along the way—but always mindful of the location of the twins and their safety. He felt that his personal responsibilities were, first, to always protect the twins and, second, to keep a close eye on Mia's backpack and to protect it from potential loss or even worse, a thief.

Finally reaching the circular driveway in front of their home, which also doubled as the perimeter of a large koi pond, Andrew suggested that their search for their father should start in the backyard in the garage.

Being that this was a Saturday morning and their father's day off from his responsibilities as chief of veterinary services at the city's zoo, he most enjoyed his free time catching up on back issues of veterinarian trade magazines or, if weather permitted, working in the yard. This weekly reading ritual was always best completed while he swung from a bench swing that he had built himself that was attached to the ceiling of the wide porch that was protected from the elements and slurped grandmother's homemade lemonade.

While cycling past the kitchen's bay window, the twins were able to observe their mother attending to her indoor herb garden but were unable to see any sign of their dad outside.

"Mom!" Mia cried out, sounding exasperated. "Do you know where Dad is now? Is he inside the house with you?"

"No, sweetie!" called back the twin's mother. "I believe he's in the garage, repairing something or other with all those fancy tools of his. Is there anything wrong?"

"No! We found an injured fox in our meadow. I think he has a broken leg!" Mia shouted back with an anxious look on her face. "We need Dad to take a look at him. Why don't you also come out to the garage and see for yourself?"

"Well, get out of the rain! And, Andrew, why don't you have your jacket on?"

"What are we going to tell Dad?" asked Andrew while dismounting his bike and walking it in the direction of the garage.

"Hey, hold up! What do you mean, what are we going to tell Dad?" Mia asked. "We're going to tell him that we found a fox and we think that he might have a broken leg."

"Have you recently suffered head trauma?" Andrew asked.

"Not to my knowledge," Mia barked back sharply. "Why would you make such a crazy remark? What are you thinking about with that pea-sized brain of yours? I'm surprised that you're thinking at all, being that you're out of practice in that department?"

"No, silly! I'm talking about what happened out in the meadow," whispered Andrew, lowering his voice so that no one could overhear him. "Mia, look into my eyes, because I need you to hear what I'm saying." He drove his hands into the back pockets of his blue jeans.

"Why are you whispering?" questioned Mia. "We're not in church or in the library. We'll tell Dad that we saw: Whiskey chasing the fox, and he must have stepped in a hole or run into a large rock in the tall grass, and we think he broke his leg."

"No! No! You moron," Andrew interrupted with irritation flashing in his eyes and with obvious frustration in his voice. Mia remained silent even though she thought that he sounded like the scrape of rough sandpaper on wood.

"I'm not talking about the fox! You nut case! I'm talking about the angels, and being able to talk to animals," cried Andrew, forgetting about lowering his voice, then immediately covering his mouth with his right hand when he realized that he was now almost shouting, as Mia was observing her brother's annoyed disapproval.

"What do you mean, what are we going to tell him?" Mia stubbornly continued. "Is this somehow supposed to be an unannounced pop quiz? We're going to tell Mom and Dad the truth," as if Andrew were suggesting that they should do anything else but be completely candid with their parents, especially under such extraordinary circumstances.

Andrew understood fully that for Mia such an omission of the full truth would be tantamount to dishonesty for her; it would be just like an outright lie in her mind. Mia had always had an intense sense of moral and ethical integrity.

"Sure! That's a great idea!" responded Andrew as he shook his head trying to fight against the nausea rising in his stomach. "And after we tell them all about the angels and being able to talk to the fox and Noah, we'll tell them how we also came across some aliens from outer space. And how they took us back to their mother ship for lunch and tried to sell us a set of encyclopedias to better do our homework." His blue eyes were intensely staring into Mia's, his face alight with nervous concern.

"What aliens? Now you're being ridiculous." She blew out a breath. "I didn't see any aliens!" Mia replied with a puzzled expression frozen on her face.

"And we're not going to see any freedom either," he said with his eyes steady on hers. "That is not until after your friend White Dove graduates from college, gets married, and names her third child after you. That's because we'll be in a padded cell!" responded Andrew sarcastically. "If they're going to believe us about seeing and talking to our guardian angels, they will most certainly believe us about aliens from outer space."

"I don't believe that," Mia said so firmly, so decisively. "They're going to be happy for us. So what are you talking about, Andrew?" asked Mia. "You're not suggesting that we lie to Mom and Dad, are you? Maybe you should be locked up in a lunatic asylum! I'm not going to lie." She scowled at him. "Because that would be lying by omission, quoting Sister Mary Grace. It's deliberately misleading. And it's going to eventually fall like a house of dominoes," stated Mia emphatically.

"I believe that's a house of cards or rows of dominoes," corrected Andrew automatically.

"Whatever you want to call it, it will all be coming down and falling on our heads," cried Mia.

"I don't care what you believe. I'm telling you the truth. You can think what you want, you obviously do. Besides, I'm not talking about real lying, just not telling the whole truth, that's all, at least initially," suggested Andrew. "Anyway, not until we figure this out and all of its consequences. You're just going to have to follow my lead in this. Remember, I'm your oldest brother and wiser."

Mia listened for a moment, but anger touched her face. "What are you talking about? You're my only brother, and yes, you're older, but only by three minutes and fifteen seconds," she muttered and took the opportunity to snarl as she glanced back at her brother. "How much wiser do you think you can become in that little time? I'll tell you how much. About the same amount as the thickness of an ant's eyelash! Besides, girls mature faster and are smarter than boys their age, at least by two full years. Everyone knows that!"

Andrew leaned in close for a little face-to-face persuasion. "And who came up with that old wives' tale? A bunch of females with their psychobabble? Look, you should admit, it's going to sound ridiculous, and you know it. This is going to be simply impossible for a reasonable adult to believe. We can't prove any of it conclusively, and we're going to look like fools. We're not going to lie. We're just going to have to leave a few parts of the story out. What I refer to as the wise CYB standard, cover your butt. A tactic that I've developed into an art form with some success in the past." He scowled at Mia while he tried to make the acronym CYB his own.

She hesitated at first and didn't bother to muffle a snort. Then after taking a calming breath, she responded, "Andrew! I can detect your annoyance and impatience with me about this, even beneath your natural charm, but that's being dishonest—and I'm being sarcastic about the natural charm," protested Mia. "We've never been dishonest, and the thought of it tries my patience, and at the moment, I seem to have none. So don't go ballistic on me now and get your knickers in a twist. All I see is that you're just giving me more of your psychobabble. And remember, we'll always remain best friends to each other, so cut me some slack." Mia's easy expression slid away, leaving her face cold.

As his eyes got larger, he blinked and refocused. "Oh no! What about that cookie jar you picked up, trying to squeeze that last cookie out of it, and broke it when you dropped it on the floor, and not going to Noah's defense when it was assumed he broke it while trying to get a cookie? I don't remember your conscience bothering you then for not stepping forward and telling the truth," Andrew reminded Mia. "Your track record for the truth is not all that impressive now, is it?"

"Maybe I didn't immediately tell them, but I eventually did, didn't I? And you can consider that a rhetorical question," Mia quickly responded, sounding annoyed. Her stomach shimmied, but her voice stayed steady.

"And that's exactly what I'm saying here. We just hold back a little, and we'll eventually tell them the whole story—like you did about the cookie jar," responded Andrew.

"Okay, so I held back a little then, but only once, and I had a guilty conscience until I told them the whole truth. I don't want to go through that ordeal again," replied Mia.

"Yeah, you did, two years later. And what about the time you told Daniel that we were related to Mel Gibson?" Andrew snapped right back with a cold, hard stare.

For the first time, frustration leaked through. "Well, we're all descendants of Adam and Eve, aren't we? Therefore, we all must be related to each other, one way or another," Mia said defensively. "Besides, what are we doing here, trying to get help for this fox or going to reminisce about my whole life? Are you sure this is a good idea, Andrew? Are you very sure? We're walking a thin line. It sounds more like linguistic camouflage to me, covering up the truth."

"Yes! I'm sure. Dead sure." His eyes flickered with annoyance and walked away, which was his way of ending a conversation that no longer furthered his agenda or held his interests.

Hey, what about me? asked the fox. *Are you going to introduce me to your father or not? If not, maybe someone could loan me one of his medical books, and I'll set my own leg.*

Realizing that they all were still in the rain, Andrew and Mia pushed their bikes under the garage eaves. Mia carefully picked up the fox from her basket, where he had remained nicely wrapped in Andrew's jacket, and she gently carried him into the side entrance of the garage while Andrew was calling out for their father.

Mia thought not telling their parents the whole truth was a bad idea. She felt that this omission was eventually going to come back and grab them by the throat and violently shake them, but for the moment, she would play along with her brother's not-so-bright idea.

As Andrew and Mia entered the garage, Andrew was still gnawing on the problem when he turned and realized that their mother had exited the house and was following them into the garage bearing hot chocolate and homemade cookies for everyone. Andrew turned to Mia, shaking his head slowly, indicating not to mention anything about angels.

"If you're looking for me, I'm over here, son," muttered their father as he continued to perform some sort of preventative maintenance on a power tool.

He was fastidious about his tools, as well as with his working area. He had always maintained a strict vigilance about cleanliness and keeping every tool well-oiled and in its precise location in the garage, always so tidy and clean, meticulously so, just as he scrupulously maintained his clinic at the zoo. He lived his philosophy: "If you take diligent care of your equipment, it will never let you down when you need something from it."

"Dad, Andrew and I found a baby fox in the fields," Mia called out cheerfully and offered him to her father. "And we think that he may have a broken leg. We brought him home as quickly as we could. I told him that you would help. Please, Dad, he is in a lot of pain and can't walk and really needs your help."

Quickly taking the wrapped fox from Mia's arms and placing him on top of his workbench, Dr. Brooks, in an understanding voice and without trying to frighten Mia, answered, "Princess…you know what I've always told you and Andrew about picking up wild animals. It can be very dangerous, especially when they're injured or scared. They can carry diseases. And like all wild animals, they're unpredictable. They can bite, and they can easily scratch you," reminded her father. "They must always be handled with appropriate equipment and protective clothing, but most of all, with the proper training. I know that a small fox may look cute, innocent, and cuddly to you, but it's still a wild animal. Although I must admit, this one seems to be very cooperative…as though someone has tranquilized him. I find that quite fascinating!"

"Well…you might say that he has been," replied Mia with a little discomfort in her eyes.

Andrew, with his system already jittery from nerves, shook his head violently from side to side outside his father's and mother's views, indicating…no! Then passing his right hand with a flat palm pointing downward, back and forth rapidly in front of his throat, saying, "Stop! Don't go any further!" Mia understood her brother's gesture and remained silent as she could see in his big, troubled eyes that he was calling out to her to please stop until they could agree on a course of action. And although the air was foaming with Mia's frustration and energy, she communicated to her brother with a nod of her head to stop talking.

"What do you mean? You might say that he has! What have you done to him? Did you do something to him or feed him something?" requested their father as he removed Andrew's jacket from the fox after he put on a pair of safety gloves so that he could give him an efficient cursory examination.

"Oh…that's not what she meant, Dad." As Andrew searched for a suitable metaphor, his adrenaline shot up, and his pulse hammered. "She means that she calmed him down by just talking to him. We all know how Mia in the past has always been able to calm Noah down when he starts to misbehave," Andrew quickly responded with a smile. His smile had always been a handy weapon, and he used it now, keeping his light-blue eyes friendly. His face was thin, sharp-angled, and would probably be termed scholarly as he aged. "Oh, and we did give him one of Mia's homemade cookies. You know how a homemade cookie always makes everyone more agreeable." He took a cookie and a cup of chocolate from his mother.

"Yes! She does have a knack for it, especially when she has a treat in her hand," their mother responded, continuing to pass out cookies and hot chocolate to everyone as they all started to laugh.

As the fox's legs became visible, Dr. Brooks was able to observe a large amount of swelling and tenderness in its right front leg.

"Well, Princess, I can't say with absolute certainty, but I think your diagnosis is probably right. It does appear that it's a broken leg," declared her father. "But we won't know for sure or how serious it is until we get him to the clinic at the zoo and confirm it with x-rays."

Still realizing how calm and relaxed the fox remained without any logical explanation throughout the cursory examination,

Dr. Brooks could not help but once again comment, "Are you sure you didn't give him anything to calm him down beside a cookie? It's extraordinary how patient he's remaining."

Stepping in front of Mia, Andrew eagerly responded, "It's just that he knows we're trying to help him, and he's grateful, that's all."

"Oh! And how do you think that he knows that?" replied Andrew's father. "He's a wild animal and most probably never had any real contact with humans before. So how would he know that you're friendly and wanted to help him? I suppose that you just walked up to him and told him so. And he, being a trusting kind of a guy, not only understood you but also believed and trusted you."

Mia was about to open her mouth to speak, and Andrew could see in her body language and eye contact nothing but trouble. Not taking any chances that she might reveal their encounter with the angels, he quickly jumped in again. "Well, Dad, maybe it's just instinct." He flashed his patient, good-humored smile and being very defensive with his theory. "You always told us that all animals have natural inborn instincts that can't be explained, haven't you?" He knew that he was in trouble and needed help. "And after Mia slowly and calmly spoke to him in her persuasive voice, he just instinctively knew that we were there to help. We all know how good she is about it." Andrew concluded with an exaggerated, indrawn breath and a shaky exhale while he just stood there with desperately hopeful eyes. He was hoping with optimism that his response would suffice as an acceptable answer.

"If it's instinct! I only wish that all my other patients at the zoo had equally developed instincts," rejoined his father. "Boy, wouldn't that make my work so much easier? Maybe I should hire both of you as patient advocates, and it wouldn't hurt if Mia brought along a batch of her cookies to share with the other animals at the zoo."

"So what do you say that we try to immobilize his leg and get him to the clinic so that we can get his leg x-rayed?" suggested Dr. Brooks. "Meanwhile, I will try to place a temporary splint on his leg. Mia, why don't you continue to avail yourself of your most useful talents and keep talking to him? It unquestionably does seem to soothe his anxiety."

CHAPTER 3

*W*hile Dr. Brooks disappeared into the storage room in the rear of the garage to search for a travel cage to safely transport the newly found fox to the dispensary, Andrew grabbed Mia by the elbow and led her to the side of the garage farthest from their parents, where he felt more comfortable in not being overheard.

Andrew's teeth bared in a snarl, showing little patience for his sister, as his eyes narrowed and focused on hers, trying to read her mind and failing badly. He then leaned forward and loudly whispered into Mia's ear if that was humanly possible in his state of mind. "Mia! What in the world are you thinking about? Have you fried a few circuits in that muscle in your head that you call your brain? I'm going to speak in simple terms for you, because that's how you talk to mental patients. You almost gave us away! Are you deliberately placing my patience in jeopardy?" His mouth tightened briefly as he overdramatized his rebuke.

Mia hesitated and then decided to speak her mind. "Well, I'm terrible at lying," she reiterated, "so cut me some slack. Because I don't have much experience at it," Mia stubbornly continued. "Why are you having trouble shaking hands with the truth?"

"How soon we forget. Don't you recall the Mel Gibson incident we just talked about a few minutes ago," Andrew said almost at a whisper, trying not to be overheard by their parents. "And why are you having trouble shaking hands with reality?"

She scowled at him even as the blood poured under her skin.

"Mia, from now on, let me do all the talking. Just follow my lead, okay?" cried Andrew. "Sometimes I think Julius Caesar's brain scan would register more brain activity than yours, and he's been dead for over two thousand years!"

"You mean you want me to be perfectly quiet like a good little sister, don't you?" suggested Mia with total exasperation showing on her face, then going mute dramatically but remaining icy as she stood fuming.

"As quiet as a worm hiding in a bird's nest," replied Andrew, infuriated with her. "And stop sulking, it's not working for you," he continued as his blue eyes flashed angrily at his sister.

"Okay! Okay! I get the message," she said, not needing to hear any more of his amusing analogies and rolling her eyes. "I'll try to be a little more careful!" acknowledged Mia as she slipped her hands into her pockets. "But obviously a little of my emotions are bleeding through, because I have some—unlike yourself." Her eyes were fierce, brilliant, and filled with emotion. "Besides, guilt clouds logic."

But Mia's comment did nothing to improve Andrew's temper.

"Hello, hello," a voice called out cheerfully. "Is there anyone in the garage?" a girl's voice was heard.

"We're all in here, White Dove," returned Mia, recognizing her best friend's voice. "We're all in the garage."

"There you are!" White Dove responded as she and her younger brother Rain Cloud entered the garage. Mia and White Dove exchanged light hugs and double-cheeked air kisses. "We saw both your parents' cars in the driveway, so we knew you were at home, but no one answered the front door."

"Oh, it's probably because I saw Mom working in the kitchen and invited her to join us in the garage. So there was no one in the house to hear you knocking on the front door. But look! Andrew and I found this little fox with a broken leg in the field, and Dad is trying to set it. Isn't he remarkable-looking? And you'll never believe what happened to us."

Andrew, quick thinker that he was, speedily stepped on her foot to prevent her from going any further, and started bellowing with an expression of utter fear on his face. "Oh! It's just a baby fox with a broken leg that he injured when Whiskey was chasing him on our property, but Dad said he's going to be fine."

"Oh, I want to see him," White Dove exclaimed, obviously intrigued, with her beautiful large hazel eyes that resembled antique golden coins.

"Ouch! Andrew, get off my foot, you fat cow! Do you want Dad to set two broken feet?"

"Oh! Mia, I didn't see you there. I'm so sorry," Andrew answered back immediately.

"What do you mean you didn't see me? Are you blind? Maybe you need Mom to examine your eyes, but she may find one of my fists in one after I relieve you of several teeth," she responded with a low throaty growl. Beneath those cool blue eyes, violence was bubbling.

"I thought you said earlier that I was your best friend?" responded her brother, tilting his head to the right.

"Well, best friends have their limitations or can be replaced!" She turned her head in White Dove's direction, with her eyes looking into hers.

Mia heard a snicker and then turned to her brother again with a glare. "What are you grinning at?"

"Oh! It's your way with words again. I do so admire your way with the English language. Daniel Webster would be so proud of you," responded Andrew.

"Oh, now that's convincing and reassuring," Mia said sarcastically. "How would you also like a fat lip? I'm sure that would make my swollen foot feel a lot better."

"Mia, that's no way for a lady to talk! What's wrong with you?" interrupted her mother. "Your father and I have taught you better. I don't want to hear any more arguing in here while I'm in the kitchen, getting more hot chocolate and cookies for our guests." She exited the garage for the additional refreshments.

Mia saw Star suddenly appear behind her mother as she reentered the garage, carrying a fresh tray of hot chocolate and cookies, revealing herself only to Mia and Andrew. She addressed Mia, "Please think twice before you say anything rude to your brother. It's much nicer to be gracious and humorous than discourteous and sarcastic. So play nice. You're a very intelligent and beautiful young lady, but

I'm here to also remind you that we expect wonderful things from you, so please don't disappoint us."

Taking Star's advice, Mia replied to her mother. "I'm sorry, Mom, I really didn't mean to be so rude to Andrew. It was kind of like an accident," Mia apologized softly.

"Oh! I'm sure that it was, like it was an accident when Germany marched over France and occupied it in the Second World War!" Andrew retorted. Mia gave him a bitter look, dragged a hand through her hair, and walked off to the side, muttering and biting her lower lip.

"And that goes for you too, Andrew," interjected his mother. "Be respectful to your sister. You both are so dramatic and such exaggerators when you argue with each other. And you're setting a bad example for your friends. I'm sure White Dove and Rain Cloud don't act this way at home."

"No, Dr. Brooks, it's pretty much the same with us at our home, to tell you the truth," White Dove added to the conversation as she was shaking her head. "When Rain Cloud isn't tripping over his own feet, he has at least one of them in his mouth, saying something foolish."

"Oh! Fine, was that you attempting to say something sarcastic?" Rain Cloud said as he frowned into White Dove's eyes with arrogance. His dark eyes narrowed and darkened, focusing on his sister's face. "So let's get it out on the table." He now drew his lips together at the sides so that they wrinkled and formed a semicircle to express his intolerance of his sister's remark. He was looking mean enough to chew on rocks and spit pebbles.

"No, I wouldn't call it sarcasm, Dr. Brooks. It was too truthful to be sarcastic, it was more fact than mockery," responded his older sister as she walked over and stood by Mia. Looking directly at her brother now, she continued, "The family is just grateful that he tries to appear as a human being on occasions when we're out of the house."

"See how she treats me, Dr. Brooks?" Rain Cloud turned to face Rachel. "Like an imbecile chewing on a bone." His stance transmitted annoyance. "She doesn't even have basic social skills." He flicked a glance over to her, seeing her grinning. "She always wants to and thinks she sounds mature, but in reality, she comes off sounding grandiose and self-absorbed!"

"Yuck! And ouch! See what you two started, Mia? An epidemic of being rude to your sibling!"

"I didn't start it, Mom. Remember, it was Andrew who started it by stepping on my foot. If anyone started this outbreak of the plague, it was Andrew." There was a sneer in her voice, light and disdainful.

Star just placed her hands over her face, trying to conceal herself as she shook her head back and forth.

Mia understood her concerns and tried to redeem herself to Star. "As always, you're right, Mom. The four of us should be more tolerant and respectful of each other. Right, Andrew?"

Andrew also felt Star's disappointment in them and responded, "Yes, we wouldn't want anyone to be disappointed in us. So I say, from now on we should all act like adults, especially to one another."

"Well, that would be a lovely change of events," his mother responded. "Can I hold you to that?"

"Absolutely," exclaimed the twins in unison, as they so often did. And they all started to giggle.

"I don't know how you two do that," stated White Dove. "You two can always say the same thing at the same time."

As the twins' father returned with the traveling cage, he asked, "Did I miss anything?"

"Oh, nothing more than an interesting recreation of World War II," revealed the twins' mother. "But we may have just signed a new peace treaty."

"Well then, I'm glad that I wasn't in the war zone! What do you say, let's pack this little guy up safely and get him x-rayed?"

"Can we come along?" requested White Dove, flashing her eloquent wide, soft, hazel doe eyes, which were almost impossible for anyone to refuse. "Mia told us yesterday that there are several new arrivals in the nursery which we haven't seen yet. I especially want to see the two new little panda bear twins and their mother. They were all over the local and national news this week. I so want to see them. I find pandas fascinating, and hopefully the stories that we are hearing are true and that the pandas will be able to remain here at our zoo on a long-term loan from China."

"Well, I have to admit, they're going to be one of the most popular attractions this summer, but they're so new that we can't even get close to them yet. At this stage, the mother is very protective. We don't even know if they're male or female yet. That's going to take a while. I guess we will be referring to the babies as twins instead of *him* or *her*. We have the mother and her babies in a special enclosure for now, with a large glass viewing window, so that if we're lucky we may be able to sneak a short peek at them. But we can't count on it. What we do have, though, are a couple of video cameras in the enclosure 24-7 to capture the total experience. We're documenting everything we possibly can about the babies, and the natural instincts of the mother for how she protects and provides for them. It's a research project of love, and all of us on staff are really excited about it."

"We still would like to try to see them," White Dove pleaded her case skillfully, working those beautiful hazel eyes of hers artfully.

"Well," answered Rachel, "let's see what your parents have to say about it. We need to make sure that they don't have any prior family plans for you today. It's wouldn't be right for us to presume anything, because the last thing we want is to interfere with them, right?"

"They don't have any plans," Rain Cloud quickly jumped in. "Dad is working on his stamp collection, and Mom is sewing on her quilt, and I'm sure that she plans to be working on it all day, so for sure they won't mind."

"You may be right, but I think that it would be imprudent to assume so. We'll need to check with them for sure. Take my word for it. Parents want and need to know where their children are at all times, and speaking as a mother..." She stressed it again by repeating, "At all times."

As White Dove reached into her jacket pocket, retrieving her phone, she suggested, "Okay, I'll call her on my cell."

"No, that's okay, I'll call her. I've been wanting to talk to your mother all morning anyway. I need to bring her up to speed on a couple of projects that we're both working on for the church and your school. What's wrong, White Dove? You seem worried about something. Do you not want me to talk to your mother?"

White Dove spoke in a quiet voice as her eyes began to droop. "I hope not about my brother and me." The room suddenly went silent as a crypt in a country church.

"No! Why would you think that? Is there something that you're particularly concerned about? So do you have a guilty conscience about something, White Dove? Do you have any deep hidden secrets you want to share?" Rachel asked musically, with a wide smile on her face, looking humorously satirical with very suspicious eyes.

"No, I just don't want you to think that Rain Cloud and I were really fighting. We just like to kid around a lot, but we weren't really serious," White Dove responded as she lowered her head, cowering a little while, looking straight up with her eyes.

"White Dove, I was only kidding you. You're not in any trouble," stated Rachel, giving White Dove a reassuring hug. She then walked to a corner of the garage so that she would be able to hear clearly on her cell phone. She reached into her pocket to retrieve one of two cell phones that she always kept within arms' length, one personal and the other for hospital business.

"I hope your parents let you go with us," Andrew said, looking in Rain Cloud's direction. "The zoo has the best lemonade and Italian sausage dogs in the world."

"I know," whispered Rain Cloud. "We just got our allowances this morning, so let's try to get White Dove to pay for them. She gets more than I do because she's older. I've tried unsuccessfully to base our allowances on grades, but I'm told that with age come more responsibilities. Therefore, it entitles more spoils."

"What are you talking about? How is that going to change anything? I've seen her report cards, and she always gets all As, just like the rest of us," questioned Andrew.

"Yah, but this time she received an A-minus for gym. She catches and throws a ball like a girl."

"What are you talking about? Maybe you haven't noticed, she is a girl, you nut," as Andrew placed his hand on his forehead, shaking his head vigorously back and forth.

As Rachel returned to the group, she stated, "We have liftoff! Your mother says that you two belong to us for the rest of the day, so let's get a-moving."

As they were all loading into the SUV, Mia could see Star and Simon standing next to the rear door leading into their kitchen. And after a flicker of hesitation, she glanced over at Andrew for confirmation that she wasn't hallucinating, and that he also could see them. Andrew only nodded and gave her the most pleasant of smiles in return to indicate yes, he indeed did.

"How is he doing, Princess?" Mia's father asked as he carefully drove past the meadow en route to the zoo.

They were almost at the exact location where the twins first discovered the fox.

Suddenly the twins noticed Star and Simon waving from the shoulder of the road. "Look, mom, look!" Mia was trying to wave back when Andrew grabbed her arm to restrain her.

"Look at what, sweetie?" Mia's mother started to focus outside the car. "I don't see anything."

"Oh, this is where we found the fox, mom," answered Andrew quickly, so smoothly covering Mia's slip that it was barely noticeable. But still it made him grind his teeth with a stern look at Mia. He continued trying to change the subject and at the same time tried to be unruffled and persuasive.

"Oh! Look over there, on the right side." As everyone turned east looking out the windows, they noticed both Whiskey and Brewski still up to mischief, this time chasing free-spirited birds in the meadow. The weather had turned into a light rain. "At least they're on their own property this time, and they're never going to catch those larks. They're way too fast for them!" But both Mia and Andrew couldn't help but continue to stare at their guardian angels who somehow remained completely dry in the rain until they disappeared in the distance. It did relax the mind and soothe the spirit just knowing that their guardian angels would always be available to them. But nonetheless, Mia was going to have to be more discreet as Andrew directed his eyes steadily on hers.

"You're not ever going to learn, Mia, are you?" Andrew leaned over and whispered in Mia's ear.

"Leave me alone, Andrew. It was an accident." Mia pouted, returning his whisper. "You're still making my system jittery with nerves!" It was obvious that she was quite distraught and anxious, with anger touching her face.

"Yah, you have more accidents than are reported to Triple-A all year. How can you be so smart without ever having to study yet be so stupid at the same time? It's not fair to the rest of us. Have you ever been diagnosed as bipolar?"

"I've never been diagnosed as anything but gifted," her voice cold as February as she thrust her hands into the pockets of her coat before she could pull her hair out by the roots. "You better be more civil to me or you're going to disappoint Simon," whispered Mia.

"Mia, I asked, how's the fox?" repeated her father.

"Oh! He's fine, Dad. He looks like he's just trying to get a little sleep," replied Mia, keeping a vigilant eye on the little fox while holding the small travel cage on her lap.

"You forgot, didn't you?" questioned Andrew.

"No, I didn't!" And Mia cleared her throat as she added, "Forgot what?"

"Didn't I tell you not to say anything," Andrew reminded Mia, still clenching his teeth and looking with irritation at her.

"He asked me a question. You don't want me to be disrespectful, do you?" snapped Mia, sounding annoyed and with friction in her voice.

"Remember, a worm in a bird's nest! Just remember, as quiet as a worm in a bird's nest!" Andrew reminded Mia grumpily.

Mia ignored the sarcasm.

"What are you two whispering about?" asked White Dove. "Are you keeping secrets?"

"What secrets?" asked Andrew. "We don't have any secrets. We're just trying to come up with a name for the fox, that's all."

"We want to help," eagerly offered Rain Cloud. "I bet with all of us we can come up with several clever names." And for the rest of the ride, several witty names were proposed.

As Dr. Brooks stopped in front of the security gate of the employees' private parking lot, he entered his key card into the appropriate slot, then waited for the electric black metal gate to slide open along its tracks. The first thing that he noticed was that there was an unfamiliar light-blue van parked in his assigned spot.

"That's strange!" remarked the twins' father. "Someone's parked in my space."

"Well, it is your day off. Maybe one of the other veterinarians is using it today, thinking that you wouldn't mind. It is the closest space to the office," remarked his wife. "Do you recognize the van?"

"No, I don't think so," David replied quickly. "And no, I don't mind, but I'm familiar with the cars of everyone on staff at the clinic, and I don't recognize this one. Although it must belong to someone who is an employee, because you can't gain entrance to this lot without an employee's security card to open the gate. I guess it's not important," Dr. Brooks continued. "I'll just park in Dr. Michael's spot. I'm sure it will be okay. He told me that he'll be out of town this weekend visiting family."

Andrew and Mia, followed by White Dove and Rain Cloud, walked briskly ahead of their parents through the extensive grounds between the employees' parking lot and the veterinary clinic. They also needed to traverse several alternating openings and gates separating different fruit and vegetable gardens that were assigned to different school groups in the area. Lastly, they approached a beautiful two-hundred-year-old tree in front of the clinic busily trying to rejuvenate its prespring leaves. Dr. Brooks followed last, carrying the travel cage containing the small fox.

As Andrew opened the front entrance door into the lobby of the clinic, the twins' father walked up to the employee-only side door and scanned his thumb in the biometric lock. As the door opened, Cecilia, the clinic's lead medical technician, turned to see who was entering and cried aloud, "Well, good morning, Dr. Brooks! We didn't expect to see you today," with pleasant surprise on her face.

Simultaneously and presuming that the greeting of the day was addressed to themselves, both David and Rachel cheerfully returned

Cecilia's greeting and then turned to each other and started to laugh uncontrollably.

"I'm sorry, I should have said, 'Good morning, Doctors,'" Cecilia corrected herself while joining in with a giggle. She quickly walked over to Rachel and the twins, her movements both graceful and efficient, giving each a fond embrace as pleasure and excitement rushed to her face.

"Well, that's quite a welcome!" declared Rachel.

"That's because we haven't seen you on the grounds since the employees' Christmas party, and it's always exciting for me to see you and the kids. And knowing how busy you always are at the hospital, you must have had to bribe someone to get the weekend off," continued Cecilia. "Or did you have to shoot someone?"

"No, if I had shot someone, I'm sure that they would have forced me to stay in the emergency room and treat him before they arrested me and carried me away to the dungeons in shackles. People can be so unreasonable at times." Everyone laughed uncontrollably again.

"But yes, I sort of have the weekend off. Unfortunately, I'm still on call at the hospital," responded Rachel jovially. "So let's all keep our fingers and toes crossed that there are no cardio emergencies this weekend!"

"And I remember you two from the Christmas party." Cecilia focused on White Dove and Rain Cloud. "You two beat my daughter Kristin and me in the three-legged race. You two were faster than the wind."

"And who's your other little friend?" Cecilia asked as her attention focused on the small traveling cage that David was carrying.

"Oh!" replied David. "This is why we're here today. Andrew and Mia found this little injured red fox on our property this morning. It looks like he'll need an x-ray to confirm if he has a broken leg. And if it's what I suspect, he'll need some tender loving care for the next couple of months. Then we should be able to release him back to his natural home with Mother Nature."

Always eager to pick her father's brain and constantly having a natural thirst for answers as if it was ingrained in her, Mia asked, "How can you tell what kind of fox he is? You said that it was a red fox. Is that a certain kind of fox?" She really wanted to know the reasoning of how her father came to that conclusion.

"It's really not that tough, Princess. It doesn't take a crystal ball," responded her father, always enjoying the precious moments spent with his two children, especially when they were genuinely inquisitive. It always pleased him enormously to see their thirst for information regarding the animal world.

"Although there are only about ten species of true foxes," Dr. Brooks continued, "there are basically only two that are predominately common to this area—the red fox and the gray fox. The thing that makes it a little difficult is that they both can be identical in size and color. The European red fox was originally imported to the United Sates from England somewhere in the 1760s, if I remember correctly. The gray fox, on the other hand, has always been native to the United States. And what mostly makes them distinguishable from one another is that they have different habits."

"What do you mean by different habits?" Andrew asked curiously with an avid interest in his eyes totally focused on his father.

As his father's gaze now shifted from Mia to Andrew, David continued answering questions. "Well, the red fox feels more comfortable in open areas, where it can look in all directions for any possible predators," Andrew's father responded, delighted to see how both twins were always genuinely interested in nature and its complexities. "It likes to run and is very intelligent. The gray fox, on the other hand, does not like to run. It likes to live in dense areas, and if pursued, it will hide down a hole or even climb up a tree. In fact, it's the only member of the dog family that does climb easily."

"Dad, now you're pulling our legs! A fox is from the dog family and can climb trees? It's hard to believe that a fox is in the dog family. And if it can climb trees, shouldn't it be more in the squirrel family or maybe in the chipmunk family?" Mia replied as it was obvious that she found her father's comments not only questionable but also hilarious. "I thought normally only cats and monkeys could climb trees. Maybe we should try to teach Noah this trick."

After several minutes of contemplation, Andrew, after everyone had a chance to chuckle and laugh about Mia's comedy club routine, continued to ask, "But, Dad, that still doesn't answer the question!" as he interrupted. "You didn't see his habits, so how do you know that this one is a red fox?"

His father's brows lifted at the question. "Oh, that's because I guess I only gave you half the answer. I should have mentioned also that it's not that tough when you can also see the bottom of his feet. Here, look at the pads on his feet. The key difference here is that the gray fox has larger toes and footpads while the red fox has a larger amount of hair between its toes, therefore making just a small part of its pads visible. So now knowing that, what kind of fox do you think he is?" asked his father.

Looking at Andrew with a comical smirk on her face, Mia stepped in and confirmed her father's opinion, struggling not to show her surprise at this tidbit of information. "He looks like a red fox to me!"

"Well, thank you, Miss Know It All," responded Andrew. "Being that you are so knowledgeable and obviously know everything about red foxes, I'm sure you can tell us how old he is?"

"Good question," responded Mia as she slowly turned to her father, hoping that he would quickly answer the question, negating the need for her to respond.

"I would say, in comparison to a human's life, he looks like he would be a young teenager, just like the two of you will be when you turn thirteen in July," Dr. Brooks responded.

"That's about what I would've said too," Mia agreed, confidently nodding.

"Maybe so," Andrew said sarcastically, looking into Mia's eyes, "but don't you ever forget, I'll be a teenager before you will."

"Only by three minutes and fifteen seconds," Mia responded quickly and irritably, with a sarcastic tone in her voice.

"It doesn't matter by how long. I'll still be a teenager before you will," insisted Andrew.

"Maybe so, but it has been scientifically proven that females are two years more mature than males, so that would make me one year, eleven months, twenty-nine days, twenty-three hours, fifty-six minutes and forty-five seconds older than you are," Mia quickly snapped, with a smile as sharp as broken glass and a no-doubt-whatsoever in her voice.

"I think you're reading way too many of Mom's *Cosmopolitan* magazines," Andrew said, unimpressed.

As Cecilia returned from the radiology room, she advised Dr. Brooks that the x-ray room and the x-ray technician were clear and ready for the patient.

Turning to Cecilia, Mia asked, "What do you think, Cecilia, are girls more mature than boys?" trying to obtain her support.

There were a few seconds of contemplation. "I think, I'm going to take my mother's advice"—she gave a delicate shrug—"and keep my opinions to myself," Cecilia wisely answered with a humorous smile on her face. "I can clearly see this is a no-win situation if I weigh in on this sibling infighting."

"Well, what do you say we get started and get this little fellow x-rayed?" David said as he carried the fox into the x-ray lab with his x-ray technician.

Looking at Mia, David suggested, "Why don't you also come along, Mia, and continue to talk to the little guy while we try to position him in place for a clear x-ray? We need him to not move for a couple of seconds. Being that he seems to respond to you, Mia, do you think you can get him to cooperate?"

"I'm sure I can if I promise him another cookie," responded Mia. "He seems to love them as much as Noah. What do you want him to do?"

"See if you can position him on his left side just for a couple of seconds and then step behind the security wall," David asked. "If you can't, then we will need to sedate him."

"Let me try first, Dad," asked Mia. And looking to the corner of the room, Mia saw Star and Simon standing, patiently observing Mia's confidence. Focusing on Mia and without anyone being able to hear her other than Mia and Andrew, Star, in a soft tone and nodding, told Mia, "Go ahead. Speak slowly and softly. He'll understand you. He'll do what you ask of him."

Taking a cookie out of a plastic Ziploc from her backpack and showing it to her new four-legged friend, and looking into the fox's eyes, Mia began to speak slowly and softly, "If you want another of my delicious homemade oatmeal cookies, lie down on your side and don't move."

Why can't I have the cookie first? asked the teenage patient.

Reaching out very carefully, Mia aided the fox to his side and responded, "First the x-ray, then the cookie," then she slowly backed up behind the security wall.

Humans, thought the fox, *I can see that they always want their own way.* But also wanting the cookie, the fox decided to go along, to get along, and to get the cookie.

As soon as Mia stood behind her, the technician immediately took the x-ray. During the process, with Mia's help, the technician was able to take a series of four x-rays from four different angles, and then Mia gave the little fox his anticipated reward.

David was still baffled. "I can't believe how you did that, Mia. The fox not only listened to every word you said but did everything you told him to do. He must have really wanted that cookie. But what I don't understand is how a wild fox was able to understand your directions. It's not like you raised him as a pet. He is a wild fox with probably no prior contact with a human."

"What can I say, Dad? It's probably a gift," Mia responded as they returned to the examining room.

Andrew, overhearing his father's question to Mia as they entered the examining room where Rachel, Cecilia, and he were waiting for them, immediately stretched his neck and started shaking his head violently back and forth indicating "No, don't say it."

"Probably a gift given to me from you and Mom," Mia continued.

Andrew lowered his head and shoulders with a sigh of relief. *Mia is going to eventually give me a heart attack, if not a stroke,* Andrew thought. *God only knows if I'm going to survive this ordeal!*

Cecilia spoke up and volunteered to go to the developing room and assist the technician. A few minutes later, she returned from the x-ray developing room, handing the series of x-rays to David. As everyone immediately started to follow Dr. Brooks into a large examination room, Mia asked her mother, "Will we be able to see the results now and know how seriously his leg is broken?" The amusement in her face now turned to worry.

"Oh, absolutely," Rachel responded with a brilliant smile. "We should know in just a few minutes." Seeing the anxiety on Mia's face, she attempted to alleviate her concerns. "I wouldn't worry too much about him. He's in the best of hands. Between your father and Cecilia, he will not only receive the best of care but will be treated like royalty." Everyone crowded around the x-ray viewer that was mounted on the wall. And as her father switched on the lamp, Mia said a short prayer that there wouldn't be any serious complications.

"Dad, please! Don't keep us in suspense," Mia protested in anticipation of learning the results. "What's the verdict?"

"Well, it's clearly a fracture," declared Dr. Brooks. "Fortunately, it's just a simple fracture and easy to treat. In fact, it appears to be an incomplete fracture."

"What does that mean?" Andrew asked his mother, being that she was now closest to him. As he had no idea what to do with his hands, he just stabbed them into the pockets of his pants.

"In terms easy to understand, it means that the fracture does not include the whole bone. The bone is only partially broken, like when you break a green stick and it's not completely broken in half. It's very common with young patients because their bones are still relatively soft and pliable," responded Andrew's mother.

"Well, Dr. Brooks, would you like me to assist you in treatment?" asked Rachel with a humorous tone to her voice, as she flashed him one of her perfect smiles that he always loved.

"Oh! Indeed, I would. It's not every day that I get a leading cardio-surgeon in the clinic assisting me in a veterinarian procedure," responded David humorously. "But I'm not sure I can afford your talents."

"Can you afford an Italian sausage dog with a medium lemonade?"

"It sounds like high finance to me. I'll have to check with my savings at the Zoo's Employee Credit Union," responded David with a smile that almost exposed all his white teeth.

"And for sure, we're going to also need the talents of Mia and Andrew to relax and calm down the patient." David now looked at his wife and declared, "Rachel, I want you and Cecilia to see this, because you're not going to believe your eyes! Mia has this extraordinary ability to tranquilize our patient here by just slowly and calmly talking to him. It's as though he realizes she has nothing but good intentions and love for him. And he freely submits to her care. I only wish that I had this natural ability. You both know as health professionals how hard it is to get your patients to cooperate even when you have a good history in working with them. They seem to think that a patient is like a customer—they are always right even without a medical degree hanging on their wall! Okay, Mia, I want you to do your magic or mojo and make our patient calm and secure so that we can set his leg."

"Your wish is my command, Father." As Mia walked up and stood next to her father, she started to talk slowly with a gentle voice, "Now you know that we are here to help you. We are not going to hurt you. My father is a good and kind veterinarian. My mother is a wonderful and loving doctor. They both help and cure sicknesses and injuries in both humans and animals alike. So we need you to just lie there and let them do their work, and everything will be over in no time, okay?"

Do I get another cookie for being a good patient? asked the fox.

"I can tell by the look in his eyes, Dad, that he wants another cookie for his cooperation," Mia spoke out, not wanting to give any indication that she had heard the fox's request. "I tell you what, little guy, if you do exactly what you're told, I'll give you another oatmeal cookie."

As the fox reclined on his side, he gently lifted his head and looked directly into Mia's eyes, and in a voice that only Mia and Andrew could hear, he said, *I trust you, and if you say to also trust your parents, I will. I know deep in my heart that you only want the best for me, so I'll just lie here and behave myself, okay? I just want you to know that I really need my leg. My favorite thing to do is to run in the meadow with my friends. So please help me and remember what your mom said about treating me like royalty. And don't forget my extra cookie!*

"Trust me, little guy. My dad told me that in just a few short weeks your leg will be as good as new and you will be able to return to your family and run with your friends in the meadow. I would never lie to you. You're in the best of hands."

The fox was fully comforted and, with Mia's loving words, placed his head flat on the table and became fully cooperative.

"Have you ever seen anything like this before?" asked David.

"I have to admit, no, I haven't, and this is truly amazing! Mia, you have a gift. You have to teach me your charisma," asked her mother.

"I'm not sure if you can be taught this gift," stated Mia. "I think it's more of something that is given to you as a gift."

David realized that even though he worked almost daily caring for animals, this day was special because it was a whole family experience, and moments like this should always be cherished.

With exhilaration in her voice, Cecilia was asking everyone to gather around closely. "I want a picture of this for our bulletin board, for this is surely a Kodak moment." She felt a warm sentimental carnival atmosphere. "And I'm sure that the zoo's editor would want a copy to publish in our employees' newsletter."

As the twins stood quietly by White Dove and Rain Cloud, they closely observed their mother and father rendering medical treatment to the small fox's leg. They couldn't believe how lucky they were in having such wonderful parents. They couldn't be any prouder. God gave them more than their newly bestowed gifts; He had also given them stable, loving and supportive parents.

"They do excellent work, don't they?" whispered Andrew to Rain Cloud as he was surprised to find that both Simon and Star had reappeared and joined them at their sides. Although no words were spoken, it was obvious that both angels were invisible to all in the room. There was no clue to the twins' parents, Cecilia, the twins' best friends, and to the other staff members throughout the clinic that they were in the presence of two heavenly bodies ensuring that all went well. All that needed to be communicated to the twins was accomplished by both angels smiling, enormously pleased, and bowing their heads in approval of everyone's excellent work. And there was no one the twins admired or wished more to emulate in the entire world than their loving parents.

CHAPTER 4

*A*fter a good twenty minutes of tender loving care by the two gentle, good doctors, Cecilia, under the observation of the Four Musketeers (Mia, Andrew, White Dove, and Rain Cloud), as they were known on the school campus, kindly placed the fox into his own cage for rest and recuperation. "Well," stated David, "the prognosis as before remains the same. All that is needed is about six to eight weeks of TLC, no weight on the leg, a good nutritional diet, and good friends to keep him company."

"Well, I can see three of the four requirements will be easy to meet here at the clinic," responded Mia. "I feel comfortable that he will receive nothing but excellent food in conjunction with a proper diet, and medical treatment from your staff, Dad. And for the last one, the four of us can keep him company. But how are you going to keep him off his leg? Are you going to prescribe crutches? No! I have a better idea. We'll make him a wheelchair, and he can push himself around." Everyone started to giggle.

"You're not too far off the mark, Mia," commented David. "I thought that we could fabricate a device similar to a wheelchair but more like a skateboard. But instead of sitting on it, he will have to place most of his weight on his chest and stomach to ride on it. And then he can push himself around on it with his other three good legs. I've made a couple of these devices before in the past, and they work pretty well with a little training and practice."

"I know exactly what you're talking about, Dr. Brooks! I've seen one of those devices on the Animal Channel," declared White Cloud energized. "The story was about this dog that was run over by a car, and his hindquarters became paralyzed. They made one for him, and he was really fast with it."

"Well, I'm sure that this little fox will probably be able to out-run you on it," snickered Rain Cloud. "You run like a girl who looks like she never knows where she's going." He then quickly flashed one of his well-known smiles of sarcasm, attached with plenty of charm.

"You're not going to let it go, are you? You're just not going to let it go that I got an A-minus in gym last week, are you?" White Dove addressed her brother with a frustrated frown and fists clenched at her sides, her eyes bulging in a flushed face.

"Well, it's not my fault that you run and throw a ball like a girl," her brother responded without hesitation as he couldn't control his chuckling.

"And when you're about sixteen or seventeen, I bet you're going to love having a sister so that she can introduce you to all her good-looking girlfriends." Mia stepped in, rolling her eyes as she commented.

The room took a quick direction into silence. You might say the room turned church quiet.

"Well, all I have to say is we had an excellent team administering this medical procedure," David changed the subject to jump-start the conversation again. "Do I see any volunteers interested in helping me construct this so-called wheeled crutch skateboard? On second thought, I think we can just call it a mobility device!"

"Why can't you just use one of those that you've already made before?" asked Andrew.

"It's not as easy as it may seem, and that's because a new one has to be constructed and tailored to each particular animal." David, as was his modus operandi, started talking with his hands to show height and length of the device. "It needs to be customized to meet each animal's body length, as well as the length of their legs. There is not much of an issue about their weight, but that's the reason why we just can't use another animal's apparatus. It's kind of like when an astronaut is measured from head to foot, his seat needs to be tailor-made to accommodate his size, height, weight, leg, and arm reach in the spacecraft when he goes into outer space. He needs as much leg room as he can get but also still have the proper arm length to reach all his controls while buckled up in his chair."

"So who wants to help? Who can I count on?" David asked with the thrill of adventure in his voice.

"Well, since we've already assembled such an outstanding medical team, let's not reinvent the spacecraft again. We can't break up a winning combination now!" declared Rachel. "I don't see why we won't also make an outstanding prosthetics team. We should all be able to contribute. I bet that if we pool together all our individual talents, we can come up with the Rolls Royce of wheeled crutches." Now Rachel started to talk also using her hands, mocking David, in combination with one of her well-known endearing smiles.

"Yeah," responded White Dove, "we should all be included. One for all, and all for one!"

"Does that mean that I can be one of the Musketeers?" asked Cecilia. "There is no way that you're going to keep me out of this adventure, so count me in."

"Of course, why would you think anything else?" David spoke up. "We undoubtedly have the best medical team known to science thus far, so why would we want to make any substitutions now?" David exclaimed enthusiastically. "We need to keep our A-Team on the playing field," He looked directly at Rachel with a wink from his smiling eyes.

"Then we share the exact conclusion," Rachel quickly concurred, "that the result of this sensitive procedure was not only a complete success but performed by the best surgical team in the country, if not the entire world! Therefore, it is settled. This team will remain intact and proceed with the fox's rehab." Rachel was being intentionally overdramatic and whimsical. "Now can I presume that you will reciprocate and assist me in treating one of my patients needing surgery?" Rachel continued jovially, obviously indicating that she was also enjoying the moment.

"Are you crazy, Doctor?" David burst out laughing. "Why do you think I went into veterinary medicine in the first place? Not only do I get to practice excellent quality medicine with the most advanced scientific knowledge available to me, the best staff and equipment at my side, but I also don't have to worry about malpractice suits, with those notoriously high premiums. Why, I've never even had to deal with a patient talking back to me with a complaint of service. If anything, our patients have done nothing but show their love and appreciation for everything we've done for them. No! I only work on animal patients who appreciate their doctors."

As everyone joined in the levity, Rachel laughingly admitted, "I guess you're right, as usual. We 'people doctors' must be gluttons for punishment!"

"Now that Rehab has been taken care of, can we take him home with us today? And then when he's fully recovered, we can return him back to his family," Mia asked, with her eyes lighting up with excitement.

"Whoa! Slow down for a minute, who's Rehab?" requested David, making an educated guess that she was referring to the fox.

"Oh! Andrew and I got together to name the fox Rehab because Mom said it best that we will all be working toward his needed rehabilitation," replied Mia, softening her expression. "So we thought that Rehab was a great name for him."

"Princess, we can't take the fox home, I mean Rehab. It's far too soon. What's best for him is for him to stay here at the clinic until he has fully recuperated," replied her father, trying to be sympathetic. "But I agree that Rehab is a great name for him."

"But, Dad, it was Andrew and I who found him. He knows us best. Like you said, we've bonded with him. You know we'll take loving care of him. You said that he needs to be surrounded by his friends," Mia pleaded her case, staring intently at her father with her big beautiful blue eyes for any sign of reconsideration. "Besides, don't we have to make the wheelchair what-cha-ma-call-it at home?" Mia stepped forward closer to her father with a morose face and jammed her hands in her pockets to keep from squirming from disappointment.

"Oh, Princess, you know I don't like to say no! But we must think and do what's best for the fox. I'm sorry, what's best for Rehab," David stated, pleading for his daughter's best judgment to emerge while still trying to ease her disappointment. "He's going to need care for the next six to eight weeks, maybe more. We'll need to assess whether he'll be able to return to the wild. He may no longer be able to run as before. He must be able to run from his predators and hunt for food on his own. We have a great workshop here on the property where we can construct his skateboard apparatus. Besides, you'll be in school most of the day. Here, he can be cared for 24-7 by a highly trained staff. Now, you do want what's best for Rehab, don't you?"

Mia, not being able to hide her disappointment, acknowledged. "I know you're right, Dad. But it's hard to just leave him behind because I want to help too. We all want to help. And what about his family? They must be worried about him too. I would be worried about Andrew if he didn't come home from school on time. Well, maybe that's a bad example," she exclaimed as she was making a goofy but humorous, half-cocked smile that she was well known for, especially when she was making a cynical joke about her brother. Then she turned in Andrew's direction, looking and waiting for his reaction. "But he would have probably just found some extraterrestrials who forced him back to their mother ship for lunch while trying to talk him into buying a set of their encyclopedias, you know, to help him with his homework." Andrew struggled to maintain a straight face as he tilted his head, trying to figure out where Mia was going with her comments. In fact, Mia continued, "I'm placing him on notice now that if he ever comes home late from school, he'll find that his bedroom is rented out for a little extra cash!"

Although Dr. Brooks always appreciated the twins' fun and loving rivalry, he tried to bring the situation back to reality. "If you both have finished your little sibling bonding dance, can we return to Rehab? Now look, Princess," David continued in his most sympathetic voice, "I know you want to help, especially being that he was initially your patient first. And I really don't understand fully why, but he seems to be very comfortable around both you and your brother. So I'll tell you what we'll do. Let's make a deal. On weekends, with your mother's permission, I'll bring you and Andrew to the clinic, where you can help in nursing him back to health. And when his leg is completely healed, we'll make the assessment together if he can be released back in the meadow where he can rejoin his family and friends. Okay? Is that a good compromise?" the twins' father asked, anticipating a successful reconciliation.

"Well, I guess that will be okay," responded Mia slowly after she used her way of working through a problem thoughtfully. "It does make more sense than him being in a small cage by himself in the garage. But if you find that he needs us, we can come here after school. We can do our homework here too. Okay, do we have a deal?"

"If it's okay with your mother, we have a deal. Shall we seal it with a handshake?" replied David, extending his right hand out to Mia.

Rachel nodded, expressing her firm agreement without giving a vocal comment.

"No," answered Mia, "fathers and daughters don't shake hands. They seal a deal with a hug and a kiss." She wrapped her arms around her father's neck, giving him a tender kiss on the cheek and whispering in his ear, "Dad, you always seem to know just the right things to say, don't you?"

Turning to his mother, Andrew gave his mother a thankful and welcomed hug and kiss. Andrew then stepped back and humorously said to his mother, "Well, Dr. Brooks, I congratulate you on your excellent medical skills. We're very happy with the quality of your work and will recommend you very highly to all our sick and injured friends and associates we find in the meadows."

"Paying friends and associates, I hope? They're the best kind!" exclaimed Rachel as she nodded animatedly.

As everyone was enjoying the moment with laughter, Mia walked over to Cecilia. Not wanting to leave her out of the celebration, Mia also gave her a big hug and thanked her for all her help. Then with her irresistible eyes and more of a plea than a question, Mia asked, "Cecilia, we have a special bond with Rehab, so could you please keep an extra eye on him for us? I feel that he's going to miss us locked up here all night. You know that he's still just a baby? He'll probably be a little scared in here with the other animals that he has never seen before. I'll tell him to be extra good and do everything you tell him to do. Just talk to him very slowly and calmly, and hopefully he'll understand everything you're saying. Okay?"

With an enthusiastic smile, Cecilia quickly replied, "Of course, I will. I'll make sure that he gets nothing but our red-carpet treatment that we reserve only for our most important patients. He'll be placed in our nursery with our other babies. There will be staff members always with him there 24-7. We'll make sure that he's well fed and gets plenty of water and rest and, most of all, tender loving care from the entire staff. And maybe, with your father's permission, on the weekends, when you're not personally caring for Rehab, you and Andrew can help me with some of the other babies we have in the nursery?"

Hey! I'm here in the room too, cried out Rehab. *I'm no baby, and I'm no scaredy-cat either. I'm a teenager. You remember, something that you won't be until July. So stop it with the fearful act. I'm fearless. In fact, the other animals around this joint should be nervous about me being here and should be placed on notice. They better hope that I don't escape from my lockup. Because there is a new sheriff in town, I'm the man around here who can place the hurt on them and put them on the sick call list. Yeah, they're the ones that should be frightened, if not petrified, because there is a canine ninja warrior red fox in the house!*

Mia looked over to Rehab, lowering her head and shoulders and looking right into Rehab's eyes with a scowl on her face. *If you can read my mind, like I can read your mind, I'd quit the rebel act. It's not working for you. Or you can forget about the tender loving care and the great food treatment bit. So I expect you to conduct yourself in a mature and gentlemanly fashion. Do you understand me, mister?*

Hey, buddy, I'm just saying that I'm injured and hungry, not frightened, that's all, replied Rehab. *No need to knock me down and kick me to the curb. So tell me, what's on today's menu?*

"Mia, Mia," Cecilia was still trying to get her attention, "did you hear what I said?"

"That would be great!" Mia and Andrew quickly responded in unison, much like the way they've always had the ability to do. "Can we, Dad? Oh, please say we can! You always said that we need proper training to handle wild animals. Well, here is our big chance!"

"Well, my immediate reaction is, I should probably give this a little more thought. But with your and Andrew's sense of responsibility and being aware of your thirst for knowledge and adventure, I don't see why not. If it can help stop both of you from constantly searching for and finding every sick and injured animal in the wild, here at least I know that you will be safe and under proper supervision. If your mother agrees and if Cecilia is willing to supervise being that she is the one in charge of the nursery unit, I have no objections. But may God help Cecilia!"

Immediately turning to their mother, both Andrew and Mia, without verbally saying a word but with their puppy-eyed look saying a thousand words for them, Rachel replied, "Well, I don't know how I can refuse. Besides, I think the opportunity will be a great education extension and nothing but a positive experience for the both of you to enjoy."

Now both parents faced Cecilia and asked, "Are you sure you're willing to take this on?"

"What about us? We want to help too!" exclaimed Rain Cloud. "We want to volunteer too. Who more than we Native American Indians has a better history and reputation for the caring of animals and the environment? Our tribe considers it courageous when we are compassionate champions of humanity in these causes. Our customs and heritage dictate for us to do so. It gives us a sense of purpose, a focus. It makes us whole. Please don't leave us out." He smiled, bringing small dimples to life at the corners of his mouth.

"Well, since you put it that way, how can I refuse?" replied David. "Did you ever think that you may have a calling as an attorney? But we'll need permission from your parents and Cecilia as well."

"An attorney?" Rain Cloud replied with dancing eyes. "No! But I'm always open to new things to think about!"

As the Musketeers were jumping for joy and giving each other large high fives, Rachel added a big *but* to David's offer. "You must first complete all of your homework and responsibilities at home. You must always, without any exception, follow all instructions carefully by everyone on staff, and never do anything on your own without asking permission first. And of course, White Dove and Rain Cloud must get their parents' permission as David said."

"Not a problem!" Andrew exclaimed exuberantly, with the rest of the Musketeers concurring to all the terms. "Now we can learn the things that excite us the most and do something rewarding at the same time."

"I think this is going to work out just fine for everyone," Cecilia declared. She now attempted to place her arms around the shoulders of as many of the Musketeers as she could, trying to show an obvious consent of approval. "We always seem to be short-handed around here. And with your genuine concerns for the best interests of animals, and with your natural abilities to get them to respond to you, yes, I think you're all going to be a big asset around here. Yes, it's going to be a win-win situation all around."

Mia and Andrew were now noticing that both Star and Simon were standing behind one of the examination tables. With soft and gentle smiles on their angelic faces, they were nodding in unison to indicate their approval and support of the Musketeers' new responsibilities.

With a humorous smirk on her face, Mia suggested, "I think we may still surprise you even more on how helpful we can be and how eager we'll be to learn from the staff. This is a win-win situation for us as well. We'll be doing the things we love to do in helping others, especially when it relates to the animals."

"If the response by Rehab to you is any indication, I think the animals are going to love having you around as much as we will,'" responded Cecilia. "I may have a PhD in animal behavioral and psychology science, as well as in animal husbandry, but I must confess that I learned a thing or two today!"

"Well, now that you're all here," Cecilia stated, addressing the Musketeers, "would you like me to show you around and explain what some of your duties will be? I would especially like to introduce you to the new babies that have arrived since the Christmas party. I'm so excited that you will be working with us here in the nursery!"

"Cecilia, I have another great idea!" cried Mia. "Why don't we ask your daughter Kristin if she would like to join in working with us? She can be another Musketeer!"

"Oh! I think she would love the idea. She's always asking if she can come to work with me. That's if your father thinks that it would be okay? He is the one in charge of the clinic and would have to place his stamp of approval on all our activities."

"I was thinking the same thing," David promptly replied, "and was going to ask you the same question, Cecilia. I know how fond Kristin is of the animals. We should think about initiating a whole new program for them, not only with duties and responsibilities but with rewards and privileges to encourage new membership. We can come up with a board to help create a program and lesson plans, with volunteers from the staff to teach. We should even be able to get the local school boards to jump in and give school credit to students that participate. I'm sure that we can recruit staff throughout the zoo to volunteer to be either on the board or give classes. The more that I think about it, the more that I like the idea. From just the top of your head, Cecilia, what are your immediate thoughts?"

"I love the idea!" exclaimed Cecilia. "Let's do it!"

"Can I be on this board?" asked Rachel. "I want to participate."

"Absolutely!" David said with enthusiasm. "And just think of all the classes that you're so qualified to teach, not only as a doctor but with your skills as a surgeon."

"I think I'm going to call Don to see if he can bring Kristin to the clinic," stated Cecilia. "I'm sure that Kristin will be disappointed if she is not included as a charter member in our program."

"Why don't you do that while I give Dr. Steward a heads-up on what we're planning to do? I'm sure that he will be in agreement and lend us his total support. As our zoo's director, he always wanted us to start some kind of a community outreach program. He even was asking for volunteers to start some kind of an animal awareness program for the community. You might say that this is just what the doctor unknowingly had in mind."

"Well, what do you kids think?" asked Rachel as David and Cecelia stepped out of the room. "Do you like the idea?"

"You have no idea, Mom, how much I love it! And I know that we can get other students from our school to join, even students from other schools in the area. They all don't need to be from Holy Family, right?" asked Mia.

"Right! You heard your father. He said that Dr. Steward wanted participation from the whole community. I think that this program will fit that scenario very nicely," responded Rachael.

"We love the idea too!" chorused the Musketeers enthusiastically. White Cloud added, "I'm sure that everyone would want to be kept up to date not only on the new baby pandas but with all the other animals that live here as well."

"Well, Kristin is on her way. Don said that they should be here within fifteen minutes," offered Cecilia as she and David returned together.

"And I just had a brief word with Dr. Steward on the phone," added David, "and he loves the concept. He said that something like this is exactly what he had in mind. And he's positive that we will not only receive total support from all the zoo's other department heads and their staffs but also expects the total support from the entire board of directors."

As everyone was giving each other high fives, Mia casually walked to the back of the room to stand next to Star while Simon was intrigued with some of the exhibits on the north wall. Mia was still in total awe and amazement of Star with a mixture of wonder and respect. And without saying a word but only thinking to herself, she was asking her, *What do you think*?

I've just received a very warm embrace from God Himself, responded Star. *He continues to be exceptionally pleased with you and your brother, and so am I. Although I'm not so sure about all the playful bantering with your brother*, continued Star, *I think that if I were you, I'd tone that down a little.*

Okay, I'll give it a little more attention and try to behave a little more like a lady in that area, promised Mia, *but that's going to be hard for me. Will you please ask Simon to ask Andrew to do the same thing? It would be even harder if he doesn't reciprocate.*

Suddenly the clinic door swung open, and Kristin ran in. Mia and Kristin hugged each other like they hadn't seen each other in fifteen years, then grabbed Andrew around the neck, dragging him into a group hug.

As Kristin looked up, she recognized White Dove and Rain Cloud. "I remember you two—you beat my mom and me in the three-legged race at the Christmas party."

"Oh yeah, I remember that," stated Rain Cloud, "I'm sorry about that."

"I'm not," said Kristin, "we had a wonderful time! It was only a race, but we want a do-over next year."

"You got it, but don't expect a different result," stated Rain Cloud, looking into her large emerald-green eyes with a smile.

"So what's the new idea?" asked Kristin. "Dad only gave me a limited idea of this new plan because Mom didn't go into any details on the phone. But what I heard in the car ride, I really liked."

"We're staffing our own new group of Musketeers!" shouted Mia.

Kristin started to laugh hysterically. "That's really funny because Dad said that you guys were starting a new Club of Musketeers. My first thought was that we were all going to Disneyland. But he rarely gets anything right."

"Since we're all here, why don't I give everyone the grand tour?" suggested Cecilia. "If it's all right with you, Dr. Brooks?" She was making it sound like more of a plea than a question.

"It sounds good to me," replied David, looking in Rachel's direction. "You didn't have any other plans, did you?"

"Only in collecting my promised salary for working on Rehab," responded Rachel. "I believe it was in the form of an Italian sausage dog and lemonade."

"Never let it be said that I reneged on a deal." David laughed. "Why don't you give everyone the grand tour, Cecilia, and I'll return with Italian sausage dogs and lemonades for everyone."

As David left the clinic, Cecilia faced and addressed the group to start her presentation. "Since everyone has had the opportunity of being here before, let me start by saying welcome again. But before we get started, let me get just a little technical so that you can have a deeper understanding and appreciation of the clinic."

"But before I start, I think this is a great time to make an announcement." Cecilia faced her daughter. "Before I started my shift this morning, I had a meeting at school with a certain principal."

"Was it about me?" Kristin asked. "If so, I didn't do anything wrong. I promise you, I didn't do anything wrong." Bright smiles turned to worried frowns and questing glances furtively exchanged among the Musketeers.

"Why is it that when a parent talks to a school principal, the child always assumes the worst? No, Kristin, you are not in any trouble. In fact, it wasn't even your principal that I was meeting with. It was with Mia's and Andrew's principal that I was talking to. Starting Monday, you'll be attending Holy Family! Someone moved, and there was an opening, and we were first on the waiting list. I know how much you wanted to go to the same school as Mia and Andrew. So now it will happen."

Suddenly Kristin's face changed from concern to exhilaration. "Oh my god, Mother!" Kristin exclaimed. "This is wonderful news." Additional hugs were exchanged. "But, Mom, at Holy Family they wear uniforms. I'll need uniforms."

"Don't worry about uniforms, Kristin," Rachael told Kristin. "New students don't need to wear a uniform during their first week. Besides, you can share a few uniforms with Mia until you can pick up a few of your own. The important thing is you will be attending Holy Family. I'm so pleased! Welcome to the family." The room got a little misty in the excitement, but after a few moments of emotion, the now five Musketeers turned their attention back to Cecilia to start their indoctrination.

"As you entered through the main doors, you could see that there are several corridors leading to a series of other rooms and labs each painted in white. Many have recycled glass tiles glazed with a grayish-brown substance called truffle. Soft reflective LEDs create a soothing cloud of light, and acoustical drop ceilings conceal miles of wires while cameras and movement trackers monitor the passage of all who come here, humans and animals alike.

"Our clinic is one of the largest in the state, if not the largest in the nation. It was built by a bioresearch company that went bankrupt late in construction, and with rare exceptions, the original design is unequaled in the world. It is ideal for what we do here. In fact, it is a veterinarian's dream! We can look out energy-efficient solar tinted windows that no one can look in, and high-performance monitors control the environment, so precisely we have our own customized climates. Dehumidifiers remove moisture from the air before chillers cool it, preventing condensation and an inconvenient phenomenon known as indoor rain. Robots and special sophisticated filters suck in and scrub away pathogens, chemical vapors, and accompanying awful odors.

"This clinic is cleaner than most human health-care clinics. The interior treatment rooms and labs that you will see are ten times more sterile than a hospital or operating room. We are not only one of the premier veterinarian clinics in the world but one of the finest teaching facilities producing the most qualified veterinarians in the country. We have several polysensorial labs and various lecture rooms, and we're equipped with the latest technology dedicated to theoretical and practical training in veterinarian science. We have an extensive virtual and traditional library of over ten thousand volumes of textbooks and training manuals dedicated to veterinarian subjects. We also have the most innovative communication tools, making it possible to consult veterinarians all over the world and of course access to the internet from over 350 computers in the clinic. There isn't a zoo in the world that isn't familiar with Dr. Brooks's work as a large animal surgeon and the eleven books that he has authored. Dr. Brooks receives on an average day over fifty requests from other veterinarians to consult with him on their patients. Without the help from other veterinarians under his tutelage, he would never be able to accommodate these requests and still complete his own work here at the clinic. Now you know why our employees are so proud and honored to work at this facility under the supervision of Dr. Brooks.

"We have the world's largest x-ray and CT scanning equipment known in the profession with the most qualified technicians to operate them, only because we need to accommodate and serve the largest patients in the world. We also have a large staff of diverse doctors and technicians just as you would find at a large medical hospital, like the one where Dr. Rachel Brooks works. We even have pathologists and a team of investigators to determine the cause of death when we lose an animal or when a dead animal is brought to us from outside agencies such as from small animal hospitals and animal shelters. Most people think we just care for and feed our animal friends, but we accomplish much more than that!

"I see that Dr. David Brooks has returned with our lunch, so let's stop here and enjoy it while the food is still hot. Then we'll start with the tour of the clinic."

CHAPTER 5

*A*fter Andrew, David, and Don inhaled second helpings and with contented stomachs all around, Cecilia asked boldly, "Musketeers! Are we all ready for the grand tour?"

"Only if I can go with them!" replied Rachel. "I want to see the new babies!"

"That goes double for me," added Don. "Cecilia is so tired when she gets home that she seldom updates us on the new arrivals. Kristin and I must read about them from the employees' newsletter each month. She's a bad, bad wife." He humorously stared down Cecilia.

"I don't believe that you just said that in front of the children," replied Cecilia. "I would never consider saying anything that mean about you. I just love you too much. No matter how much someone would try to pry out of me or pay me to say anything derogatory about you, I would never say anything to embarrass you. Go ahead, just try it. Try to bribe me. I won't say anything like how you just love to wash and polish that big red fire ambulance at the fire house and how you won't even turn on the lawn sprinklers to wash the dirt off the family car. Go ahead and twist my arm behind my back or pull my front teeth out with a pair of rusty pliers. I won't say anything like that about you. Because I just love you too, too much."

"Mom, you just squealed on Daddy." Kristin laughed with the rest of the Musketeers.

"Oh! Did I, sweetheart? It must have accidentally slipped out!"

"Well, don't beat yourself up about it, Cecilia. Accidents happen every day. So let's get started," Don suggested.

"I want to see babies," Rachel said jubilantly. "David, are you tagging along with us?"

"No thank you, I don't think so. I work here at least five days a week, and being that I'm the publisher of the employees' newsletter, I know only too well what's in it. I think I'll complete a little paperwork while I'm here, and Dr. Steward asked me to drop by his office later if I had time. It'll also give me the opportunity to kick around with him a couple of ideas about our new concept. So there's no reason for Cecilia to hurry through the tour. Go ahead and give them the million-dollar tour versus only the 100,000 dollar one! Maybe Cecilia can show you around inside here first. Then I'll try to catch up with you guys later, and maybe I'll tag along with you so we can all visit the panda habitat together. I know that's where most of your interest is going to be focused. But don't direct all your attention to seeing the pandas so that you lose the opportunity to enjoy all the other exciting things going on all around you. I realize how exciting it is to see the baby pandas for the first time, and we consider ourselves so fortunate to have them here! But give the other babies a chance to steal your hearts! Maybe Cecilia will give you the opportunity to hold a couple of them. Once you do, it's almost impossible to put them down. But please, take your time and learn as much as you can, and I'll be back shortly. I'm sure that Cecilia is going to show you several things that you will find extremely interesting. If it's okay with everyone, I'm going to excuse myself now, but I will be back with you shortly. Is that okay with you, Rachel?"

"Oh, that's fine with me, David," responded Rachel. "I'm sure that Cecilia will not only be extremely informative but also very entertaining. You're leaving us in good hands."

"Dad, we're not interested in just the pandas even though I'm sure we're all wanting to see them. But you know I love all the animals, and I want to see them all!" responded Mia.

"Great! Then we're all on board," replied Rachel, "because I want to see them all too!"

As David left the clinic, Cecilia started her presentation with the Musketeers eager for adventure and anticipating a day to remember.

"I can't think of a thing that I would rather do more than to give the Musketeers a close, up-front, and personal tour of the nursery,"

Cecilia began enthusiastically. "In fact, it's almost feeding time for some of the babies. You'll find that the chimps are always hungry."

"As everyone is aware, the panda babies are not in the clinic's nursery. Those babies are housed with their mother in a new special multimillion-dollar panda exhibit that was constructed especially for their needs. It was created to mimic the exact temperatures and humidity as their native environment in China where they live in real time. In fact, the lights turn on and off at the exact same time as if they were in their natural terrain in China. For all they know, they are in China!"

"So you are playing a trick on them?" asked Don. "They actually think that they are halfway around the world?"

"Yes," replied Cecilia, "we do that so their natural mating, eating, and sleeping habits will not be affected. We don't want to change their normal behavior or confuse them when it comes to the care and feeding of their babies. We need to study and document everything that they do and don't do. Being that they are an endangered species, we need to learn what we can do to raise their birth rate."

"That's very interesting, Cecilia," responded Rachel. "You are not only teaching the guests of the zoo, but the staff is also learning as much as they can! I find that fascinating."

"Yes!" Cecilia continued. "This is one place where we all feel that education is a never-ending task. So on that note, let's continue the tour. To accommodate the bear lovers, we have built their habitats in the same area for the guests' convenience. In fact, as in most zoos in this country, we usually locate the same types of animals together when possible. But our primary goal is keeping ecosystems together. It is felt that when you keep a group of interconnected elements together geographically, in our case plants and animals, the guests can experience those natural communities more vividly. We also design habitats as accurately as possible to their regions in the world, keeping buildings and landscapes in harmony with those regions increases the visual impact and enhances our goals. Our walkways are our way to separate regions and even continents from each other. As you will be able to see, we designed a small park as the transition from one continent to another. This allowed us to keep the great panda bears a

short walk away from our exhibit of the Alaskan brown bear population, which includes our renowned Chester.

"So before we go outside to see our mother panda and discuss
the latest news on her babies, let's walk over and first get familiar
with the babies that we have here in the nursery." With her right
hand extended, Cecilia gestured to an observation window in the
upper portion of the east wall where the enclosed nursery was easily
seen. There were several nursery staff members caring for some of the
newborns, with gleaming natural light filtering in from several of the
one-way glass side windows. "As you can see," Cecilia continued, "the
staff is feeding, cleaning, weighing, and interacting with the babies.
This is where the Musketeers will come in. This is where I envision
we can train all of you to work alongside our regular staff in performing their daily protocols."

"How long do you think it will take for you to train us, Cecilia,
to work with the babies?" asked White Dove.

"You should think of it more as never-ending. You—no, we—as
I said earlier, are always learning new things every day. I'm constantly
learning new things about the wonders of animal behavior and how
to best serve our clients. That's why I love my job so much! I'm so
lucky to have two families. My first love will always remain with
my husband and daughter, but my second family is our wonderful staff and the animals that we care for. That's why this is going
to be such an awesome day for me. I'm going to enjoy both my
families together! But back to the tour, as Rachel knows only too
well, new medical techniques are being developed every day. After
our Dr. David Brooks and the senior staff evaluate them very closely
and give their final approvals, we adopt and implement them. So
your Musketeer training will be like what Walt Disney said about
Disneyland—it will never be completed!"

"I can see where the nursery is because I can see it through
those windows on the far side of the reception area, but I don't see
an entrance to get in. Where are the doors?" inquired Rain Cloud.

"Oh, that's because it's very important to enter first through our
locker room," answered Cecilia with an easy smile. "So just follow
me, and I'll show you why we must enter through there."

Escorting the way to a door clearly marked "Employees Only" then opening a secondary security door leading into the employees' locker room, Cecilia began to explain to the group the protocol on entering the nursery. "We never open the second door without making sure that the first door is completely closed. That way, we can be assured that no animal accidentally escapes from the nursery. Even though they may be babies, always keep in mind that they can be extremely fast for being so young." Cecilia meticulously explained the rationale and the necessity for everyone to always conform to the same policy in order to enter the nursery.

"We need to sanitize ourselves first. So follow my example, and I'll show you what you need to do. Every time, without exception, when we enter the nursery, and before and after the handling of any of the animals, we first need to scrub up by washing our hands and arms with this special antibacterial soap. Then we need to put on a clean white lab coat over our regular clothes or wear hospital scrubs, and finally, over the lab coat or scrubs, a sterilized blue paper smock." Smiling at Rachel, she said, "I know that I'm not teaching you anything that you don't already know, and much better than I do—but please bear with me."

"Oh! I'm not bored," Rachel reassured her. "Everyone here must really understand the importance of these procedures. I can't concur more ardently in their importance! Please continue and pretend that I've never heard this information before. Sanitation is imperative. The last thing we want to do is expose the babies to a virus that they aren't immune to. Don as a fire paramedic and myself as a doctor daily follow these same precautions, precautions that we all need to exercise at all times. We all must take things quite seriously when working with people as well as with fragile animals, such as these beautiful babies." Everyone could clearly see Don nodding in agreement.

"So you're telling us that every time we enter the nursery, we need a new blue paper smock?" responded White Dove. "You must go through a lot of blue smocks." She raised her eyebrows and tucked her hands into the back pockets of her jeans.

"Oh, more than you realize," answered Cecilia. "It also applies when you handle a different baby from a different exhibit. So every time you move from one exhibit to another, you remove your old smock, sanitize your hands and arms again, and put on a new sanitized smock. We need to always be cognizant of this protocol so that we can prevent cross contamination. And I noticed, White Dove, that you put your hands in your back pockets. Everyone must be mindful that once you're sanitized, you can't put your hands in your pockets until you leave the nursery. That's one of the reasons why I prefer the medical scrubs. They have no pockets, and that's the reason why we always have plenty here in the locker room in all sizes."

"Oh my god!" commented Rain Cloud, "that could mean you will need hundreds a month." His eyes blinked, widening in surprise.

"I'd say more like hundreds a week!" replied Cecilia. "We have a large staff of paid personnel and volunteers. You wouldn't want us to lose a baby because someone was lazy about the protocol, would you? I know that your mother could explain the need for this protocol much better than I ever could and the importance of personal hygiene and decontamination before and after touching any of the babies," Cecilia continued as she looked in Rachel's direction.

"Oh! I couldn't have said it any better," responded Rachel. "Time and expense are inconsequential when it comes to the life and safety of one of the animals. Every life is precious. And it's equally important to sanitize yourselves again when you leave the nursery to go home, to protect yourselves, families, pets, and others from the bacteria of the animals that you may have interacted with here in the clinic. These essential protocols give me an idea that I should write a lesson plan tailored to the new Musketeer Program as one of my first duties as a member of the teaching staff."

"That's a great idea, Rachel!" Cecilia responded. "We have an SOP manual, which means standard operating procedures, for our staff, but like all manuals, they need to be constantly updated. As a surgeon yourself, I'm sure that David would love for you to consider our policies and update them."

After everyone thoroughly washed and dried their hands, Cecilia continued her orientation while answering individual questions.

"And like I said, we always wear a white lab coat or scrubs," Cecilia continued as she walked over to a coat rack with an assortment of lab coats on a near wall. "I don't think your husband would mind if you used one of his coats." She pulled off a freshly laundered white lab coat from the rack. "Besides, I see it already has your name embroidered on it." Everyone laughed, reading the embroidered letters: "Dr. Brooks, Medical Staff." "And as for the six of you, including Don, it looks like we have more than enough extra lab coats on our volunteer rack. In fact, you're all old enough to wear one of my extra jackets," she said, noticing that both boys were about the same size as she, and the girls couldn't be more than an inch or two shorter than herself.

"I must admit, I'm excited to be able to share these special babies with you," Cecilia explained, "because as you know, they are not on exhibit to the public and they are so precious to work with. But first, let me introduce you to my assistants in case you don't remember them from the Christmas party."

"This is Dr. Julie Harrison, my right hand here in the nursery and an essential member of our staff. She not only specializes in the primates but also enjoys working with the koala bears. She has earned two PhDs, one in microbiology and another in zoology. She also interacts with the other department heads and supervisors throughout the zoo."

"She has a PhD just like you do, Mom," stated Kristin.

"Yes, in fact, we both graduated from the same university, but four years apart, so we never knew each other until your father and I met her at a zoological convention two years ago in San Diego. She impressed us so much that Dr. Brooks offered her a position here with us on the spot, and thankfully, she accepted. In fact, we stole her from another zoo in the state of Washington that offered her a job there, but before she said yes, we enticed her to accept a job here with us in the nick of time."

"And I have never been so happy in my life," acknowledged Julie. "It was the best decision I ever made! Working here with Cecilia, and with your father," she was looking in the direction of the twins, "and the rest of the staff has been a dream come true for me. My parents along with my two sisters and their families even moved out here so that we could all be together. I even met my husband, Albert, here.

Like your father, he is a veterinarian and works with the rhinoceroses, hippopotamuses, and water buffalos. He's working in the park here today. Maybe you will run into him sometime today working with the animals that he cares for."

"Do all of you work with only certain animals?" asked Rain Cloud.

"No," replied Julie, "most of us are cross-trained to work with several varied species of animals. That way, we can help each other out when needed. It's just that we all have our favorites and may specialize in certain areas."

"Does the rest of your family work here at the zoo?" asked Andrew.

"Yes, several of them," answered Julie. "My sister Stefani, who is two years older than I, and her husband, Larry, both have master's degrees in hematology and work in our lab. She and Larry are two of our experts in blood diseases, along with blood relationships and ancestries of our animals," she commented with a smile. "My oldest sister, Donna, and her husband, Philip, are architects and work at a large architectural firm in the city. My father, George, is a lawyer who knows and sometimes works with your grandparents."

"It's a small world, isn't it," replied Mia, "that your parents know my grandparents?"

"Well, maybe not all that small, but small enough, I guess. It seems more than a coincidence that our friends and family can and do know each other in the normal course of their lives."

"Can we come back later and work with you and the monkeys?" asked White Dove. "And maybe even with the koala bears?"

"I would love that! I have several babies that I feel you would love to meet," replied Julie. "Maybe you can come back around their feeding time. Two hands never seem to be enough!"

"You can count on us, Dr. Harrison. We would love to feed the baby monkeys!" the group all agreed.

As Cecilia continued her orientation, she would periodically stop and kick around some ideas that would come to the top of her head and ask for the group's response. Several promising ideas came from the group as they worked themselves throughout the clinic.

Even Dr. Harrison thought it was a terrific idea for an outreach program and wanted to volunteer and participate. She was eager to contribute her ideas to the new Musketeer concept.

Though it was only in its infancy, the concept did not lack in support and motivation from the staff as the group moved from station to station.

"So we can count you in as a staff employee to help on this project, Julie?" asked Cecilia.

"I would love to," replied Julie. "I think that it would be a joy not only for the kids but for all of us who work here at the zoo. Count me in! And please don't forget to come back so you can help me feed the baby monkeys and the two koala babies their milk formulas."

"That's a deal," answered Mia. "We'd love to hold the babies! They're all so cute!"

"And if you all remember correctly from the Christmas party, Julie's sister Stefani has two children—Sydney, who is eleven, and James, who is twelve. I'm sure that they would also love to become Musketeers. Do you know, Julie, if either Stefani or Larry is working in the lab today?" asked Cecilia.

"No, both are off today, and they were planning on going to visit with our parents for the day. But there is no doubt in my mind that both Sydney and James would be interested in becoming Musketeers. Larry and I will catch up with them for dinner this evening. May I ask them to join the program? But I can tell you now that yes, they will be interested!"

"Absolutely," Rachel quickly answered. "The more, the merrier. I just love how this idea is growing! I'm getting more and more excited! All the adults need to sit down and start a plan. Maybe David and I can host a dinner party at our home and brainstorm."

"I'm always up for a good dinner," replied Don. "I can always think better on a full stomach!"

"Don, you just wolfed down two Italian sausage dogs and a gallon of lemonade! How can you be thinking about food so soon?"

"That was more than five minutes ago, and a man must eat. Besides, I'm still a growing boy, and I need my protein," exaggerated Don.

"That would be good," replied Cecilia, "but unfortunately, you've been growing horizontally instead of vertically."

"That's cruel, Cecilia, that's just so cruel. Are you implying that I'm getting to be a little overweight? I'm not overweight per the stringent fire department standards. I'm just wearing a fat shirt, that's all. I haven't gained more than two pounds during the fourteen years that we've been married."

"Well then, you wouldn't mind trying on the suit that you got married in?" asked Cecilia.

"No, I wouldn't. It's just that it went out of style and I donated it to Goodwill," answered Don. "And what happened about only saying favorable things about each other in front of the children? How soon we forget."

"The Goodwill, how convenient," responded Cecilia. "I'm sure they will find someone small enough to look quite handsome in it, and about saying only favorable things about each other, I was only saying that the few extra pounds you put on gives me more to love about you. In fact, you would make a great Santa Claus next year, and you know how much Santa Claus is loved. You see how favorable I was." She began to reintroduce the rest of the nursery staff to the Musketeers. They all could clearly recall meeting each other and had only the fondest memories of the holiday adventure.

"Mom, why are these babies here in the nursery instead of being with their mothers?" asked Kristin, looking with concern at her mother. "I always thought that babies were best cared for by their biological mothers, like the way you take care of us when we're sick."

"Normally, that's true," replied Cecilia. "Some of the babies' mothers are here in the nursery with them. But there are always exceptions. It could be that for some reason a baby was unintentionally separated or abandoned by its mother. It could be that for some reason the mother couldn't care for it because one of them became too sick or injured where it might be life-threatening. Sometimes babies are sent to us from smaller zoos or rehab centers because we are better staffed or experienced to handle their particular needs. Or like your fox Rehab, some caring person finds an injured animal and then brings it to us to nurse it back to health. There can be several good reasons, but those are the most common."

"So then not all the babies in the zoo are here?" asked Rain Cloud, with the sound of concern in his voice and a hard, focused look in his eyes. "Some are with their mothers?"

"Of course, most are with their mothers! Could you imagine if we had to house all the babies in the zoo here in the nursery, especially the larger animals, such as giraffes, water buffalos, hippopotamuses, rhinoceros, elephants, etc.? Especially having to tolerate the odors of the camels?"

Everyone, without exception, started to laugh hysterically, especially Andrew, closing his eyes and pinching his nose closed with his right hand to indicate experiencing an extremely noxious odor. "I can remember vividly one Saturday coming in from home with Dad because a camel was sick. He had the worst odor I've ever smelled in my life, so I'm not interested in working with camels again!"

"That can be an unpleasant problem," agreed Cecilia, "but when the health of an animal needs to be addressed, we always accept any challenge necessary for the comfort of the animal."

For the next several hours, while Dr. David Brooks was meeting in Dr. Steward's office discussing the merits of the program, Cecilia and the staff introduced every baby in the nursery to everyone while fulfilling their every fantasy by letting them hold and help with their care and feeding.

The type and size of each baby dictated what type and amount of food each received. Everything was either weighed on a scale or measured by measuring spoons, including their nutritional supplements. All facts, observations, and health conditions were meticulously recorded in each baby's personal medical folder. Nothing was ever left to chance or memory.

The Musketeers, as well as Rachel and Don, could not have been more pleased or excited to participate in the experience. It was not only fulfilling but gave them all a profound sense of community, and no one realized the time passing or even gave it a thought.

"I'm terribly sorry that I'm so late. The time just got away from me!" David said apologetically as he entered the nursery. "Paperwork,

paperwork, paperwork! It seems like the zoo runs mostly by paperwork. Paperwork that is both extensive and mind-numbing! And I had an enjoyable conversation with Dr. Steward. He is completely on board with the new concept of the Musketeer Program. The best part was that I initiated the appropriate forms to get the program started and had human resources make all you volunteer IDs and name badges for your lab coats."

"Late! I even forgot that you were gone," replied Mia, then stopping to think about what she had just said. "Dad, I'm so sorry. I apologize. I didn't mean it like it sounded." She gave her father a hug. "What I meant was that we have been so engrossed in what we've been doing that I didn't realize you weren't here."

"No problem, Princess!" David answered jovially. "No offense taken." He returned her hug. "It just goes to show how entertaining Cecilia and the babies can be."

"Unfortunately, I can't take any credit for it. It's the babies!" replied Cecilia. "Once you start working with them, your mind is totally oblivious to anything else."

"Well, who's ready to go outside to see the new panda habitat?" asked David, knowing full well that everyone was going to take him up on his offer.

All hands immediately shot in the air as Don answered verbally, "Time is a-wasting!"

As David walked the group to the panda area, traversing back and forth through a maze of animal exhibits and large clusters of park guests, he started giving them a little background information on what they were about to see for themselves. Unfortunately, because he was recognized by several of the guests, he and Cecilia were answering a series of questions imposed on them. Zoo guests were asking directions to particular animal exhibits. What did certain animals eat? He was even asked by one adult guest if they had any whales on exhibit. He just smiled and told him, "Sir, this is a zoo, not an aquarium. We have no sea mammals or fish on display. I wish we did, but we made a deal with the city's aquarium across town that, if they didn't display any tigers, lions, elephants or bears, we wouldn't have any whales, sea lions, or fish."

Everyone started to laugh, even the guest who was the butt of the joke. "Well now, that makes a lot of sense to me now that I think about it, Doc," the guest replied, still laughing at himself. "We also came to visit the pandas, if that is a safe question to ask."

"As a matter of fact, that is exactly where we're headed, to give a private tour, so why don't you and your family join us?" David suggested.

"Oh! We would love to," replied the guests' wife. "Are you going to be the tour guide, Dr. Brooks? We recognize you from your speaking engagements and from numerous newspaper articles about the splendid work you and your staff do here at the zoo. I didn't actually think that we would have a chance to meet you and your family. If you have any time, I would love to hear more about your Zoological Society program here at the zoo. We would love to become members."

"Oh! I would love to explain all the benefits you would be able to take advantage of as members of the zoo. First, you would have free access to the zoo 364 days a year—we are only closed on Christmas Day. We have individual packages, but for you, obviously, I would recommend the family package deal. You would receive our monthly *Zoo News* publication. There are always several articles written by our staff, including articles from our research scientists with color photos updating you on an array of interesting topics. Articles featuring the animals of the month along with the zoo's new baby arrivals. And one night a month, we reserve a 'members-only night' with special tours throughout the zoo, on which your questions are answered by our highly trained staff."

"And," interjected Mia, "on 'members-only nights,' they have lectures in the auditorium, not only by the zoo's staff but also by special invited national experts. You really get to learn a lot on these nights, especially when it's my dad's turn to speak."

"I would quite agree," answered the guest's wife. "I'm a teacher at my children's elementary school, and I heard your father speak there one day on tortoises and other reptiles. And he brought in several beautiful specimens as visual aids. Your father captured the interests and hearts of both students and teachers alike. We're all looking forward to having him back on campus."

As the small group continued their journey to the panda habitat, Dr. Brooks ran into many other guests who also had questions to ask until their small group grew to well over a hundred before they reached their destination.

"Probably no animal in history has gone so far toward capturing the hearts of human beings as the plumpish, clumsy, but lovable-looking creatures called the Giant Panda. Many debates have taken place as to whether pandas are really bears or are in fact giant raccoons, which they also resemble in many aspects. But after several genetic analyses that have been recently carried out, zoologists have determined that the giant panda is closer genetically to bears, whereas the red panda is closer to raccoons. Later, we'll visit the red pandas, but we'll leave that for another day."

"Are the red pandas kept near the giant pandas?" asked Kristin.

"No, sweetheart," answered Cecilia. "They're housed in a totally different area of the zoo near the raccoons. We'll be able to see them on another day, okay?"

"That's fine with me. Now that we've started the Musketeer Program, we'll be back over and over again."

"That's right," answered David as he continued talking as he walked.

"What's this about a Musketeer Program?" asked the schoolteacher. David then gave a small description of the future concept of the program and suggested exchanging contact information, so Cecilia could get back to her and some of the others in the group about further details.

"Once I get back to school and talk about this program with the other teachers, I'm quite confident that you will have more students interested in this Musketeer Program than you anticipate!" answered the teacher. "I'm very much in support of it, as I'm sure the entire school board will be. The community needs more of these types of outreach programs."

David thanked the teacher for her support, promised to forward zoo literature once it was printed, and exchanged business cards with her. Then several others who also wanted more information on the program were reaching for their wallets and business cards. It was evident that there was going to be tremendous interest by parents and their children in the Musketeer Program! Trying to get back on track, David returned his focus to their journey to the panda habitat and occasionally looked back to see that his crowd of spectators was increasing by leaps and bounds before he could reach their destination. He decided that he was going to need a PA system to accommodate his audience and used his radio to order one from the audio department.

"As I'm sure that you are all aware, these pandas are on a long-term loan to the zoo from the Republic of China. Since there are so few captive pandas, the Chinese government has officially banned hunting them and only rarely permits their export. They control the panda population as efficiently as humanly possible to protect and ensure their existence in the wild for all future generations to enjoy. They live mostly in remote and almost inaccessible parts of the eastern Himalayan Mountains close to the Chinese-Tibetan border. Baby pandas are very small when born, with a weight of around five ounces. Now there are going to be many things that you are going to want to learn about pandas, but there is no way that I can explain everything you'll like to know about them in one tour. But I'll try to explain as much as I can today, okay?"

David continued discussing and answering questions from the group for the next two hours. He provided panda facts on both the adults as well as their babies. He discussed how pandas are named, how they mature, their size and rate of growth. He talked about their diet of bamboo and wild plants.

Mia asked how long pandas live. David's response was, "The giant panda typically lives around twenty years in the wild and, fortunately for us, over thirty years in captivity. The oldest captive so far was a female named Jia Jia, who died in 2016 at the age of thirty-eight."

"So they live longer in zoos than they live in the jungle?" asked Andrew.

"That's right, son, because they don't have any predators in zoos. They get all they want of their favorite foods, plus added nutritional supplements, free health care, and plenty of friends to come and visit, wishing only the best for them. The same goes for all our other animals that live here in the zoo. They all live longer and healthier lives in captivity. The staff throughout the zoo considers them like family and gives them all TLC. You might say like the same care and treatment you and Mia get at home."

Suddenly, all the night lights on timers started to light up, and David immediately looked at his wristwatch. "Oh my goodness, it's already 6:00 p.m.! I think we should now call it a day and think about what's for dinner."

As the small crowd moaned its disappointment in unison and started to break up and dissipate in all directions, Mia pleaded, "Do we have to, Dad? There is so much more that I want to see and learn about, and the zoo stays open until 10:00 p.m. on Saturdays." Hoping that Mia's plea for a continuation would prevail, the group held its breath for the answer.

"Well, I guess we can call off dinner if no one's hungry," David said, attempting to sound serious and trying to create his best face showing unconcern for food, looking at no one in general. "Should we call off dinner and continue the tour?" He again looked at his watch, suggesting in jest, "I have the keys to the place, so we can continue to your heart's content."

The parents, having more rational minds, began to realize that they did in fact need to consider feeding their families and should continue this awesome adventure at another time. Hesitantly, while stammering, the children acquiesced after being promised that they would return to continue their quest sooner rather than later.

"Now that you mentioned it, Dad," Andrew now comically entered the conversation, slowly looking up, then closing his eyes, moving his head slowly from side to side, "I see this vision of hot baked pizza, just freshly out of the oven. Now, I see this Italian chef and smell the aroma of freshly grated Parmesan cheese as he sprinkles it gently over the center of the pizza. Then he tenderly hands it to a courteous waitress who promptly serves it steaming hot to our table."

"Yes! Pizza for dinner is my vote," proclaimed Mia, thinking quickly.

"I'll second that motion," answered Cecilia, laughing, hoping for an invitation, as she was nodding energetically.

Even the other guests enthusiastically responded that they too would enjoy a hot pizza on a chilly night and were asking for suggestions for good Italian restaurants.

"That works for me!" declared Rachel. "As much as I hate to leave these adorable animals, I can hear my stomach rumbling for groceries. I think we should call White Rose and Running Bear, tell them that we're on our way for dinner, and if they would be interested in Italian, have them join us at Dominic's." Now she looked directly at Cecilia. "And I'm just presuming that you, Kristin and Don, would be joining us, because I wasn't going to accept no as an answer!"

"Are you kidding me?" answered Cecilia laughing. "You think I'm entertaining a death wish? Dominic's is Don's and Kristin's favorite restaurant. And I love their lasagna."

"Well, I guess that settles that! Italian dinner it is," replied David, completely satisfied with everyone's reactions. "Dominic's always sounds good to me."

"Sounds great to us!" responded the Musketeers with their thumbs high in the air. "But we better order extra for Noah." Andrew laughed. "If he smells pizza on our breath when we get home and we don't have anything for him, we'll all be sleeping in the doghouse tonight."

"I think I'll call Joseph and Cynthia now to see if I can tear them away from stamps and quilts and meet us at Dominic's for dinner." Rachel was directing her comments to White Dove and Rain Cloud.

"Wait, Dad! We can't leave until we say good night to Rehab. He's going to think that we have abandoned him," protested Mia.

"Okay," replied David, "we need to pass the clinic to get back to the parking lot anyway. We'll all stop to say good night to him before we leave."

Mia noticed that Simon winked at her in approval, and Star placed her hand on Mia's shoulder to comfort her. Mia was surprised that she could feel the pressure and warmth of Star's hand. She looked up and greeted Star's smile with one of her own. Mia was so happy and felt so secure and safe knowing that she had such a close relationship with her guardian angel.

"Why don't you take Kristin in your car, Don, and go directly to Dominic's?" Cecelia suggested. "I need to go back to the clinic to pick up my purse and my car in the employee's parking lot. I'll meet you at Dominic's, okay?"

"That's okay with me," responded Don. "If we're a little late, it's because I need to stop for gas."

"We'll walk back together to the clinic, Cecilia," instructed David. "I need to pick up a couple of things from my office while the kids can say good night to Rehab. And then we'll all meet at the restaurant."

"And I can call White Dove's and Rain Cloud's parents to see if they are free and interested in Italian tonight," contributed Rachel.

As they entered the clinic, the twins saw that Rehab noticed them immediately as they were walking in his direction. His head jerked up and his eyes were focused on their hands.

Okay, where is all this tender loving care you were talking about earlier? I haven't felt any TLC since you left me here alone hours ago with nothing to eat, Rehab directed his comments to Mia.

Mia shook her head no, she wasn't buying it, and whispered, "What are you taking about! You were never left alone. I see a whole staff of personnel here. And are you saying that you had nothing to eat since we left? And what were you expecting? Someone to tuck you in and kiss you good night?"

Well, that would have been nice, answered Rehab. *Foxes need to be loved and appreciated too. And okay, they did feed me, and I have to be honest, it was pretty good grub. There just wasn't enough of it, and I didn't get any dessert.*

"Dessert! Foxes don't eat dessert!" answered Mia. "Are you trying to tell me that you have pastry chefs in the woods serving you chocolate cake and pumpkin pie?"

Of course, we eat dessert! I prefer berries, strawberries, blueberries, raspberries, and yes, I like pumpkin when I can find it, answered Rehab.

"Okay," replied Mia, "I didn't think about fruit. I know that they have all sorts of fresh fruit and vegetables here in the clinic. The monkeys are given fruit, as well as the turtles and other reptiles. Now that I think about it, a lot of animals are given fresh fruit. I just didn't think of it as dessert. So Andrew and I will find you some and bring it to you. I'll even kiss you good night on the nose, but no more complaining out of you. We have already told Cecilia that you are going to behave yourself and be extra good, and in return, she promised to take extra loving care of you and give you the royal treatment. Don't make liars out of us! We'll come back as soon as our parents let us. But the last thing I want to hear from Cecilia is that you were uncooperative, up to mischief, or being a hooligan to the other animals. Do we understand each other? Rehab? Yes, I'm talking to you, mister! Do we understand each other?"

Yah, yah, I understand you. I'll be the poster boy of civility. When you come back, the rest of the residents here in the clinic will probably vote me in for mayor. So don't be late for my swearing-in and inaugural address and ball! Rehab shouted out as everyone left the clinic for Dominic's.

CHAPTER 6

$\mathcal{A}$s the group reached the employees' parking lot, David looked over to his assigned space and noticed that mysterious blue van still occupying his assigned parking space. "Cecilia, do you recognize that blue van in my parking space?" David asked.

"No," she replied, "no, I don't. I don't even think I've ever seen it before. How long has it been there?"

"I'm not sure," answered David. "It was there when I arrived this morning. I was going to inform security, but I got so caught up with the Musketeer scenario and the tour that I forgot to follow up. Maybe I'll call them on my cell on the way to Dominic's."

During the drive to Dominic's Ristorante, there was total confusion in the vehicle as everyone was talking over each other with ideas about what to order at the restaurant. Rain Cloud was even making the case and trying to convince everyone in the car that he could taste his dinner from the back seat. He went so far as to say that he was actually experiencing how his taste buds were talking to him and making him salivate. Andrew, not to be outdone by Rain Cloud, was talking about how his sense of smell was so powerful that he could smell the Italian aromas emanating from the restaurant from four blocks away. White Dove was taking about how she was already experiencing eating her fourth slice of pizza. All David could talk about was spaghetti and sausage. Rachel was commenting on how freshly baked bread always made her heart respond emotionally with song, and she didn't care what anyone ordered as long as she got to taste a couple of bites from each different dish at the table.

As David was pulling into the parking lot of Dominic's, he noticed Don in his rearview mirror right behind him. As both families were exiting their vehicles, Don was clearly heard saying, "And with plenty of sausage and pepperoni," as he ran his tongue around the outside of his lips with his eyes as big as a frog's.

"With extra cheese and double the mushrooms," Cecilia replied as her lively eyes started to dance.

"Mom, you can't order pizza from the parking lot," Kristin stated, after which the group started to laugh hysterically. "You have to wait until we're seated at our table!"

"Are those the house rules, or are you giving me a hard time because I didn't let you take home one of the baby turtles?"

"No, Mom, do you see a waitress on roller skates out here in the parking lot to take your order?" answered Kristin.

"Maybe not, but it does sound like a clever idea. Why don't you look for a suggestion box inside and submit it? Although I do smell Italian garlic bread with Parmesan cheese."

"Well, if you think it smells good from the parking lot, just wait until you taste it!" exclaimed Rachel. "Do you know Maria?"

"No, I don't, but I do know who she is. Normally, Don just picks up takeout on his way home from work, and we eat at home with our shoes off," answered Cecilia.

"Then I'll have to introduce you. Maria supervises all the baking. She makes the best Italian garlic bread I've ever tasted, and there is nothing else even in the ballpark. She also is known for her variety of hors d'oeuvres, such as prosciutto wrapped around melon or figs and so many others. Oh! If you haven't tried their vast selections of ricotta crostini, then you have lived a deprived life! I can see that we're going to have to broaden your horizons tonight."

The entire Brooks family nodded in agreement as they all continued to laugh, and David led the way to the entrance.

As each of the Musketeers was pushing and shoving, trying to be the first through the door, and Rachel was pleading for a little more decorum, she was able to hear clearly: "*Buona sera* [good evening], Dr. Brooks. *Benvenuto* [welcome]!" Luigi exclaimed enthusiastically and distinctly with his enormously obvious Italian accent.

Walking briskly over to the Brooks family as they entered the restaurant's reception area, Luigi greeted them at the door. Luigi gave each and every member of the family a large traditional Italian hug.

"As always, *il piacere è tutto mio* [the pleasure is totally mine] to see you and *tu tala tua famiglia* [your whole family], for you have no idea how much it *ravvivare* [brightens up] my day to no ends to see you coming through my humble front door!"

"Oh! I don't think it's any more of a pleasure for you than it is for us being here," replied Mia as she tried to imitate Andrew's earlier antics by gently closing her eyes and raising her head, taking a slow, deep breath, enjoying the delicious aromas wafting from the kitchen.

Everyone could not stop laughing as Mia portrayed herself as a culinary epicurean. "You have always been such an intelligent and beautiful child, Mia! I have always considered you and Andrew as two of my own," responded Luigi appreciatively.

Always reserving the best table for special guests, Luigi addressed everyone at once. "Please, your favorite table just happens to be free. Let me seat you, and then I'll let Maria and the *bambinos* [kids] know that you're here. They will be very *contento* [happy] to see each of you."

"Luigi," Rachel replied, "there will be two more at our table. Congressman Yanez and his wife the mayor will be joining us."

"Oh! This is no *problema* [problem]. *Antonio, stiamo andando ad avere bisogno di diverse sedie supplementari* [Anthony, we are going to need additional chairs]. Chairs are a-coming up. It is always a good thing to see the good congressman and his *attraente* [lovely] wife the mayor. This is even more good. The sun is very bright today," answered Luigi in his very strong, broken English, along with his entertaining Italian accent.

Luigi then quickly disappeared through two large hand-carved swinging doors leading into the kitchen. As quickly as Luigi disappeared, a young man's head with light-brown hair cut ruthlessly short over a sturdy square face appeared. As he looked through the same doors that Luigi used to enter the kitchen, this young man tried his best to remain incognito. His lively eyes the color of chestnuts sharpened and focused on Mia. *Oh! She is so adorable*, he thought to himself. *I need to think of something special to do for her. I need her to notice me this time.*

But realizing that he wasn't carrying anything, he immediately made an about-face and reentered the kitchen. Ten seconds later, he reappeared briskly carrying a large tray containing two large baskets, each one containing Italian bread sticks and freshly baked garlic Italian bread, buttered, and topped with a special family Italian seasoning and Parmesan cheese. Also, on the tray was their well-known house seasoned oil and vinegar for bread dipping, with an extra dish of freshly blended garlic butter. He so wanted desperately to impress. His every gesture expressed a dignity and love for his work.

Rachel, seeing Luigi's son approaching their table, said, "Cecilia, please allow me to introduce you to Andrea. He's Maria's and Luigi's son. He also attends Holy Family with the kids but one grade ahead of them. And don't let his boyish good looks fool you. This young man is a great up-and-coming chef in his own right and is indispensable to his parents in the running of the kitchen." Andrea's face now became keen and narrow and a little flushed, showing a little embarrassment from the compliment in the presence of Mia but hoping that she was paying attention to her mother. As he started to smile again, he was unable to prevent a display of two small dimples at the corners of his mouth while focusing on Mia with his peripheral vision. He didn't want to appear to be looking directly at the girl of his dreams.

"Well, it's a pleasure to meet you, Andrea," Cecilia said as she extended her right hand to him.

"Oh! The pleasure is all mine, *signorina* [young lady], I assure you." As Andrea set his tray on the table, he gently took Cecilia's hand with both of his, lowered his head in reverence, and respectfully responded, "Any friend of the Brooks family is most certainly welcome as a friend of the Dominic family." Andrea spoke in a beautiful smooth voice, with a hint of an Italian flavor from the old country, although he had only visited Italy twice in his life to visit his grandmother, uncle, and two cousins.

"Oh my goodness!" exclaimed Cecilia. "Not only good-looking but also so charming. Do you also speak Italian?"

Without saying a word, Andrea started to blush like a ripe Italian tomato and then answered, "But of course, *signorina*. Our whole family is fluent in Italian."

David immediately stood as he observed Maria and two young girls approaching their table. Rachel nodded in Andrew's and Rain

Cloud's direction, indicating that they too should follow David's example in standing to show respect for the approaching ladies. Andrew started to stand, nudging Rain Cloud's arm to indicate for him to also stand. Rain Cloud was first startled but, after noticing David and Don standing, understood the gesture and stood.

"Oh, Dr. Brooks…" There was genuine joy in Maria's voice. "I was so happy to hear from my husband that all of you came for dinner. We never see enough of you."

After politely excusing himself, Andrea returned to the kitchen.

Rachel addressed Maria, "Please let me introduce you to one of David's colleagues, Dr. Cecilia Shaw, and her husband, Don, and their lovely daughter Kristin. And these two beautiful young ladies are Anna, who is Maria's and Luigi's daughter, and Katarina, their niece from Tuscany, Italy. Of course, all the kids know each other from school."

"It's such a pleasure to have you and your family with us, Dr. Shaw," Maria replied. "It's always a joy to meet any of Dr. Brooks's friends." After Maria exchanged her usual big hugs and kisses with Rachel, David, and the twins, she asked everyone to please be seated.

After the pleasantries were exchanged, Andrea returned through the doors carrying a tray with nine glasses of water, then immediately did an about-face, and again returned to the kitchen, talking to himself. *How dumb can I get? I must concentrate more on what I'm doing. It's important that I get everything just right!* His eyes shrank, blinked, and then transformed as he told himself that he needed his mind to refocus. He didn't know when he might get another opportunity.

This time retrieving nine Waterford crystal glasses from the store room, he filled each with sparkling water instead of the ordinary bottled water that was customarily served. He then topped each glass with a thin slice of fresh lemon and a sprig of mint, hoping that Mia would notice the extra effort. Andrea then immediately returned to the Brooks's table as quickly as he could, and of course, he served Mia first.

Andrea had never felt confident while in the company of Mia, always feeling awkward and off balance. He never knew exactly what to say or do in her company, although he had always been considered by everyone to be very articulate. He felt awkward and got tongue-tied whenever he tried to talk to Mia. Apparently, this affliction only surfaced with her; he never had any problems talking to anyone else nor with any of the other girls at school, only with Mia. But of course, as Andrea started again talking silently to himself, *no other girl in the world has such big, beautiful, dark-blue eyes, with golden blond hair, and the face of an angel like Mia.* As he trained his eyes on hers, he lightly brushed his fingers through his hair and felt the tension at the base of his neck. She was magnificent; she could stop his heart! He then tilted his head to change the angle of the natural light. With the light now glowing behind her hair, in his mind and heart he knew that even Michelangelo couldn't perfectly sculpt that glorious face on any piece of marble.

Hearing his father, Andrea again returned to reality and stopped his daydreaming about Mia.

"Andrea…" Luigi looked at his son. "Could you please get us *quattro* [four] wineglasses, and *tre* [three] pitcher of our best root beer for everyone else?" Then turning his attention to Dr. Brooks and displaying a bottle of wine, Luigi continued, "David, I must share with you a new shipment of *vino* [wine] we just received from my *fratello* [brother] Francesco, Katarina's *padre* [father]. As you know, he manages our *famiglia's* [family's] vineyards in Tuscany, which inarguably produces the finest *vinos* [wines] in all of Italy. But this crop of grapes, I tell you honestly, David, this crop produced such a Chianti that even exceeded all of our expectations."

"We'd love to taste it," responded David, "but we'll need six glasses if we're going to share. Do you think it is possible for you and Maria to take a few minutes to enjoy it with us? In fact, it has been such a long time that we shared a full meal together. Do you think it would be possible now? It would be such a pleasure to have a relaxing dinner with you and the family and catch up, and it would give us the opportunity to share our friends with you."

"But of course, my friend," Luigi responded with a smile on his round but distinguished face. "Anna, my lovely dove, *due* [two] more wineglasses, *per favore* [please]. And, Andrea, *ancora un po di sedie* [some more chairs]."

"And three more root beer glasses?" Anna replied, hoping for an invitation to join the Musketeers, as her shapely nose wrinkled.

"But of course, the three of you need a break. Besides, I don't want to be reported for violating any child labor laws," answered her father, grinning and enjoying his own joke. Then he noticed Cynthia (White Rose) and Joseph (Running Bear) entering the restaurant. "Anna, *due* more wineglasses. And, Andrea, ask Antonio *stiamo andando as avere bisogno di sedie supplementari, per favore*. And I'll get more *vino*. I see a party tonight in the heavens."

Just behind White Rose and Running Bear, Dr. Brooks noticed several other families entering the restaurant whom he recognized, many of them from the group at the zoo to whom he had just given the tour. He waved at them as they were being seated throughout the restaurant, and he told himself that, when time permitted, he would walk over to each of their tables and thank them again for visiting the zoo, and also for taking his advice in trying Dominic's. He was certain that they would be impressed by the excellent food and the quality of the service if this was their first time to experience the restaurant.

White Rose was a trim woman with sable-colored hair waving back from a quite lovely face. Running Bear was slightly taller than average height, slim built, almond brown eyes, with a quick smile and plenty of charm. He was so loved by his constituents that he had hardly any competition for his US Congress seat in his last five elections and was easily recognized in the community. As for White Rose, she rarely had an opponent running against her in her four terms as mayor and was regarded as one of the most accomplished mayors in the state.

Andrea quickly disappeared through the kitchen doors and ran upstairs to the family's spacious living quarters to wash up and change into a not only clean but a new white chef's jacket that he was saving for such an occasion. He needed to be spit-polished for this special circumstance, as he started humming to himself while grooming.

"Oh, look! There are Michael and Brenda with the kids." David waved to get the attention of the sheriff and his wife entering through the doors, with Daniel and Jennifer tagging behind.

"Andrea, *ancora un po di sedie per favore*. Anna, more root beer and glasses. We're going to need to move some more tables together," exclaimed Luigi. "This is a very good day!"

"Let us all help," suggested David, as all the males stood and started to move tables together.

"Such a wonderful day," bellowed Luigi in his distinguished tenor voice. "What a wonderful day!"

Andrea, upon returning to the table, did not return with the standard stemware and pitchers that were normally used. Why, of course not! He would never consider anything for Mia other than their best crystal and their finest bone china. Why, he even polished and set their table with sterling silver—stainless steel would never meet his standards, not for Mia! He was very methodical in his work, on how he set the table, every spoon, fork, and knife in its proper place.

Maria, noticing Andrea's extra effort, winked at him showing her approval for his extra attention to detail. As everyone was enjoying their beverages and engrossed in pleasant conversation, David realized that they had forgotten to order their pizza. "Not to worry, my friend," Luigi responded with a large smile, which then immediately turned to laughter, "Luigi, he knows what you like, the house special pizza with extra cheese and mushrooms. I also *prendersi la libertà* [took the liberty] to order for you just a few extra side dishes that I'm sure you will enjoy."

So as they were waiting for their feast, they began to talk enthusiastically about the activities of the day, including a report of the injured fox and the formation of the new Musketeer Program. They discussed their exciting adventures of working with the babies in the nursery and seeing the new giant panda exhibit. Everyone was interested in all the details—how the listeners would have enjoyed being there themselves! Andrea, Anna, and Katarina were all in agreement that they also wanted to be included as Musketeers.

This was the first opportunity that Cecilia had to lean over and ask Rachel about the beautiful display of a large Dutch oven sitting over an artistically designed open fireplace located in the center of the dining room. "Rachel, what a beautiful fireplace that is in the center of the room! Do you know anything about its significance? It seems to me that it has a story to tell."

"Yes, the Italians are passionate about their food, where it comes from, and how to prepare it. Here at Dominic's, their menu can take you on a culinary journey through the regions of Italy with their specialty dishes. The family very seldom takes shortcuts. They treat their food as an extension of the way they live: social, approachable, and above all, surrounded by family and the people they love," answered Rachel. "Italians learn to appreciate food when they are young children, and eating is one of the major pleasures of the day, no matter what the day of the week or time of the year. Fine dining to them is eating at home surrounded by friends and family. The kettle or cauldron, or what the kids and I like to call a witch's kettle because we are always able to find a delicious witch's brew potion in it, is actually full of the soup of the day. When you order a main course, you are entitled to help yourself to a bottomless cup of the soup to your heart's content. Let's ask Andrea about it and what's in it today. He knows about every innuendo of its significance."

"It is so beautifully displayed," commented Cecilia. "I love the brick barbecue base and granite countertop. And what a beautiful stainless-steel hood. So what you are saying is we can just help ourselves to the soup bowls and spoons on the countertop and ladle soup to our heart's content?"

"That's exactly what I'm saying!" Turning to Andrea, she asked, "Andrea, would you please tell Cecilia about the kettle of soup at the fireplace?"

Even though there was the typical room full of voices, the clattering of dishes being picked up by the busboys, the scraping of chairs upon the Italian tiled floor, Andrea attempted to answer the request. "Oh, soups are such an important part of Italian cuisine. We serve a variety of soups every day, but we always have a soup of the day in the center of the room. Our soups vary in consistency from light and delicate to a hearty main meal soup. Unlike the French with their elaborate puréed soups, the Italians prefer to let the natural flavors of their raw ingredients speak for themselves. Texture is always apparent—Italians rarely serve smooth soups. Some may be partially puréed, but the identity of the ingredients is never entirely obliterated. As I'm sure you know, each region of Italy produces its own characteristic cuisine. That goes double for their soups. Minestrone is known worldwide and consists of a variety of tastes, flavors, and aromas of which few other countries can boast. It is our best seller because it's bursting with flavors. Each region in Italy produces its own characteristic recipe for it. Probably the best-known version comes from Milan, where my mother is from. My father is from Tuscany, and the recipe is a little different.

"Regardless of the version, we're passionate here about its preparation, and we expect and demand only the best quality and freshness of ingredients as most important. Because these ingredients are seasonal, they are at their best in quality. The soup for today is my mom's version of minestrone. However, all versions are full of vegetables and are delicious, satisfying, and bursting in flavor. Today, I prepared the soup with a variety of ingredients, and with the love and care that I was taught by my grandmother." Then Andrea named them one by one. "May I serve you a bowl?"

"Why yes! I would love a bowl, thank you so much."

Andrea excused himself from the table and, turning back, asked, "May I serve anyone else a bowl of soup?" This time, he worked up the courage and looked directly into Mia's beautiful blue eyes. "Mia, may I please serve you a bowl?"

Mia looked up and said, "Yes, I love minestrone soup! Did I hear correctly that you prepared it yourself today?"

"Yes, I did," answered Andrea. "I hope that you will enjoy it."

"I'm sure that I will, Andrea, as I have always enjoyed all the other dinners that you have prepared for our family when we eat here."

What! Andrew was asking himself. *She noticed from before that I had prepared several of their dishes in the past, and she liked them!* His heart was racing like a Lamborghini race car crossing the finish line in first place.

"May I help you, Andrea?" asked Mia. "I can carry a tray also. I love to help Mom in the kitchen when she cooks. I like feeling useful while my brother just likes to sit at the table and be waited on. I have made it a habit to serve him last if he doesn't help!"

"Of course, you can help, if you let me become a Musketeer," answered Andrea.

"Deal," replied Mia as she stood looking for an empty tray.

Several of the adults at the table in fact also requested a bowl, and Don, finding an empty tray, stood up this time and started squeezing through the spaces between tables to help Andrea and Mia with the task.

Cecilia turned to Rachel. "That's so odd for a thirteen-year-old boy to have such an infatuation about food that way."

"Oh! It's a lot more than a boy having an infatuation with food. He has a passion to become a serious chef. It's more of a badge of honor for him, and he works very hard at it. His grandmother was his first inspiration, and Andrea started helping her in the kitchen when he was about six and has never stopped since. He wants to attend the Barilla Academy in Italy. It's known worldwide as the best school in the art of Italian cooking and for preparing professional chefs in the Italian restaurant traditions. He believes that to be successful in the kitchen you must have the ability to think on your feet, to make adjustments as you cook. He also feels that a lifetime of experience isn't the only prerequisite for being a great cook, although it does help. He feels that the knowledge of the science of good cooking is essential—that's why he wants to attend the Barilla Academy. You should take the time and talk to him or one of his parents about it. He's a fascinating young man. When he comes over to the house, he never asks if he can help me out in the kitchen. He always comes prepared with his chef jacket, washes his hands, ties a clean kitchen towel to his side to keep his hands clean at all times, and starts working. I've never seen anything like it. The only thing that I've seen that resembles it is when a surgeon prepares for an operation: all his tools impeccably sterilized, determined, confident and focused, where he has visualized doing the operation repeatedly in his mind and compensating for every adjustment that may be required. Andrea says that an empty pan is his canvas and his motto is 'It's time to be inspired.'"

"How sweet is that!" responded Cecilia. "You have to admit, Rachel, we all have such talented kids! We are so blessed."

Talking to David, Luigi offered to be a sponsor of the Musketeer Program. He stated that the city's Chamber of Commerce was always looking for civic projects to get involved with, and as the current president, he was certain that all the other business owners in the area would love to contribute to such a worthwhile program. "But I would love to donate all the required monogrammed lab coats! The owner of the company that designed and monogrammed our chef jackets is a member of the chamber. I know that he would be more than willing to help in the design of a Musketeer Patch and donate all the necessary monogramming. I'll talk to him in the morning so that he can get started designing the patch. He also has a son and daughter who I'm sure would love to participate. The only problem is that they are both in high school. Do you have an age limit, David?"

David thought for a moment while looking at Cecilia and Rachel. "No, we didn't even think of an age limit."

Cecilia cocked her head to the right and said, "There shouldn't be a maximum age limit. A student is a student, and this program shouldn't be limited to just the clinic. I'm sure that all the other different areas of the zoo would love to have Musketeers to learn and help them in the care of the animals. They would all be great public relations ambassadors for the zoo."

Rachel wanted to weigh in, "I think that's a great idea. We'll just have to decide on a minimum age, say about ten or twelve years of age? We need to have the board and the zoo staff decide the parameters of the program. That can be decided on another day."

"But I'm not going to let any of the parents get away so easily," continued David. "I can only see wonderful things happening for our kids when all their parents participate in supervision or being on the board of directors. That goes for you, Luigi, and to you, Maria." Now David was looking back and forth to Michael, Brenda, Joe, and Cynthia. "I'm sure that the rest of you are all eager to participate. Rachel, Cecilia, and Don have already agreed."

"Do we have an option? That sounds more like a rhetorical question," teased Brenda.

"Now tell me, how can any of you deny a learning experience for the kids?" David laughed.

"Yes! It was a rhetorical question," confirmed Joseph. "Count all of us in."

"Oh, you're so good! You are so smooth, David, playing on our emotions and our sense of parenthood. But it works for me!" Cynthia declared. "As Joseph said, you can count us in. If there is anything that I as the mayor can contribute, my staff and I are available to you."

As everyone looked around the table, they could see that all were nodding in agreement.

"Good then, we have two businessmen, a mayor, a US congressman, a sheriff, the editor of our local newspaper, a clinic supervisor, a fire paramedic, and six staff doctors. Well, that's a good start, and I didn't even have to twist any arms!"

"And if you give me the information, I would love to write an article for the newspaper," suggested Brenda.

"You see, that's why we need you on the board! You can be actively involved and get all the information and all the updates firsthand."

"David, we should also ask your brother, Shawn. A pediatric dental surgeon would look good on the board...and Sister Mary Josephine, the kids' school principal; Monsignor Percarsic, the pastor of our church; and of course Dr. Steward, the director of the zoo. That should be a good start," suggested Cynthia. "With your ability to convince everyone of the program's merits in education and sense of community, not to mention your ability to give everyone a guilt trip, how in the world would anyone be able to turn you down?"

They all were laughing so hard that everyone in the restaurant turned and focused on their table. Almost everyone recognized the leaders of their community and just smiled in their direction. One of the members of the chamber remarked, "Luigi, you're going to have to tell us what's so funny. We all love to laugh!"

"Albert, maybe you shouldn't have asked, because you're one of the people I need to talk to, and tonight is as good a night as any to talk about it," replied Luigi, now standing at the table. "I'll be at your table shortly, so don't try to get away!" Now he was talking in a lower voice, "I'm sure you all recognize Albert Gilbert, the owner of several car dealerships, as I'm sure he'll love to be a sponsor in the program.

He's big in working with kids in a variety of different sports leagues at the parks. Kids and their programs are just what he likes to do in returning good will for his success in the community. David, maybe you'll like to talk to him with me, okay? He has, on several occasions in the past, donated a new car to be raffled as a fund-raiser for youth causes. What better cause than this one?"

"Absolutely! In fact, all of us here at the table know Albert personally. We all have bought a car or two from one of his dealerships!"

Luigi, still standing, addressed his patrons. "We're so sorry for interrupting your dinner, just good friends having an enjoyable time! So for your inconvenience, dessert for everyone on the house!"

Charlie, the local plumber, answered, "For free dessert, you can interrupt us anytime, Luigi! I'll have a piece of your tiramisu!" Now everyone in the restaurant started to laugh as they began to shout the desserts of their choice.

Looking at Giovanna, the hostess for the evening, who was standing at the entrance of the dining room wearing a beautiful off-white evening gown and was greeting the guests as they were entering the restaurant, Luigi instructed, "Please, Giovanna, inform the waiters—free dessert for everyone and a generous portion of our home-made tiramisu for Charlie!"

The twins were now able to spot Star and Simon standing near the entrance into the kitchen, giggling, enjoying the day's events.

David and Cecilia were thrilled to see how quickly everything was coming together. David asked Cecilia to remind him to invite every employee at the restaurant, at their leisure, to stop by the zoo for a VIP tour whenever their schedules permitted and emphasized to Luigi that no one would be excluded.

Cecilia, trying to be discreet, casually started to look at the place settings on the tables around them and couldn't help but notice that their table was obviously more elegantly arranged than any of the others. Then leaning over to Rachel, she whispered into her ear, "I just can't believe the extra service we're getting. I can't help but notice how Andrea has such a cheerful attitude and how much he loves working with people. It's easy to see how some day he will be a great success."

Rachel smiled and responded, "Oh, you haven't seen anything yet! And I don't think you would, if it weren't for Mia." She lifted her brows, unable to conceal her amusement.

Not understanding at first and with a puzzled look on her face, Cecilia noticed a variety of expressions crossing over Andrea's face. With curiosity and puzzlement, Cecilia turned to Mia. And suddenly it struck her, it was now obvious that Andrea was beaming with joy as he was looking at Mia, trying desperately to impress her. Impulsively, a smile started to grow on Cecilia's face, and turning back to Rachel, she whispered, "Puppy love, right?"

Still with a smile on her face, Rachel nonchalantly nodded in agreement and whispered, "Puppy love, and Mia still has no clue."

Now Andrea stood up and, lowering his head in respect to everyone seated at the table, asked politely to be excused because he had duties to fulfill in the kitchen.

Cecilia immediately asked, "Andrea, are you leaving us so soon?"

"Oh! I will soon return. There are a few things that I need to attend to in the kitchen. I had the staff prepare some of my signature dishes, and I just want to see if any adjustments need to be made to meet my standards. The kitchen staff are excellent, but it doesn't hurt to check with them every now and then."

As soon as Andrea cleared the kitchen doors, Maria, who was sitting next to Rachel and Cecilia, said in her low Italian voice, "He told me that he wanted to be assured that this meal is prepared perfectly, so he wanted to take charge himself and finish preparing a few of the dishes personally. When it comes to the Brooks family, how would you say? He is a perfectionist?"

Cecilia turned to Rachel and winked. "Everything is so perfectly clear to me now." She raised her voice so that others might hear and looked at Maria. "My mouth is already salivating—that soup was excellent! It's hard to believe, but I do…that Andrea made that from scratch. I can't wait to see what else he has in store for us, but I feel that it's going to be delicious!"

Andrew was the first one to realize that several waitresses were approaching their table with not one but six extra-large specialty pizzas and announced loudly, "Dinnertime."

Mia looked over to White Dove, rolling her clear blue eyes, "Musketeers, be ready to be impressed!"

Then a tidal wave of waiters and waitresses was coming, one after another, with an assortment of side dishes of antipasti, soups, lasagna with marinara sauce and porcini mushrooms, veal breasts stuffed with spinach *pistou*, ravioli with squash and chestnut filling with a sauce made with garlic and fresh basil, and a variety of seafood dishes. It got to the point that David had to beg Luigi to stop.

Andrea exited the kitchen, and gently removing a half-eaten pizza that was sitting in front of Mia, replaced it with two decadent platters that he had on a serving cart. One of the platters consisted of garlicky grilled jumbo prawns with lemon sauce, and the second platter contained Andrea's specialty, slowly braised short ribs served over polenta.

Noticing the smile on Andrea's face, Cecilia looked over and whispered to Rachel, "Must be Mia's two favorite dishes?"

"Her most favorite Italian dishes," confirmed Rachel.

"Do I dare help myself to a couple of the shrimp?" mused Cecilia.

"Wasn't it you who told me earlier that you didn't believe in death wishes?" asked Rachel. "You can try it, if you don't mind a fork in the back of your hand! Besides, I've already patched up one patient today, Rehab. I wouldn't want another patient at the dinner table."

"Oh look, Rachel, doesn't that chicken parmesan look delicious? I think that I would rather have some of that instead of the shrimp. Besides, I just had my nails done, and I think that a fork sticking out of the back of my hand would spoil the effect!"

"Good choice, Cecilia. But don't worry, there is no way that Mia can eat that much shrimp and ribs. There will be plenty to go around. I just normally let her help herself first."

"You do know, Rachel, I'm never coming back here again without you and Mia. Even kings don't experience elaborate meals like this!"

There was an amazing number of wonderful dishes, much more than they would ever be able to eat. But it seemed that as quickly as the dishes arrived, they were served and just as quickly eaten. At the end of the meal, everyone had to admit that a dinner could never be so satisfying and the conversation never as enjoyable as when it's seasoned with love and shared with family and friends.

David was also grateful that he managed to circulate throughout the restaurant to personally thank again all the diners who had followed them to Dominic's from the zoo. He made it a point to shake everyone's hands, especially the children's, telling them that he was looking forward to seeing them again at the zoo. And all the patrons that he addressed felt that David was genuinely sincere and speaking from his heart.

"It's hard to believe how delicious all the dishes are," Cecilia exclaimed. "I have no idea how I would ever be able to describe them to anyone. I don't believe the dictionary contains the words to describe the tastes and aromas of these dishes. The veal breasts stuffed with spinach *pistou*, the pork loin with fig and prosciutto stuffing, the shrimp sauté with garlic and lemon, and my very most favorite, the lasagna with marinara sauce and porcini mushrooms. These are foods that only kings and presidents get to eat. I feel like nobility today! Please, Maria, give…"

"Well," interrupted Maria, "he's right here sitting at the table! All these dishes were mostly prepared by Andrea's own hands. Most of them are his own recipes that he came up with using his skills and imagination. His father and I are so proud of him and his enthusiasm," continued Maria with such sparkling bright eyes. "We are enormously proud of both our children and of course also of Katarina. I'll fight with anyone who says she is not our own daughter, and Francesco, he is going to have a very hard time trying to take her back to Italy!"

The three children lowered their heads, beaming with pride, listening to such high praises from Maria, but Andrea couldn't help but look in Mia's direction to see if she was paying any attention. She was, as Mia also echoed how much she enjoyed each and every bit and was looking forward to the leftovers.

Then Mia looked over to Andrew and, seeing the quantity of empty dishes in front of him, couldn't help but pull his chain. "How in the world could you just plow through a double-crust large pizza with the works all by yourself? Why aren't you pig fat?"

"I guess it just comes from enormous strength of will and great metabolism. And what are you talking about? I saw you attack those platters of shrimp and ribs. You ate like a condemned man on death row eating his last meal. If you hadn't stopped, you would have been the one leaving the table 'oinking' all the way home."

"As always, Andrew," Mia snickered, "you have such a talent for exaggeration." She scowled at him, pretending to ignore the sarcasm.

The table couldn't help but erupt in laughter.

Although Andrea spoke very little throughout the dinner, it was obvious to everyone, except to Mia, that he enjoyed every second of the meal, for the young prince had his best meal sitting at the same table with his fairytale princess. His eyes started to dance, and his heart throbbed to the sound of music in his head.

"Now that we're here all together, I want to make a special announcement and invite everyone at the table to Andrea's birthday party in July." Maria was attempting to talk over everyone, with her beautiful, creamy, rich Italian voice. "He will be fourteen, and I think that we will have it here at the restaurant."

"Oh, I have a suggestion," replied Rachel. "Why not have it at our home? We can have a barbecue next to the pool, and the kids can go swimming. It's such a beautiful area that was designed for parties, and we hardly ever take advantage of it enough."

"Are you sure, Rachel? Wouldn't this be such an inconvenience for you? I know how little time you get off from the hospital."

"It would absolutely be no problem at all! And it couldn't be any rowdier than the party we're having here tonight. By July, the weather will be beautiful outdoors. In fact, I'm sure of it, and I love the idea. Can we count on it?" Rachel asked with a brilliant smile. "David and I are always looking for an excuse for a good barbecue."

"Well, okay, if you're sure. But feel free to cancel if it becomes inconvenient or you find that your work load won't allow it," answered Maria.

"Well then, that settles it." David expressed his delight in total agreement. "It will be the best barbecue of the year!"

The Musketeers gave it their personal approval with cheers. It was like thunder that echoed and echoed and echoed to the highest arches of the ceiling. For now, there were only ten Musketeers, but the recruiting season had just begun. In just one day, their ranks more than doubled. The twins could now see their angels clapping behind them in total approval.

Andrea was in a daze. *What just happened here, a birthday party for me at Mia's house? No! I must have not heard it right. No! This can't be true, can it?* Then he looked in Mia's direction. *She is so beautiful. How did genes decide to mix themselves all up, then combine and create such serious beauty? It doesn't seem quite fair to the rest of the population,* Andrea thought.

As they were all feeling content and enjoying each other's company, the waiters and bus boys cleared the table of used dishes and replaced them with a variety of desserts. There were dates and melon wrapped in prosciutto, slices of an assortment of fresh fruit, freshly made Italian *gelato* (ice cream), and of course, the house specialty, a decadent tiramisu, to only name a few.

Then suddenly, the table was unexpectedly interrupted by the beeping sounds of several personal cell phones. Everyone began frantically searching for their cells, each hoping that it wasn't theirs that was interrupting the celebration.

"Unfortunately, it's me!" cried David, looking a little somber. "It's from Paul Chapin, the chief of security at the zoo."

"No! It's me," replied Cecilia. "It's the nursery trying to get in touch with me."

Michael also reached for his cell phone. "It's central dispatch. Please excuse me, I have to take this."

"Well then, it looks like they're trying to reach all of us," responded David. "I wonder what's going on. It must be serious for the office to call both of us, Cecilia." Turning to look at Rachel, David continued, "I guess the only way we're going to find out is to answer the calls."

"If you need some privacy, please feel free to use my office," suggested Luigi. "Our home is always your home."

"Thank you, Luigi," responded David. "That might be best." And David left the table due to all the laughter and clamor typical of a large dining room area. Cecilia and Michael followed close behind.

"Well, that was unfortunate," commented Rachael tongue-in-cheek, "but it does gives us an opportunity to get a head start on the desserts!" With a large smile on her face, she reached for a slice of tiramisu. And as the others at the table started to laugh, Andrew reached for a bowl of gelato crooning, "Come to Papa, little guy."

Returning to the table with Cecilia and Michael at his side and with a serious look on his face, David announced, "I hate to break up the great party we have here, but Cecilia and I have to return to the zoo. It was Dr. Steward on the phone, and they desperately need Cecilia and me back on the property. Apparently, some of the primates have escaped from their enclosures, and they are creating total chaos at the zoo."

"I have been notified of the same thing. I have several units responding to assist in any way we can, and animal control has also been notified for their assistance. Just tell me what we can do to help," added Michael.

"We need to return to the park as soon as possible, Michael, before I can evaluate the situation and determine if any help is necessary," responded David. "But it easily could get extremely dangerous and out of control because there are still many guests on the property, and pandemonium is probably at hand. The guests could be in danger if they interact and try to help in capturing the animals themselves. They have no idea how strong and dangerous primates are. Even the small monkeys are enormously strong for their size."

"Dad!" Mia's eyes flashed like supernovas. "We forgot all about Noah!" she exclaimed with concern in her voice. "We can't go yet! We have nothing for Noah!"

"Not a problem!" Andrea quickly spoke up. "I know that Noah is never too far from your thoughts, so I've already prepared a special treat for him. I'll go get it from the kitchen."

While Andrea quickly ran to the kitchen to retrieve it, Luigi and Maria along with Anna, Katarina, and some of the staff were hurrying to gather the leftovers in carryout containers. Some of the entrées had not even been touched. "There are plenty of leftovers for everyone to take home for bedtime snacks," suggested Luigi. "Just give us a couple of minutes to box them up."

"May I have the bill, Luigi, please?" David handed him his credit card. Don, Michael, and Joe were also all reaching for their wallets.

"*Canto* [bill]? What bill? You bring joy to my house, and you ask for a bill? Please, David, I know you only too well that you would not try to shame me in my own house intentionally. In my home, there is never a bill for you, my friend. Please go and attend to your emergency. We will take care of everything here."

Andrea quickly returned with Noah's treat and handed it to Mia and, leaning forward with his eyes on hers, whispered to her, "I made it exactly the way Noah likes it, with plenty of extra meat."

Seeing Mia's face light up with gratitude, Andrea couldn't help but grin as she thanked him.

As always, finding her to be impossibly gorgeous with those eyes so bold and brilliantly blue, Andrea for the first time felt very confident and satisfied with himself. He had finally scored some points with her, which brought pleasure and a sense of euphoria to him.

Before scrambling to the parking lot, David apologized to Luigi for the emergency and for having to eat and run. "We'll have to come back and continue our conversation at a later date." As David was politely excusing himself, the Raphael, Shaw, and Yanez families were thanking the rest of the Dominic family as well for their gracious hospitality.

CHAPTER 7

*M*ichael was right on David's heels as they quick-stepped to the parking lot. As David was sliding behind the wheel, Michael asked if there was anything extra that he could do to help with, just anything at all.

"You know there might be, now that I'm thinking about it. You think you can dispatch your mobile emergency command and control unit? Because it's Saturday, the zoo has extended hours tonight. When we left to come for dinner, there was a massive overflow of guests still in the park. We're not only going to have to lead them safely out of the park, but we also must cordon the perimeter to make sure that, if any of the primates do breach the walls, we'll be able to track them. So I feel that a couple of units will not be enough. You're probably going to have to use your entire complement of available units. You may even have to call in some of your off-duty deputies for crowd and evacuation control. Since we know at least a couple of primates are loose in the zoo, knowing human nature, it seems reasonable to assume that some of the guests at the zoo might want to be local heroes and attempt to catch them themselves. And that would not only be extremely foolish but very dangerous! They will not only place themselves at significant risk in their attempts but will undoubtedly agitate and make the primates even more dangerous. Primates may look harmless, but they are still unpredictable wild animals—not to mention extremely powerful!"

"I'm responding myself," replied Michael. "We'll set up a field command post on site, and that way, we can expedite any assistance you may need. We'll not only be on location to back you up, but I can assure you that every department resource will be available to you. I'll get Henry Lockheart, the superintendent of animal control on the radio to commit all his resources as well. We'll give him a section in the command and control unit to coordinate his personnel. As you know, he has a unit well-trained for such an occasion. They have special equipment, including specialized nets and tranquilizer guns, if needed to subdue large animals such as primates. With all our combined expertise, we should be able to contain the situation. If not, we can call in any other assets from the city, county, or state agencies to assist as needed. I know that your zoo staff has been trained and is prepared for such emergencies. I don't want you to think that we might get in your way or take over your control. You and Dr. Steward have full authority. We're here to back you up and secure any additional resources you require. Just tell me what else you may need. In fact, why don't you ride with me, and we can brainstorm ideas on the way?"

"Go, David," Rachel said, "and take Cecilia with you in the sheriff's vehicle. Being that both Cecilia and Don have their cars here, I can drive Cecilia back here to pick up her car after the emergency is over. I think that Don will probably take Kristin home with him. Cynthia has already said she wants to go to see if she will need to activate a team from the mayor's office to assist you. So I'll invite her to go with the kids and me. I'll meet you at the zoo in case you need any medical backup assistance. It seems reasonable to me that some of the park's guests might get hurt in the evacuation, especially with this inconsistent and unpredictable weather from tonight's storm. I'd like to be there in case any of the guests are injured by trying to capture the animals on their own, or just slipping and falling on the wet concrete sidewalks running to or from the animals."

"Okay then, let's get a-moving," was all David said.

As David and Cecilia left in the sheriff's vehicle, the rest of the dinner party was left behind standing in the parking lot. Rachel was easily able to read the concern written all over Cynthia's face. After the twins were settled in the car, Rachel turned to the mayor and asked, "Cynthia, I also saw David's concern. After all these years of marriage, I can read him like a book. I'm feeling apprehensive that he may need all our help. What resources can you think of from the mayor's office that David might need?"

"It will all depend on the situation and what David feels that he needs," responded the mayor. "The city has enormous assets! All that David needs to do is make a request for them. Everything that the city can provide will be at his disposal. All he needs to do is just name it. But without further information, we're groping in the dark. Without being there and being updated on the problem, I can't tell how serious the situation is at the moment. I think that we both need to get there as soon as possible ourselves so that we can evaluate what needs to be done."

"But if the primates are out of their habitats and running around scared in the park, it can be serious," Rachel expressed her concerns. "Primates are so powerful to begin with, and if they're scared, it's safe to assume that their adrenaline is running in high gear, so they could be three times more powerful than normal and the guests three times more susceptible to injuries! So I agree, I think that neither one of us we will know for sure until we get there and assess the problem."

"Then we better get there to see how we can help," agreed the mayor. "I'm prepared to approve and release any of the city's assets that may be required."

"I suggested to David that you should ride with me so Joe could take Rain Cloud and White Dove home with him. I know that we don't have the luxury of a black-and-white to ride in, but I do have doctor's license plates, and we may even pick up a police escort. I'm sure we can make good time even though we need to be vigilant in this weather."

Now turning her attention to her husband, Cynthia asked, "Joe, thank you for being so patient. Would you mind taking the kids home as well as making sure that Brenda and her kids, Daniel and Jennifer, get safely home? I'm going to ride with Rachel to the zoo. I'm sure that the situation may be more serious than the report we just received. Rachel and I both have a feeling that we shouldn't take anything for granted. Call it a woman's intuition!"

"Of course, I don't mind," responded the congressman. "I was just going to suggest that to Rachel myself. The four of you go ahead to the zoo and take care of the problem, and I'll see that everyone gets home safely in this wicked weather. If I had the room, I would have suggested to take the twins as well."

"That's okay, Joe," replied Rachel. "It would be a lot easier to utterly eradicate the common cold than prevent Mia and Andrew from returning to the zoo! You know how much kids love the zoo, but with the twins, you can triple that interest. They have such an insatiable love for animals that if David would allow it, they would sleep there!"

Even though the moon was elusive behind thick clouds and leaves were dangling in midair with the rising wind, Andrew and Mia felt very comfortable in their mom's car, being assured that everything would eventually work out for the best, especially noticing that Star and Simon were riding in the back seat of the SUV with them.

*A*t first, David, Cecilia, and Michael sat in silence in the sheriff's black-and-white, all focusing on the road and the traffic. They could hear the drumming rain striking the top of the vehicle, with occasional distant lightning flashes going off as thunder started to roll in. The rain started to pour in sheets, and dead leaves darted and swarmed in the dark like bats emerging from their dark and scary caves.

David was thinking to himself as he watched the ice-tipped rain strike the car's windshield, and it hissed like angry snakes as it struck. Finally, David was the first to speak. "I really need to get me one of these black-and-whites, Michael. We're making great time despite the weather—and without even using the siren, just the red lights. I love the fact that people just pull over to the right with no questions asked. It really makes things convenient when there's an emergency," mused David.

"Yes, but there is one thing that you must always keep in mind," responded Michael. "For every perk you get, there are ten responsibilities, and I keep reminding all my deputies of that fact. We enjoy the perks, but we can never take inappropriate advantage of them."

"Hold that thought. I'm getting another call from the park," requested David. "Okay, I understand, yes, yes, I'm with the sheriff, and we're on our way as I speak. We'll be there as soon as possible, weather permitting, Patrick.

"That was Dr. Steward, our managing director of the zoo. As I feared, there are more than the initial two primates that were first reported. An undetermined number of other animals have been reported as missing from their enclosures. There are teams of staff members trying to evaluate the situation. Dr. Steward was notified earlier and has been in charge of coordinating the efforts for the last couple of hours. And as I predicted, some of the guests are foolishly trying to help by chasing the loose primates and capturing them by hand even though they are being told to stop and exit the park. Many guests are running around in a panic, falling and injuring themselves. Still others are being trampled by other guests after they have fallen. I'm going to try to reach Rachel to see if she can meet us at the clinic and maybe even try to dispatch a team from the emergency room to set up a triage unit at our clinic to administer treatment. I've just been told that there are already over forty minor injuries reported in our first aid station, and that's only the ones that have been discovered! I'm sure that there are even more that haven't been reported. I fear, Mike, that this is going to be a long night. There is no doubt in my mind that the probabilities of someone getting seriously hurt now have just risen 500 per cent. People are inherently crazy creatures!"

Without looking over at his passengers, Michael asked, "You two are wearing your seat belts, right?"

"Of course," responded both Cecilia and David. "It's just a habit to buckle up," added David. "Especially when you have kids in the car, you have to show a good example for them."

"Good! Because you'll never need them more than now." Michael leaned forward to activate the siren. "Hang on, because we are now going code 3, red lights and siren."

As he reached above his right breast pocket to activate his mobile radio, he continued, "Control, this is Commander 1. Be advised that this unit is now en route to the city zoo, code 3. We are presently located westbound on Central Avenue passing Washington Boulevard. Please advise the fire department to have all available paramedic units respond as multiple injuries have been reported, with the anticipation of possibly many additional injuries to come."

"Roger, Commander 1. We show you now preceding code 3 and the fire department has been notified. What is your ETA?"

"Commander 1, our estimated time of arrival is approximately eight minutes."

"Roger, Commander 1. Fire department is showing an ETA of ten minutes."

"Commander 1, Roger!"

Michael couldn't help but notice that David was holding on for dear life, with his left hand holding on to the center console and his right hand tightly wrapped around the handle above the passenger door. His knuckles were turning white from squeezing on so tightly. Cecilia was equally traumatized as she was holding on tightly to the back of Michael's head rest.

"David, as well as you, Cecilia, you need to relax a little. Your adrenaline is in overdrive. We're doing fine. It just seems like we're traveling faster than we really are because of the rain. It's also because, with the siren on now, the other motorists are pulling to the right and stopping, so we're passing cars faster than normal. So just sit back and relax a little."

"Can you ever get used to this?" asked David.

"Almost, you just always must keep in mind that just because you have a siren and you can hear it loud and clear, that doesn't mean that everyone else on the road can. You must be cognizant that there are drivers out there who can't see or hear you. You must drive defensively always, especially with the siren activated. There are kids out there with their windows up and their music at earsplitting decibels, parents fighting with their kids in the back seat and not paying attention. You can see that there can be scenario after scenario. I guess you just need to relax but not be complacent."

As they continued to drive, their SUV splashed through water that had pooled in low-lying areas, and broken branches littered the streets. David's eyes were beginning to water in the glaring headlights as cars went past ignoring the siren. But Michael realized that drivers approaching from the opposite direction might not be able to hear their oncoming siren or see the flashing lights in the wind and rain, so he slowed down instinctively in this unnaturally dark night.

As they entered the park through the employees' parking lot, Michael deactivated the siren, and David again observed the unidentified light-blue van still occupying his assigned parking space.

Strange, he wondered, *I still can't imagine whose van it is and why it's taking up my parking space. When I get the opportunity, I'll ask security to check it out and have them place a violation certificate on the windshield.*

David wanted to get to his office as quickly as possible to pick up a couple of handheld mobile staff radios that were set to the zoo's internal frequencies for Michael and himself. Most employees didn't carry their own radio unless needed, but the clinic did have several backup radios in case a staff member needed to exit the clinic and attend to a sick or injured animal in the general park. And each department had their own frequency setting but could change from their regular setting to any other setting for unusual situations such as the present one. That way, all park employees could communicate with each other and could follow Michael's directions and suggestions. David directed Michael through a traversing course all the way through the park, driving in areas that were normally designated as walking zones for the park visitors only.

"And you thought I was driving crazy? You're getting me dizzy just trying to reach your office!" Michael said in a loud voice.

"Oh! You're a big boy, so just man up and suck it up! Wasn't that what you just told me a couple of minutes ago?" David laughed.

"You know what? I think I'm just going to take out a couple of your plants for that remark!" retaliated Michael.

"Don't you dare, Michael," chastised Cecilia. "Most of these smaller plants were planted by Girl Scouts and some of the staff as a merit badge project."

"Well, that changes my plans. I'll just have to find a way to force David to buy extra cookies from the Girl Scouts who volunteer at our sheriff station," suggested Michael.

"Mia already has me spending more than a king's ransom for Girl Scout cookies!" replied David.

"Well, it's either Girl Scout cookies or those Italian sausage dogs and lemonade your park is so notoriously famous for."

"You know, Michael, Girl Scout cookies it is! I'd go broke buying Italian sausage dogs and lemonade for your crew!" exclaimed David.

"Besides, we know a lot of Girl Scouts to buy them from, don't we, David?" reminded Cecilia jokingly.

"I can't believe that we still have so many visitors in the park," remarked David. "It's obvious that the guests are reluctant to respond to the park security officers' directions. It's clear that they are refusing to work their way back to the main entrance. And most of them are going in the wrong direction. They're going even deeper into the park! I'm sure they're finding the situation exciting, wanting to see everything firsthand for themselves and refusing to recognize the danger that they're placing themselves and their families in. Even adults sometimes don't use the common sense that God gave them."

"I don't understand it either," answered Michael. "It's not just the danger that they are putting themselves in. What about this miserable weather? The wind is so high, not to mention the pounding rain. Some of these parents with small children should be arrested for child endangerment! With this dark sky, what do they expect to see anyway? Well, when my deputies arrive," continued the sheriff, "they just won't be making suggestions. The guests will be seeing jail time with heavy fines for failure to obey a deputy sheriff in the performance of their duties!"

As they approached the front of the clinic, Cecilia exited the vehicle as a couple of the clinic staff members ran out and offered David and Michael extra handheld radios and rain gear. They attempted to give them a concise but unverified update as they knew it and also told them that the first-aid center was being overrun by injured guests. They said that Dr. Steward was waiting for their arrival and would be able to give them a more accurate briefing of the situation. The staff advised David that Dr. Steward, along with Paul Chapin and some of his park security team, had mobilized at the park entrance to coordinate what actions should be taken and to expedite the exit of the guests from the park.

David managed to reach Rachel by cell phone and asked for her assistance. Rachel responded and said she would dispatch an emergency unit to the clinic and that she and Cynthia would arrive in about ten minutes. David then alerted his staff to be ready for Rachel and asked Cecilia to stay at the clinic to assist her in coordinating the triage team that Rachel had dispatched from the hospital's emergency room. He told them also that there were fire department paramedics en route who shouldn't be far behind Rachel and to make room for them. They would also be working out of the clinic under Rachel's direction. David wanted his staff to understand Rachel would be fully in charge of the clinic and that they were to assist her and follow all her instructions. He made it clear that he wanted his staff to prepare ample space for her team to administer medical treatment for employees and injured guests of the park. He also mentioned that injured guests would not be directed to the first-aid station any longer but directed to and if possible escorted by staff and sheriff deputies to the veterinary clinic. David also wanted his staff to locate all working handheld park radios and make them available to Rachel's team and to the county sheriff deputies who would need them. He also asked for his staff, if possible, to extend their hours this night because everyone would be needed to work overtime. Without exception, his staff volunteered to stay for as long as needed. He also told them to call in off-duty staff members if directed by Rachel. And that, of course, everyone would be compensated at double time due to the emergency rather than the normal time and a half. David and Michael then proceeded to meet Dr. Steward and Paul Chapin, the chief of security at the zoo, at the front entrance of the park to create a makeshift ready-reaction force team. As they approached, they spotted Dr. Steward and Paul standing in the wallowing wind and now heavy rainfall.

"David, you have no idea how glad I am that you're finally here!" exclaimed Dr. Steward. "We've been in total chaos mode here at the park for the last couple of hours. I called in Henry Lockheart of animal control, and he and his men have been working together with our zookeepers. We hesitated in calling you on your day off. We thought that we could handle the situation ourselves, but things got away from us, so we were forced to call you as a last resort. Somehow, the entrance to the main primate habitat was left ajar. At first, we thought that only a couple of the primates had escaped, but then we noticed a couple more missing to the point that we now realize that most of the primates are missing and are running amok throughout the zoo!" He extended his right hand to shake hands with Sheriff Raphael. "I'm surprised how you responded so quickly, but I'm thrilled that you're here, Sheriff! I have no idea what you can do, but any help that you can provide us would be greatly appreciated. And by the way, Sheriff, this is Paul Chapin, our chief of security."

"Yes," replied Michael, "I've already met Paul many times from several training conferences and training drills." The two shook hands. "We have been conducting training drills together for the past several years, and our staffs have always worked well together. I'm here, along with all my available deputies who will be arriving shortly to assist in any way that we can, Dr. Steward. But did you say that many other primates have also escaped and not just the initial two that we were told about?"

"Yes, many more! We don't have an accurate head count yet, but yes, many more," responded Dr. Steward.

"I'm sure there's something that my deputies and I can do to help. We can at least assist in clearing the park of guests and stop them from trying to catch the animals themselves. We've been briefed by Dr. Brooks that several of them have sustained numerous injuries. We are also aware that the clinic doctors and medical staff have been slammed with seriously injured people at an alarming rate. We'll help in locating the injured and escorting them to your clinic where Dr. Rachel Brooks and her team, along with fire department paramedics, will provide medical attention. We will also direct the rest of the guests to the main entrance. Please excuse me for a moment, I'm receiving a call through my Bluetooth from my office and need to take it." As Michael stepped away to better hear his call, Paul also needed to step away to be updated on his radio.

Dr. Steward now turned his attention back to David. "David, thank you for having the foresight to bring in Rachel with a medical team. You know the primates better than anyone here. I think you're the right man to take charge. I think it best if we all follow your directions. Therefore, I'd like to place full control of this situation under you, if you don't mind. And of course, I'll remain at your side, just in case I can do anything that you may need of me."

"Well, the way I see it," began David, "our priority must be the safety of the guests. We must evacuate the entire park of all the visitors and nonessential park staff. Close down the gift shops, food court, and small booths throughout the park, and let those employees go home. We will require some employees to remain in safe locations to report sightings of any loose animals. Then our trained staff, along with the city's specialized animal control staff, who are trained exactly for a calamity such as this, can safely capture any loose animals and return them to their enclosures. Do we have at least a preliminary head count of how many have escaped? And for the ones that didn't escape, we must place them under a double lockdown as soon as possible!"

"I've just been informed that an additional five radio cars are approximately two minutes out, and another eight will be here in ten," reported Michael as he returned to David's position.

Paul returned to the group after receiving an update of the situation from his staff and walked directly up to David, Dr. Steward, and Sheriff Raphael. "I'm sorry to say that I have additional shocking news. There are now reports from my security officers that numerous other animals have been released. They have no idea to what extent, but many more. This isn't an accidental escape of an animal or two. Someone is intentionally freeing them."

"My god, what else can go wrong?" was Dr. Steward's reaction.

"Thank God, here are my units now." Michael waved the vehicles in his direction, and they came to a stop. "Let me get a head count and names of the officers and their unit assignments, and then we'll be ready for your instructions, David."

"How in the world could this have happened to us, David?" asked Dr. Steward. "I know that all contingencies had been anticipated and discussed. All safeguards and precautions had been taken. We designed and constructed the most current state-of-the-art enclosures in collaboration with the best architects in the world.

I'm confident that our enclosures are the best in the country. We have all the protocols in place to prevent this sort of thing from happening. But for someone to intentionally release the animals is incomprehensible."

"I agree," replied David with a look of bewilderment on his face. "This just doesn't pass the smell test. It's obvious that the enclosures are being purposely opened. Why? I have no idea, but we will find all the answers and who the culprit or culprits are as quickly as humanly possible and then take all appropriate actions. We'll find out who they are. I promise you that!"

"All the entrances to every habitat have self-closing double doors. We all felt comfortable that every precaution was fully taken, but first things first." Seeing that Michael was returning to their position with one of the responding deputies, David asked, "Can you tell me what your assets are?"

"Well, we are not only in decent shape but lucky as well. We were just having a shift change: mid-PM watch just came on duty as midday watch was just being released, so we have extra deputies whom we weren't expecting. Let me introduce you to Lieutenant Dale Perry, who is the midday watch commander. I've authorized him and his entire shift to stay on overtime duty until they are no longer needed. I've also instructed Deputy Chief Ronald Dickson to remain at the station to coordinate with us any needs that we may require. So we have one deputy chief, one lieutenant, four sergeants, and twelve two-man radio cars at your disposal. So just tell us how and where you want us deployed."

"I have no idea," replied Dr. Brooks. "Right now, we're trying to establish who released the animals and to prevent others from escaping. We're trying to get a precise head count on how many are loose. All we know for sure is that many of them were in habitats adjacent to the primates and are now creating havoc with the other animals. Some seem to be passive about the experience, but others are totally distressed and unhappy about the intrusion into their personal territories and fighting with each other. Somehow, we must locate who is breaching our security and setting loose our animals from their habitat enclosures. Meanwhile, we must capture the animals and return them to their enclosures. I have all the zoo-keepers trying to recapture the fugitives now. I guess my immediate thoughts are for public safety. If we can have your deputies drive their units throughout the park and escort our guests safely to the main entrance and off the property while at the same time identifying any injured guests and escorting them to the clinic, that would be a tremendous help! The zoo's staff along with the animal control team will concentrate on capturing the loose animals. Rachel's medical staff, along with the fire department's paramedics, will focus on the injured visitors. And my clinic's medical staff will attend to any injured animals. The zoo's staff that is assigned to the capturing of the animals will also give a heads-up to your command center if they find any visitors for your deputies to escort out of the park. We're getting a bunch of maps of the park to pass out to your men. Also, it is imperative that if they see a primate as well as any other loose animal, please don't try to capture them! Wild animals are extremely powerful, and it takes trained personnel with the proper equipment to handle them safely. I can't stress that enough. So please advise them to stay in their vehicles and just report their locations. Zoo personnel along with animal control will capture our escapees using proper protocols.

"So if you can get your men to direct all the visitors to the main exit, I'll get guest services to distribute complimentary admission tickets to everyone leaving the park. I also think that we should marry up one of our security officers with each of your deputies as a team to ride in their black-and-whites. Our security will be able to assist them since they are all familiar with every nook and cranny of the park. Some of the guests aren't being cooperative. They don't want to leave, and they are hiding to see all the commotion firsthand for themselves. I assume that every radio car has a public-address system, right?"

"That's an affirmative," responded the lieutenant. "I'll start pairing up the security officers with the deputies. Maybe we should place some of the guests into the buildings for safety until a black-and-white can transport them back here to the entrance. Perhaps we can also utilize your parking lot trams to reach the large groups deep into the park and transport them safely back here to the entrance. Of course, each tram would be escorted by a black-and-white at all times. What do you think?"

"That's the thinking that I like to hear," approved David. "It seems to me you know what you're doing. As sworn law enforcement officers, you have the ultimate authority over our security officers, and your decisions will not be questioned. We also have seven zoo buses available to us that we use to transport school kids to the zoo for field trips. Their regular drivers have already left for the day, but we have several employees still on premises who can drive them. Besides, they won't be driving them on public roads, just within the property picking up our guests and taking them to the parking lot. I'll see to it that all our drivers are to remain on duty and be available for your instructions. So can I leave the evacuation of the guests to you, Lieutenant? I'm sure that I'm forgetting something. I've never been involved in something like this before. If you have any questions, any at all, I'll be only as far as your radio. The only thing that I would like to add is, please inform your deputies to be aware that these animals are extremely quick and can be on top of you in the blink of an eye. I can't overstress this point. Make sure that they keep every guest and themselves at a safe distance, and just report the animal's locations. We will do the rest."

"Absolutely, Doc! I hear you loud and clear. We don't need any heroes tonight. We all want to go home safely. We'll take charge of the guests so that you can be free to concentrate on apprehending your fugitives, for the lack of a better term. I've also taken the liberty to designate a location to set up our mobile command and control unit as requested by the sheriff. That is, of course, if the location meets with your approval, Sheriff Raphael."

"That's a no-brainer. If it's okay with Dr. Brooks, consider it approved," remarked Michael.

"I concur with your sheriff, Lieutenant. If that location works for you, it's fine by me," replied David.

"And if I can request from you, Dr. Steward," asked David, "to remain here at the entrance to help coordinate the activities and the smooth exit of our guests? Who better to exercise some PR with them than you? And please remain on the radio in case we need you to send us any logistics that may be required?"

"Like the lieutenant said, absolutely!" agreed Dr. Steward. "I have no plans to leave. I'll remain here ready for any assistance that you may require, David."

"You can operate from the command post with me, if you wish, Dr. Steward," offered the lieutenant. "When it is set up, you will see that our unit contains a host of resources with all the bells and whistles we'll need. At least one of our department's helicopters automatically responds with the mobile command center unless directed otherwise. It will be our eyes from the sky. From its onboard cameras, we get a live feed that can be viewed on our monitors. Besides you and me in the unit, there will be a work station assigned to each representative from your park security, animal control, fire department, and anyone else as needed to coordinate their assets. I would also like to have someone from your staff, Dr. Brooks, keeping us updated on your activities. I will also assign your representative a phone console to work from."

"Of course, Lieutenant. I'll send you Dr. Julie Harrison," responded David. "She is familiar with every employee at the clinic. In fact, she is at the clinic now as we speak. She'll be a great asset to you. I'll have her report to you with our current list of our clinic's employees and a directory of their home phone numbers in case we need to call out for additional help."

"Yes, that will be extremely helpful. May I send a black-and-white for her now?" asked the lieutenant.

"I can see additional black-and-whites responding now," offered Michael. "And behind them are several paramedic units, along with Deputy Fire Chief Winston Dallas. Oh, and lastly, here comes our mobile command unit with two of our department's helicopters. Now we have eyes in the sky."

"I'm sure that Dr. Julie Harrison will arrive here shortly from the clinic, Lieutenant," confirmed David. "I've been advised that one of the Red Cross units is transporting her. Therefore, you will not need to deploy a black-and-white for her. In fact, I can see a Red Cross unit coming now. As I said, she will be a great asset for you.

She has a thorough knowledge of the layout of the property and a solid handle on the employees. Her primary duty is working with the primates, and she is our liaison from the clinic to all the zookeepers throughout the park. Michael, that means that this frees us to go to the primate enclosures and search for Dr. Richardson. I'm sure that's where we'll be able to find Roger now. He is our managing zoologist and the zoo's supervisor of mammals outside the clinic. Inside the clinic is where Dr. Cecilia Shaw excels. Between her and Rachel, we should be in decent shape to treat the guests that are injured, as well as any animals that may require medical attention. So if you don't have any other pressing things on your agenda, let's see if we can locate Roger and find out what information he has for us. He would have the best current understanding of our problems and how successful we've been in capturing any of the escaped primates."

As they were en route to the primate enclosures, Michael was picking David's brain for answers to a series of questions he had written down, questions that originated from his officers roaming the park. "The most frequent question," summarized Michael, "boils down to, 'Is there anything that we need to know about primates before we catch up with them?'"

"Well, you can pass on to your men that primates are tremendously strong and extremely smart," explained David. "Compared to most other animals, primate brains are large relative to their body size. Remember, they are the closest mammals to human beings. They range in all sizes and weights, from the mouse lemur, which weighs only a few ounces, to the size of Billy, our lowland gorilla who weighs over five hundred pounds. There were even larger primates that existed in the past but are now extinct."

"Well, thank God for small favors!" declared Michael. "Five hundred pounds is way big enough for us to work with. It would be nice if we knew how many escaped and what sizes they are. I would think as of now these would be the most important answers that we would like to know. But what other questions should we be asking, David?"

"Hopefully, Roger will know those answers. But also tell your men that what's compounding our problem is that primates are for the most part very clever, are generally lively, and are very successful in capitalizing on their opportunities. Most primates have adapted to an arboreal lifestyle, or a tree-living way of life. Most still usually sleep in the trees. So we should all be aware that most of them would probably be found in the treetops. Getting to the chase, tell your men to be looking up as well on the ground. Because the park is planted with thousands of trees from around the world, it may take days, weeks, if not months to locate the smaller primates and return them to their habitats! We have over three thousand acres here for them to hide in!"

"What you're saying, Doc, is that we will probably find the guests on the ground, but our fugitives will most likely be located in the trees? So we better be very vigilant of our entire surroundings and not become complacent with looking for them solely on the ground. Thank God that the standard operating procedure for law enforcement is to be vigilant of our entire surroundings. That includes not only above and below you but behind every building, tree, rock, and even underwater. You have no idea where we have found suspects! But it wouldn't hurt to remind them."

Taking immediate action and using his mobile radio, Michael broadcast, "Commander 1, to all dedicated units working the task force at the city zoo, be advised that primates love hiding in the trees. If any primates are located, do not—I repeat, do not—try to apprehend them on your own. Remain in your vehicles and advise the command post of all sightings, and wait for zoo and animal control personnel to respond. Common sense is to be maintained at all times."

"Nicely said, Commander 1," complimented David. "Let's park over there by the restrooms, and see if we can find Dr. Richardson, and hopefully we should be able to get a better understanding of where we stand."

As David and Michael exited their vehicle, they began to hear the sounds of running feet, and then someone heading in their direction. As he approached closer to their location, they realized that it was Roger huffing and puffing. But he was not coming from the direction of the primates but from the direction of the bears' habitats.

Although a relatively young man in his mid-thirties, Roger was almost completely out of breath from running the short distance from the center of the bears' exhibits to the primates' habitats where David and Michael were standing, a distance not more than the length of a football field.

"Slow down, Roger," exclaimed David, "before you have a heart attack and I have to send you to Rachel! Catch your breath, and then update us as best as you can on your understanding of our situation."

Roger tried to speak and finally found enough breath to say, "I have to get away from behind my desk and get some more exercise! We have a major problem at the Alaskan brown bear habitat. A couple of the escaped chimpanzees ran into Chester's habitat and excited all the bears that reside with Chester. Apparently, Chester, the large male, in trying to chase the chimpanzees out of his territory, somehow he slipped and fell into the V-shaped chasm between his exhibit and the retaining wall of the viewers' railing. He's standing on his feet, but his back and chest are snug against the two walls where he can't turn around. He's completely stuck between the two cement walls, and there is no way that he will be able to extricate himself on his own and return to his plateau. He's all agitated and has a great deal of adrenaline running through him. He has no respect for anyone at the moment, except for his zookeeper for short bursts at a time. She is there trying to calm his nerves, and although Chester does recognize her and maybe feels that she is trying to help him, he doesn't care nor want anyone else near him."

"Oh god!" exclaimed David. "It seems that we're going to have one catastrophe after another! Instead of getting a handle on the initial problem, I can see that the situation is moving in the wrong direction. Do you have a workable plan or any suggestions, Roger?"

"Not yet, but you're a sight for sore eyes, David! I'm so happy that you're finally here! Everyone has been advised by Dr. Steward that you are in charge. He couldn't have chosen a better man." Roger, still trying to catch his breath, spoke with both of his hands on his hips and his forehead pointing to the ground, trying to concentrate on his breathing. "I've been listening to you on the radio and knew that you were making your way to my location. I've been trying to get a head count on all the primates still in their enclosures. All the double doors are confirmed closed and secured. There are thirty-one primates accounted for, and I had their keepers feed them an extra meal to calm them down."

"Well, finally a bit of good news!" declared Michael.

"No, that's not so great," responded David grimly. "We have over two hundred primates."

"What?" Michael reacted in astonishment.

"Two hundred and fifteen to be exact," Roger interjected. "With the six that you have in the infirmary, that makes a hundred and seventy-eight at large by my count."

"I can't believe it! My family and I love the zoo, and we've been here so many times," remarked Michael, "but I never realized how many animals you must have. Why so many? A monkey is a monkey, right?"

"Definitely not," David responded with a glimpse of amusement on his face. "When this crisis is over, we need to talk. Exactly how many living primate species exist today is not clear because the number varies depending on whose research you consider. Most estimates are in the range of 230 to 270. That's because some experts group some varieties together while some others consider some varieties as distinct species, and more are discovered every year. So here at the zoo, we try to exhibit as many different varieties as possible for educational purposes. So we exhibit here at the park well over a hundred distinct species. The species that we do have need to socialize with their same species, so we, as much as possible, have a family of them together. We not only want to entertain our guests, but we take pride in the fact that educating our visitors is one of our most important purposes."

"But here is our biggest problem, Doc," interrupted Roger. "Although we have already located several of the primates, they are so traumatized that we can't get close to them, especially the chimpanzees and most of the smaller monkeys. We desperately need your advice. Several of the keepers are suggesting tranquilizing some of them. Others think that's a crazy idea, saying that it would just exacerbate the situation even further. Their concern is that if we tranquilize them while they are in the trees, we can't predict with enough accuracy where they would fall. That's if we could accurately hit them with the dart gun in the first place! They are constantly moving, and you know how difficult it is to hit a moving target. And if they are accurately hit, they will still be able to react and continue to move around in the trees before the serum takes effect. Therefore, we have little confidence that we would be able to successfully catch them in a safety net when they do fall. If we don't catch them, there is a good chance that they will be severely injured. That would be an additional headache for you and your staff at the clinic. And we all know that these animals are loved as extended members of our families and the last thing we want is to injure a family member. I tend to agree with the majority of the zookeepers to find another solution to our problem. The most logical thing to do, I feel, is to try to lure them into portable cages. But it's your call, Doc. If in your opinion, tranquilizing proves necessary, I would like for you to supervise its implementation."

"I agree. I would suggest tranquilizing them only as a last resort, and only if they are located on the ground," responded David. "Because as you know, your staff, as well as my staff, religiously makes daily contact with all the animals. They are familiar and feel safe with their trainers and caregivers. I would suggest that the personnel who work with them daily would best be able to approach them and entice them with food back into their habitats or portable cages. If not, then I would suggest trying to trick them so we can net them and, only as a last resort, tranquilize them with a dart gun."

David noticed that Roger had his left hand bandaged and asked, "Roger, what happened to your hand?"

"Oh, it's nothing, Doc. I just caught it on a nail opening a crate of melons for the chimpanzees. It's no big thing, just a small scratch," replied Roger.

"What in the world are you doing feeding the animals in the first place? I thought that you had moved up the ladder and worked behind a desk now," inquired David.

"I normally do, but when one of my zookeepers calls in sick, goes on vacation, or is on emergency leave or something, Benjamin or I pitch in and help out."

"You should have it looked at anyway the first chance you get. You wouldn't want it to get infected. Besides, we have a full complement of health technicians at the clinic. You might as well take advantage of them," insisted David.

"Doc, they have a host of other problems much more serious than a scratch on the hand. It will be fine. I've taken care of much more serious cuts and bruises by myself," repeated Roger.

"Nonetheless, have it checked the next time you're near the clinic, and that's not a suggestion!" insisted David.

"Aye, aye, Captain, your wish is my command," replied Roger comically as he clicked his heels and tried to simulate a military salute.

Now Paul approached the group to report on the security team's progress. "I hope you have good news for us, Paul. God knows how badly we need to hear some!" exclaimed David.

"I wish I did!" responded Paul. "I have half my men in the black-and-whites riding with the deputies trying to locate guests who are reluctant to leave the park and who are finding it exciting to help look for the escaped monkeys. The other half of my men are trying to close the park down before any more of our visitors are injured. I've activated our protocol in having our off-duty security staff return to the park to help. Thank God, it was in the early evening and some of the early-bird guests had already left the park when everything turned to total confusion. But because it's a weekend, we have an exorbitant number of guests today. We were apologizing to everyone for the inconvenience, and at the main entrance, we're issuing complimentary tickets for reentry at any later date to compensate for their inconvenience and thanking them for understanding. We were trying to accommodate all our visitors the best we could, but some were more difficult than others. Dr. Steward and I were assisting with these complaints and trying to smooth things over. The parking lot trams and buses are really helping. Our main problem is that some of our guests are hiding from our staff and the deputies among the trees and behind buildings throughout the park. They are finding this tragedy exciting and don't want to leave, and many are documenting everything they can on video with their cell phones."

"I know that I can count on you and your men. You have always been true professionals. But could you please emphasize to them the importance of following the instructions of the sheriff, Lieutenant Perry and their deputies in this catastrophe? I would really appreciate any extra efforts on their part," replied Dr. Brooks. "Clear and accurate information from everyone is going to be essential to assist us in our dilemma. I don't want any of your staff to feel slighted by the presence of the sheriff's department. Where our staff can only ask for cooperation from our visitors, the deputies can demand their cooperation and even place them under arrest for noncompliance. Please tell them that I'll make it up to them later somehow. But for now, I think you better prepare everyone that it's going to be a very long night with every necessary park employee on emergency paid overtime. I think that once every one of our guests is located and moved to the main entrance, our second priority should be to prevent any of our escaped animals from leaving the park's grounds. And not to mention we need to discover who it is that is releasing the animals and shut him or them down from opening any further enclosures!"

"Not a problem," Paul quickly replied. "The sheriff and his deputies will have our full support. There will be no egos interfering with what needs to be done. We have worked with the sheriff's men in the past and have always found them to be great guys and gals to work with. We have a very high level of respect for each one of them. You have my word for it. We'll play well together. I am also glad to report that all sheriff deputies and our security staff are on the same emergency frequency now and have full communications with each other and the command post. I'm now distributing all the extra security handheld radios throughout the park to most non-security park employees remaining to help with this event. I'll have confirmation, hopefully shortly, that everyone on the grounds is working together on the same frequency in just a few minutes. Of course, we also have a secondary emergency frequency reserved for special teams addressing a specific problem, and we're prepared to designate further emergency frequencies if needed."

"Great idea!" responded David. "Now that everyone has received their assignments, let's go see what we can do to make Chester a little more comfortable. If we all put our heads together, I'm sure we'll come up with a workable solution. How long has he been caught in the V-shaped chasm, Roger?"

Before David could receive an answer, he heard someone call out his name on the radio. "Cecilia, is there a problem at the clinic?" David asked.

"Nothing that we can't handle," replied Cecilia. "Rachel and the kids have arrived safely, along with Mayor Yanez. They are now settled in the clinic. Congressman Yanez has returned home with White Dove and Rain Cloud and the sheriff's family but has asked if there is anything he can do to assist. Some of Rachel's staff from her hospital have also arrived through the employees' entrance. Most of them are emergency room specialists. She has set up a triage station. They have a preplanned protocol that the hospital has developed that is used for all types of emergencies resulting in multiple injuries, such as earthquakes, hurricanes, large fires, train collisions, and virtually every other natural or human-made disaster that you can think of. They are well trained and prepared for every type of scenario. They designate which patients are treated first by this protocol, and they have already developed several stations that treat only certain injuries assigned to that station. Oh! While Don was on his way home with Kristin, he received a call on his cell phone asking him to respond as quickly as possible to our location. He tried to find a babysitter for Kristin, but with such short notice, he was unsuccessful with our regular sitters. So he brought Kristin with him. She is in your office with Mia and Andrew. Is that all right with you?"

"Of course," responded David. "That's no problem at all."

"Thank you! And I want you to know that Rachel is such a true leader! She has integrated our staff and the fire department paramedics along with her hospital staff," continued Cecilia, "and for not ever working together before, Rachel has them all working together like a fine Swiss watch. She is so incredibly professional, and Don is really enjoying himself working for her. He's also enjoying himself by referring to her only as Dr. Brooks." Cecilia smiled. "She even has him whistling as he works! You should be very proud of her. They are treating a host of injuries, from minor abrasions and contusions to serious cuts requiring several stitches. Rachel has identified several broken bone injuries and is suspicious of several others. Fortunately, we have all the necessary equipment to help diagnose and x-ray the injuries. The clinic has been divided into different sections. Some rooms are for injured guests and personnel, while other rooms are designated for the injured animals. They are also entering through different entrances. The kids have been very cooperative and are doing whatever they've been told to do by Rachel. Is there anything I can do for you concerning Chester?"

"Yes, you can. I was thinking about administering a light sedative to Chester," responded David. "Would you please draw one up for me in case I eventually decide that he may need one?"

"That's not a problem," responded Cecilia. "I'll draw one up and bring it to you."

"Thank you," David responded graciously. "By the way, Michael is here with me and would like to offer the mayor a position in the command and control unit to coordinate her activities with her staff. There she would be well informed about all the developments as they occur and could adequately respond to them quickly."

"I'll inform her about the offer," replied Cecilia. "In fact, she could overhear our conversation because you're on speaker and said yes to the sheriff's invitation. She said that she would arrive shortly at the command post."

"If you don't mind," cut in Roger. "Since I've already familiarized you with Chester's predicament, I think, while the two of you walk up there briskly, I'll just walk slowly and meet you there. Chester isn't going anywhere soon."

As Roger started to walk slowly, trying to get his heartbeat to return to normal, David jokingly asked, "Would you like me to contact guest relations to provide you with a wheelchair?"

"Only if you're willing to push me," retorted Roger. "It's hard to believe that I would be so abused and harassed by one of my best friends. Why don't you just kick a man while he's down and feed him to the hyenas?"

"Oh! I know for a fact that hyenas couldn't digest that much meat," teased David. "You're so out of shape because you don't exercise enough, and I've seen you devour all those chili dogs that you buy from the concession stand every day. Why you have such an affection for them is beyond me. You know better than that! You know that it's going to catch up with you eventually. It's already placed you in a high-risk category for a heart attack." David then placed a friendly arm around him. "We both know that those dogs are going to place you into cardiac arrest someday. What you need is more exercise and less chili dogs!"

"Well, if we're supposed to do more exercise and eat less chili dogs, why is it that exercise is so painful and unenjoyable while chili dogs taste like food from the heavens?" bantered Roger, with a sarcastic smile on his face. "Besides, they cover all the necessary food groups one needs to survive: bread, meat, chili beans, cheese, ketchup, relish, sauerkraut, onions, and they taste soooo gooood!"

CHAPTER 8

$\mathcal{Q}$uickly picking up their pace to reach the bears' habitat, the group witnessed Oscar Olson, one of the zoo's animal keepers, furiously watering down Chester with a high-pressure fire hose. Carol Lee, Chester's new trainer and primary zookeeper, was arguing with him to stop and was trying to wrestle the hose away from him. David immediately ran over to assist Carol Lee and was able to push the water stream away from the bear.

"What in the world do you think you're doing?" shouted David, not recognizing the keeper and trying to be heard over the noise of the high-pressure hose. "Shut that water off," David said loudly and not directing his order to anyone in particular. "Are you insane? What in the world is going through your mind? You're just making matters worse! You're not only agitating him further, but now he's going to be extremely uncooperative."

"I was only trying to help, Dr. Brooks," exclaimed Oscar. "I'm just trying to free him."

"Free him how? With water? The only thing that you could possibly do with water is to drown him! How could that help him? What did you expect him to do?" replied David. "He's trapped. He can't go forward, he can't go backwards, and he most certainly can't scale the wall. There's nowhere for him to go!"

"Thank you for stopping Oscar, Dr. Brooks. He wouldn't listen to me. I'm Carol Lee Palin," she said, introducing herself for the first time to David. "I'm Chester's new principal trainer and keeper. I don't want to be out of line or impetuous, and I understand that you're requesting all nonessential employees to exit the park, but may I please stay? I would like to stay behind to help Chester. I know that I'm new, but in just a short while, I've really bonded with him. I know that I can contribute something to help him."

"Of course, you may stay," replied David, moderating his voice to his more cheerful tone. "You're exactly what we need! If we're going to get Chester out of this mess, I'm sure that you're going to be our greatest asset. Do you have any suggestions? I've already ordered a mild sedative for him from the clinic. I don't want to put him to sleep, just lower his anxiety level, and make him a little more accommodating."

"Well, he likes it when I serenade him by singing Broadway songs to him, especially when I'm feeding him his favorite fruits," suggested Carol Lee. "When I was growing up, I wanted to be a Broadway star until I fell in love with zoo animals. One day I was in a great mood, so I just naturally started singing, and I noticed Chester reacting and showing he enjoyed it. Ever since then I have just kept on singing to him. But he does have his favorites, like 'If I Was a Rich Man' from *Fiddler on the Roof*, 'The Impossible Dream' from *Man of La Mancha*, 'Music of the Night' from *The Phantom of the Opera*, and most of all any songs from *Singing in the Rain, Cats,* and *The Sound of Music.*"

"Wow! That's quite a repertoire. Then let's try that!" requested David. "It should make us all more congenial."

As Dr. Brooks noticed Cecilia heading their direction with Chester's sedative, he realized that the twins were not far behind. David reacted protectively, "Mia! What in the world are you doing here? It's not safe for you or Andrew to be here. Does your mother know that you left the clinic?"

"Well, not exactly," replied Mia. "We just want to help. What's wrong with Chester?" Mia was now on her tiptoes, trying to get a better view of Chester below the viewers' railing.

"Princess, I can't have you or your brother out here. It's not safe. You two need to go back to the clinic!"

"It's okay, Dad, we're safe. We have our guar—" Mia stopped abruptly just before she said *guardian angels.*

"Dad's right, Mia. We need to do what we're told." Andrew jumped in quickly, stopping Mia from completing her sentence. "Dad always knows best." Andrew showed his irritation with Mia.

"Andrew's right, Mia," David agreed as he turned to face Michael. "Could you please have one of your units escort them back safely to the clinic?"

"I'll drive them back." Senior Deputy Foster stepped forward from a group of deputies standing next to Sheriff Raphael, all awaiting their orders. "I have my vehicle parked next to the California brown bears."

"Thanks, Darrick," reacted Michael. "We can't have them in harm's way, and please give Dr. Shaw a ride back with you. Afterward, just come back and pick up your partner. I'll assign him which area of the grounds we need you to patrol."

"And will you please make sure that they both go through the clinic doors?" requested David.

"Absolutely, sir, I'll walk them in myself," guaranteed Deputy Foster as he stepped forward.

"Thank you, Deputy. I'm so sorry to put you through the trouble."

"Not at all, Doctor. I'm happy to be of service," answered the deputy.

"David," interjected Cecilia, "I didn't know that they had followed me! I'm so sorry. I would never have given approval for them to be out here in this mess and place them in any danger. Thank God that they didn't run into any of the loose animals!" Cecilia couldn't apologize enough to David.

"It's not your fault, Cecilia," David tried to console her. "I'm sure that they didn't want you to know that they were tailing you. They have always had curious minds about everything, especially if it in any way concerns animals. They think they're immune to animal aggression and that no harm will ever come to them. They are always trying to help every animal in our meadow in total disregard for their own safety. That's how they found Rehab. If they only knew that there is no way for them to know what's in an animal's mind."

"You are so right! Since the beginning of time, man has tried to guess what animals are thinking," remarked Cecilia. "We have successfully tamed and trained some domestic animals, like dogs, cats, and horses. But we generally have only a rudimentary idea of what's going through their minds. And never more than we can guess what's in the minds of other humans! We can make educated guesses, but with most of the animals here at the zoo, we have very few clues because they are so unpredictable and wild."

"Maybe I'll call and ask my parents to go over to the house, so they can look after the kids until one of us can go home. Kristin can have a sleep over with Mia, if that's okay with you?" David asked Cecilia. "Besides, my parents are always complaining to me that they don't get enough quality time with their grandchildren. Well, no time is better than the present! I'm sure that they will even be willing to come here and pick them up at the clinic."

"Please, Dad, we don't want to go home!" exclaimed Mia. "We'll behave. I promise! We'll stay in the clinic and do whatever we're told, okay?"

"I'm not sure if I can take you at your word," responded David. "I know you only too well. You have such a propensity to help even if it's a problem way over your head. What we have here is a problem that is going to take adult professionals to solve. If I reach your grandparents, I'm going to suggest for them to come to the clinic and pick up you and Andrew and Kristin and take you home, if that's all right with you, Cecilia."

Calling Rachel on his cell phone, David offered the suggestion and that Cecilia had okayed the sleepover for Kristin.

"I think that's a great idea!" answered Rachel. "I haven't a clue how long we'll all be here. Every time I think that we might get caught up, a new group of patients comes through the front door. I don't think any of us have an idea how long this predicament is going to take to resolve itself. It's most likely that it's going to be an all-nighter. I'll call your parents and see if they can pick up the kids and take them to our house. Knowing your parents, I'm sure they will be more than willing."

"But, Dad, Andrew and I want to help!" pleaded Mia with her adorable twinkling blue eyes.

"I'm sure that you do, Princess, and I'm sure that your intentions are sincerely the best," responded David. "But this needs to be handled by adults only. There is nothing that you or Andrew can do to help."

"But, Dad," repeated Mia, "you know how well Andrew and I work with animals. We both know that we can help! You have no idea how useful we can be!"

"No, Mia. I'm afraid it's completely out of the question," insisted David. "There is no way that you can help. You just don't have the abilities to help in this kind of situation. This is not open for debate. Now, you and Andrew please return with this nice deputy to my office and wait for your grandparents to pick you up."

"Dr. Brooks, please come in," requested Dr. Steward on the zoo's staff frequency.

"I'm here, Dr. Steward," David responded.

"David, I'm receiving word from staff members throughout the park that they have located several of our escapees, and many have been injured. Apparently, they have been fighting among themselves. As soon as they can be placed in portable cages, they will be transported to the clinic for treatment. Can you please prepare your staff? Apparently, there are some with severe injuries. Julie has already contacted many of our off-duty staff members, and everyone without exception is on their way to the clinic. I'm praying that we don't lose any of our animals. By the way, Mayor Yanez is here in the command post and has approved all the overtime pay from her 'unusual occurrence' fund and has pledged all the city's available assets to us if needed."

"I understand, Dr. Steward. Thanks for the heads-up, and thank the mayor for her generosity! I'll contact the clinic. Cecilia is with me now, and I will make her aware of the latest developments about the animals. She and the staff will be prepared to receive them," answered David.

"Then I better leave now," stated Cecilia sadly. "I will advise every one of the situation when I return to the clinic and coordinate with the staff to receive the new patients coming in. I'm sure happy to hear that Julie was able to reach all the off-duty staff. We will need everyone on deck tonight!"

"Of course, Cecilia, you and the staff are going to be extremely busy tonight. Excuse me for a second, I'm getting a call on my cell from Rachel… Okay, I understand, thanks!… That was Rachel. She is saying that there are now several bite wound patients coming into the clinic. They are the guests that have been trying to apprehend the animals by hand on their own. Apparently, those are the injuries that are tying up Rachel and her staff the most, along with people slipping on the wet sidewalks, chasing the animals and injuring themselves. You and our clinic staff need to be concentrating on the incoming animals. Rachel is now requesting additional help from the hospital to handle the human injuries. I sure hope that you and Don are planning on a long night. We're going to need every able body to stay as long as possible. I anticipate unforeseen problems all night."

"You can count on Don and me, and I know that his paramedic friends are used to long arduous hours, so don't be concerned about help. We're all here for you, David, and I'm not just speaking for Don and me but for the entire staff."

"You have no idea how much I appreciate that, Cecilia. Right now, I can anticipate seeing several more broken bones and bite injuries from trying to catch these animals. The animals are scared and probably hungry because some of them have missed their evening feedings. They all have ingrained internal clocks telling them its feeding time. That's why I feel we have a good chance to recapture them with the enticement of food. Now that I'm thinking about food, I'm going to reach Dr. Steward to open our food court. We'll need to feed everyone throughout the night. Meanwhile, I think I better get back to seeing what we can do to help Chester."

Reaching Dr. Steward by radio, David asked, "Patrick, I can't believe that we are going to resolve our predicament quickly. In fact, I believe that we will be working throughout the night. I suggest that we reopen our food court to accommodate our employees. It's not only our animals who are missing their evening meals."

"I'll have the food court up and running in twenty minutes, David," Dr. Steward promised. "Fortunately, we held back many of the food court personnel so that they could, from a safe position inside the building, be our eyes in spotting any free-roaming animals and report them to the command center. I'm sure that they can get the food court up and running shortly. The fire department has notified the Red Cross, and they are also en route to help feed the troops. So everyone at their convenience can just help themselves to anything they want. If someone can't leave their post, the lieutenant said that he'll have a black-and-white deliver food and hot or cold drinks to them. I promise you, no one will go hungry or thirsty tonight. The lieutenant is now getting ready to advise everyone by radio. Everything, of course, will be on the house, courtesy of the city and the generosity of the mayor. You should notify your staff as well."

Now David turned and gave the twins a stern look. "Without another word, Mia, I want you and Andrew to go back to the clinic with Cecilia and this good deputy. Do you understand?"

"But, Dad, you have no idea how much we can…" Mia left the statement hanging, unfinished.

Although reluctant, after a short pause the twins quickly answered in the affirmative and turned obediently to comply, jumping into the back seat of the deputy's vehicle while Cecilia sat in the front passenger seat. The deputy then drove off in the direction of their father's office without a single word spoken by the twins.

On the way back to the clinic, the deputy drove downhill past a wooden bench located just in front of the trail to the African lions' habitat, where the twins saw Star and Simon sitting calmly, pointing to a shadow behind a shrub. "What do you think that was?" asked Mia.

"I'm not sure," whispered Andrew. "It appeared to be some type of a small animal, a primate perhaps. But it may have been a four-legged animal, a small deer maybe? It was hard to identify. It's too dark, and it seemed like it was trying to hide in the shadows. Look, it's starting to move deeper into the shrubs."

Evening had already lowered itself over the park, deepening the shadows of the trees and filling the air with light sounds of wild birds that flowed freely in the wind. The rain had now dropped to a light sprinkle. The automatic lighting had activated and illuminated the sidewalks, but there was little lighting inside the habitats to interrupt the animals' sleep cycles.

"We need to hurry and go back and find out," whispered Mia.

"No way!" replied Andrew in a voice as low as he could muster. "Do you want to leave your room before you become eligible for social security?"

"Then I'm coming back without you, if you're so scared. Besides, I haven't paid anything into the system, and neither have you. So we're not eligible for social security. I can't imagine anyone wanting to give you a job anyway. You're too lazy and too afraid to come out of your room and think for yourself. Do you think that Star and Simon would let anything happen to us anyway?" Mia faced Andrew with a frustrated frown.

"Mia, you really can't be thinking about going back outside once we're inside the clinic! Mom is going to watch us like a hawk, if she doesn't have the deputy handcuff us to a table or something," Andrew whispered. "It's total chaos out here, and Dad will kill us if the animals don't get to us first." Andrew began to sense an unpleasant conversation coming on. He could always tell. He was about to find out something that he wasn't going to be happy about.

"What are you talking about, Andrew? Have you been listening to me? Didn't you hear me when I said that Star and Simon wouldn't let anything happen to us? Haven't you realized yet why God sent them to us? He wants us to help save His animals. Or do you not want to help because you have an aversion to fresh air?"

"You don't really think that, do you, Mia?" replied Andrew. "Even if it might be true, why tempt the animals? Some of them are very big with very big teeth," reminded Andrew. "And now it's raining again and cold enough to see your breath! I'm sure that if God wanted to save his animals, he would have chosen someone more capable than a set of twelve-year-old twins!"

"Don't you remember that we have God on our side?" reminded Mia. "Do you want to disappoint God? After all that He has done for us! Besides, He has total control over all the animals."

"It's not exactly something one could forget," responded Andrew. "But did you hear Him personally tell you that He would protect us from all animal situations? Did you hear Star or Simon say that? No, you didn't! All Star and Simon said was that we would be able to talk to and hear what the animals had to say. They never said anything about the animals not trying to bite us, or even worse, eating us whole while they were talking to us. So my vote is for us to stay in the clinic where it's warm, dry, and safe from big hungry teeth."

"Well, that might be your vote, but it's not mine! I believe that the animals are not going to hurt us. Why do you think we happened to be here in the park at this precise moment in time? Doesn't that seem a strange coincidence to you? Why do you think God sent Rehab to us? It was because his injury would bring us here at this precise moment to the zoo to help His animals. He has given us the ability to see and talk to our guardian angels and to the animals for this reason. I believe it's exactly for occasions like this!" Mia's face was now glowing with confidence, her eyes sparkling and vibrant. "The thought of doing nothing tries my patience, and at the moment, I seem to have none with you."

Mia and Andrew, in the custody of the deputy, followed Cecilia into the clinic and found their mother right inside the front entrance with her arms folded in front of her. "You two are in deep trouble," Rachel spoke in a tone that displayed her disappointment in them. "Both of you have more common sense than to go outside and place yourselves in danger. Or maybe you don't? I want both of you to go into your father's office and wait there with Kristin for me until I can find the time to address this in more detail. Well, what are you waiting for? Go on! And I don't want to see you out of there without permission. Do you hear me loud and clear enough?"

The twins figured that their mother's last statement was a rhetorical question, and just did an about-face and walked to their father's office without saying a word.

Finding Kristin asleep on one of the two sofas in their father's office, Mia started a vigorous and passionate plea with Andrew that it was imperative for them to sneak out of the clinic and resume the task of locating and returning the animals to safety. Andrew, being the more responsible and sensible of the two, put up a convincing argument to the contrary. He insisted that they must obey their mother's demands and stay put in their father's office. "Mia! Do you want to get us in deeper trouble?" argued Andrew. "Do you want to continue to see the outside of your bedroom again?" he argued.

"Do you want to disappoint God?" debated Mia. "Because that's what we will be doing if we don't try to save and protect the animals."

How Mia somehow successfully persuaded the rational Andrew to leave the office remains inexplicable. But perhaps it was because of the powers of their guardian angels to alter situations by their mere thoughts.

"Mia, it's raining again outside, and we didn't bring any of our rain clothes with us," reminded Andrew.

"That's okay," replied Mia. "When Cecilia showed us where we could find medical jackets in the employees' locker room, I noticed that there was also protective rain clothing there that we can borrow."

As Mia and Andrew were putting on the rain gear, they found a rear-side door leading outside, and as the staff was distracted by administering medical aid to the multitude of visitors and animals entering the clinic, they secretly exited the clinic again.

"Mia, what about our grandparents? Dad was going to call them to pick us up. What's going to happen when we're not in the clinic when they arrive and start looking for us?"

"Don't worry about that, Andrew," Simon remarked. "I have a little stratagem to solve that minor problem. Your grandparents will not be free to babysit you this evening, I guarantee it."

"You can do that, Simon? You can change their plans on the spur of the moment?" asked Andrew.

"Andrew, how can you always forget who you're talking to? Of course, he can, so let's go."

"I think we should work our way back to the lions' habitat where we saw that monkey...or could have been a monkey," remarked Andrew. "It was too dark to say for sure because it was hiding in the shadows."

As the twins reached the area where they thought they had observed a primate or perhaps some type of four-legged animal earlier from the back seat of the black-and-white, they realized that they must have been mistaken or that it had moved on.

Sitting on a bench near the pathway, Andrew took the opportunity to reflect a little while Mia was deciding on a course of action. Andrew had always been a deep thinker and a fan of the many mysteries of life, much deeper than other young men of his age. Here in front of the lions' exhibit was probably his second favorite place to contemplate the majesty of life, second only to the hilltop view near their property line. This was a place where he loved to sit on the bench in solitude and absorb the fascinating view, contemplate the wildlife of the world, and reflect on the complexity of mankind's role as caretaker. Regardless of how many times he and Mia visited the zoo—which had been hundreds of times—he always found it to be breathtaking and exciting. How could he not, after all? He was sitting in what was considered to be one of the finest zoological and botanical collections in the world! Sitting here, Andrew was always reminded of the zoo's primary function, not only to entertain and educate the property's guests but to conserve and care for these exotic animals and plants.

Yes, this is most certainly a world-class park, Andrew was thinking to himself. *This is truly a well-balanced collection and accurate representation of much of the world's most exotic combinations of animals and plants.* Both African- and Asian-style villages were reproduced with painstaking designs and constructed to imitate authentic straw and adobe huts. Depicted also were carefully planned and artistically assembled hillsides, ponds, and rivers which enormously enhanced the scenery in the park.

Andrew never forgot what White Rose once told him of her people's philosophy. It made a great deal of sense to him. Men do not own the earth but are simply caretakers of it. Only God can claim ownership. And sometimes he felt that humans were in total disregard of their responsibilities. That is until he visited the park and realized that some of mankind were not. Every employee at the zoo was always conscious of his or her primary function: to care for and conserve all animals and plants in their charge.

From this vantage point by the lions' habitat, Andrew had a clear view of the African village located in the center of the park, with its four amphitheaters featuring an assortment of free animal shows and exhibits. He most enjoyed the trained bird shows, including the talking parrots and free-flying birds of prey, which always awed him with their intelligence and majesty.

Then there were always those entertaining animal shows consisting of cats, dogs, and domestic birds called Critter Encounters, which offered close-up and personal views of trained animals handled by competent, professional animal trainers. And afterward, it was always exciting to walk up and talk with the animals' very approachable trainers after each performance. In fact, this was where Mia and he would ask questions and receive numerous answers on how to train Noah.

The park was a large collage of entertaining attractions, such as the man-made Congo River, Australian Rain Forest, the Gorilla Grotto, tropical African and Asian animal habitats, the multilevel primate and bird centers, several specialty gardens, and many other enticements. These were some of the reasons that this particular zoo attracted thousands of visitors and zoologists from around the world.

As Andrew was reflecting on the beauty of the park, the automatic timed lights for this section turned from the "on" position to the less illuminating "night" mode, signifying that the park was closed. He also noticed that the electric monorail train, which transported visitors throughout the park, was still operating although the park officially closed at 10:00 p.m. Maybe it was still being used to transport employees. He loved that ride; it took over an hour to complete with its many stops where an interpreter would explain in detail what the guests were viewing. It was quiet, with open windows and with an environmentally friendly, nonpolluting power system.

Andrew always remembered what his father had told him and Mia about the first true zoo built by Louis XIV of France. He housed the wild animals in cramped, filthy cages, often by themselves, and fed them food that rarely approximated their natural diet. Their fatality rates were very high, but it was of little concern to him because the animals could be easily replaced at the time from an abundance of reserves still at large in the wild.

As the appreciation and concern for these rapidly disappearing exotic animals rose at the turn of the twentieth century, the first modern zoo was designed and built at Stellingen, near Frankfurt,

Germany. It had a small number of cages and barbed-wire enclosures; animals were exhibited in large natural-looking surroundings of artificial mountains, plains, and caves, usually with others of their species. The animals were treated with dignity, and their diets were chosen wisely. Even today, many of the older zoos still have enclosures modeled after those at Stellingen.

But this zoo was nothing like the one built at Stellingen. Here people could experience the wonders of many of the animals without the barriers imposed by bars and wire and have the zoo's staff explain and answer questions from the guests to enhance their experiences. Hopefully everyone leaving the park enjoyed a much more genuine awareness of earth's wildlife and emerged with an increased commitment to the preservation of this precious heritage.

Although the twins were so much alike, there were also many differences. Andrew was more intuitive, contemplative, the deep thinker of the two. He was the one who thought before taking action and never passed a flower without enjoying its beauty and pondering the importance of its role in the environment.

Mia was more impulsive, spontaneous, and always ready to spring quickly into action. There was always such passion in all her objectives, and she never stopped until every problem was rightfully solved. But as with Andrew, love of God, family, and animals was always her motivation.

"Andrew! Andrew!" cried Mia. "Wake up! Are you daydreaming?"

"What?" replied Andrew. "No! I wasn't daydreaming, I was reflecting. You know, in deep thought, contemplating. But what would you know about deep thought? That's something that you've never been accused of!"

"Okay, Plato! What's the difference between daydreaming and deep thought?" asked Mia cynically.

"Well," Andrew explained loftily, "daydreaming is nonproductive and a waste of time, while deep thought is the appropriate way of studying the human condition, appreciating legitimate art, acknowledging the complexity of nature and science, and the method used by intellectuals to solve the world's most serious problems. The only deep thought you've ever been engaged in is reading the headlines of those stupid tabloids at the checkout line! I'm waiting for next week's revelation: 'A modest baby, born by cesarean section, who was delivered fully clothed!'"

"So what are you trying to tell me, Andrew?" Mia responded. "That the mother swallowed the baby's clothes?"

"No!" Andrew replied, "I'm saying stop reading those crazy tabloids and start reading something worthwhile, like Shakespeare!"

"Sure, like that's going to happen!" retorted Mia. "I'll start reading Shakespeare right after I finish my correspondence course on being an astronaut performing brain surgery in outer space."

As the night's rain turned to a drizzle, the twins heard a very soft and gentle voice. Andrew and Mia recognized Star's voice immediately. "My, my, how in the world are we going to get the world to respect one another, Simon, when we can't even get a brother and sister to show brotherly love to one another?"

As the twins quickly looked up, they saw both Star and Simon standing in front of them.

"Oh! We're not fighting or being disrespectful. That's it! We're just having a little fun. It's called bantering. We always play like this when we're bored."

"I see!" answered Simon. "With all this commotion going on, you're bored?" He stood aside so that he wouldn't obstruct their view. "Do you think that you're bored or scared as much as those two over there? They don't seem to be having any fun at all."

"Andrew! There are two of the monkeys," Mia exclaimed excitedly. They could see two primates dashing across the walkway, heading in the direction of the Kilimanjaro Hiking Trail. Obviously not bored any longer, she shouted, "Let's get them!"

"Slow down, slow down there, you two," Star cautioned the twins in her gentle-hearted voice. "If you rush right in there like that, all you're going to accomplish is to frighten them even further and add to their confusion."

"What should we do?" asked Mia. "I don't want them to get lost or, even worse, get hurt."

"Do you remember what you did with Rehab? Well, the same principle will also work with these Asian monkeys."

"You told me to just lower my tone and speak softly," answered Mia, "and he'll understand me."

"That's right," responded Star. "Just this time, I'd also suggest that you approach them slowly so that you won't alarm them. Once they realize that you're trying to help them, they'll not only be able to understand you, but they won't be frightened of you either."

"I'm so excited!" exclaimed Mia enthusiastically. "I'm going to talk to the monkeys!"

As Andrew and Mia stood up, they excitedly started to briskly follow the monkeys as they scurried down the rolling and twisting narrow steps leading to the Kilimanjaro Trail, with Star and Simon right at their sides, doing what guardian angels do best: protect their wards.

As the twins were in hot pursuit of the monkeys, Andrew cried out, "Quick! Jump in the bushes!" He had noticed a pair of head-lights approaching in their direction.

"Do you think that they saw us?" asked Mia.

"No, I don't think so. It's a sheriff's car, and it looked like they were looking up, maybe for any sign of monkeys or birds in the trees. Besides, I think it's too dark for them to see us from this distance. They are easy to spot because of their headlights, so we have the advantage of seeing them way before they can see us."

"What about the monkeys that we saw? We have to follow them before they get away. I just know that they have to be lonely and hungry and uncomfortable without their friends."

Star and Simon felt Mia's deep concern, especially knowing perfectly well that both Mia and Andrew wouldn't deny any of God's creatures the relief of a rescue.

"We just have to wait until…Look, they found some other people over by the path leading to the panthers. Yes! They're driving over to talk to them now. We're just going to have to wait until they drive away."

"It looks like they're making them get in the back seat of the car," whispered Mia. "And now they're driving away. Okay, let's see if we can find those monkeys again."

"I think they went in that direction." Andrew pointed. "Over there by those trash cans."

"No! I see them behind those flowers." Mia strained her eyes and started to slowly walk in that direction, followed by Star.

"Don't forget, Mia, lower your tone and talk to them softly," reminded Star.

"Hi, little buddies," stated Mia as she started her conversation, stopping and crouching low to appear smaller and see them more at their level. "My name is Mia, and my brother and I are here to help you. Please don't be scared of us, and please don't run away from us. We wish you no harm. Can we please come up closer so that we can talk?"

Who are those big people with you? asked one of the monkeys.

"You can see them? You can see Star and Simon?" asked Mia.

Of course, we can see them! They're standing right next to you.

"They are our friends. Actually, they're our guardian angels, Star and Simon. They're here to help you as well." Mia now turned, looking over her right shoulder. "I thought no one else could see you but Andrew and me?"

"Normally, that's true. Although animals don't have individual guardian angels, they know we exist. In fact, we have special angels assigned to our nonhuman friends who also look after their best interests. Although normally they seldom see these special angels, under certain circumstances, these special angels that are devoted to wild animal life do make themselves visible to them when it is felt necessary. And because of this unusual incident here tonight at the park, Simon and I are making an exception. But please go on."

Mia now refocused back on the Asian monkeys and said softly, "There is no reason to be afraid of us. We just want to help. Would you please follow us? We'll take you where you'll be safe and be fed and can be back with your other friends."

We're not afraid of you anymore. Something is telling us that you are true friends to the animals. And yes, we'll follow you, but we're cold and hungry!

"Andrew! Isn't this exciting? We're talking to the monkeys! Now aren't you happy that we didn't stay in Dad's office? We are doing things that no one else can do, anyway that I know of. We are truly blessed!"

CHAPTER 9

"*F*or the life of me, I can't think of an easy way to free Chester," the perplexed Roger informed David and Michael. "Thank God for Carol Lee! She has been working with him and is the only one he is not lashing out at. It's obvious that he has a great deal of love for her and doesn't blame her for his predicament. But that only lasts for a brief period. Then he is reminded that he is extremely uncomfortable and wants to punish everyone else in his vicinity."

"Well, hopefully, when Frank arrives, he'll be able to come up with a solution that we haven't considered. Knowing Frank, he'll suggest some kind of elaborate production," David responded, grinning from ear to ear. "After all, his engineering degree is from MIT."

One of Roger's assistants, standing several feet away, was motioning with his arms trying to catch Roger's attention.

"It's okay, Benjamin. Come over here and join us," cried Roger as he signaled with his hand for his assistant to join the group. "There's no need to be bashful."

"I didn't want to interrupt," confessed Benjamin. "But I do want to update you on a few things."

"This is no time for formality, Benjamin," Dr. Brooks said kindly. "We're all part of a special family, so please, always feel free to speak your mind. But please tell me that you're a messenger of good tidings." Then David spotted Carol Lee in his peripheral vision on the plateau in Chester's enclosure. As he focused on her, he thought that she was a godsend. She was trying with all her heart to keep Chester distracted from his predicament and to remain as positive as he could by constantly talking to him and offering him his favorite fruits. David acknowledged her presence by waving to her, and she returned his wave. "I'm sorry, Benjamin. Please go on with your report."

"How does this go? I have some good news, and I have some unwelcome news," replied Benjamin. "The good news is that we've discovered how the primates escaped. Someone propped both security doors open at the same time, giving the animals the opportunity to just freely walk out of their habitats. At this point, I can't confirm any other new breaches. Of the hundred and seventy-eight primates that were not accounted for, ten have been spotted, but not one has been reported as captured yet. The ten have been identified as three langurs, two François monkeys, three chimpanzees, and two orangutans. Employees are still reporting in from home and are being assigned to sectors from the command post. Of the fifty-six birds originally unaccounted for, five have been spotted, but no one has a clue on how to recapture them."

"Birds! Birds have also escaped their enclosures?" David asked, totally surprised.

"Yes, Doctor. You didn't know?" replied Benjamin. "We know of nine pairs of Brazilian parrots, eleven sets of mynahs, and sixteen stork-billed kingfishers. But back to the primates, we haven't seen any evidence that any of the primates have left the property, although there have been sightings of them all over the park. But as soon as we see them, it seems that a guest or two jumps out of the shadows and tries to capture them! The guests have no clue how strong they are, especially the orangutans. It seems that every guest who has tried to catch them on their own is injured in their attempts and needs to be taken to the vet's clinic where the Mrs. Dr. Brooks assigns them to a doctor or to a fire department paramedic. After the animals escape from the grasps of the guests, they disappear in the shadows and foliage of the park. As for the birds, your guess is as good as mine! As I have said, only five have been sighted, and they have disappeared in the dark treetops, and there have been virtually no sightings of any of them again."

As they were discussing the new developments of the bird situation, David, from the corner of his eye, observed that Frank Hartman, the leading engineer who had complete supervision over the entire zoo's original construction, had arrived. Now perhaps he could begin a practical assessment of Chester's predicament and how he might be freed.

"What do you think, Frank? Have any ideas on how we're going to get Chester out and back on his plateau?" asked David.

David could still see Carol Lee on Chester's side of the plateau kneeling above him and desperately trying to calm him down. It was obvious that Chester did recognize Carol Lee, and she could give him some sense that she was there to help, but Chester was uncomfortable in his position and made it obvious that he had little tolerance for it. Carol Lee was not about to give up on him. She was determined to be at Chester's side until the situation was resolved. David was easily able to see a little of Mia's stubbornness in her and couldn't prevent himself from smiling.

"I tentatively came up with a couple of ideas while I was en route to the park, but you're not going to like any of them," responded Frank.

Focusing back on Frank, David asked, "And what might they be?"

*M*eanwhile, Mia and Andrew continued their search for additional escaped animals. Mia asked, "I don't see them anymore, do you, Andrew? I thought that I saw a couple more monkeys in those trees over there, but I'm not sure anymore." Mia pointed to an area where a clump of a half-dozen or so trees were spiraling high into the sky.

"I'm not sure either, but I think they could have gone straight ahead toward the lions' or right to the tigers' habitats or even left to the elephant ride area," replied Andrew. "Oh, I don't know!" Andrew sighed in frustration. "They suddenly just disappeared! It's so dark now, especially over there where there are dark shadows coming from the tall pine trees."

Mia, looking up at Simon, hesitantly asked, "Did you by any chance see in which direction they went?"

"I think if I were you, I'd go right toward the tigers' habitat," suggested Simon, nodding.

"The tigers!" exclaimed Mia. "Andrew, we have to hurry before they become dessert!"

Beginning to run to locate the second pair of monkeys with the first pair of Asian monkeys they were rescuing running right behind them, Mia and Andrew felt a new rush of adrenaline raising their blood pressure and producing a rapid heartbeat. "What's that?" asked Andrew as they slowed down and stopped. "I thought I saw something." But there was nothing when he looked again. Lowering their bodies to decrease the size of their silhouettes and remaining in a frozen position on the path, they tried to listen for any kind of sound, but no sounds were raised in warning or alarm. Both Mia and Andrew thought for sure they saw furtive movement, a darting shadow from the corner of an eye. Alert, they remained crouched in a frozen position, immobile, waiting, every sense alive and tingling. Even in the darkness, Mia felt suddenly exposed, vulnerable, knowing the animals had much better eyesight in the darkness with their enhanced purple vision than herself. Finally, cautiously, they decided to proceed on their way. It might have been a shadow after all. Perhaps a small bird skimming the ground in search of insects, feeding in the night.

Now that the rain had stopped, and the clouds were scudding westward, the moon was visible behind a cluster of elm trees, casting long shadows over the sidewalk. Andrew again caught a fast-moving shadow straight ahead and to the right. He asked Mia not to move. He was positive that he was not mistaken this time. Then again, movement was seen by both twins, but the shadow was so quick that the twins were unable to distinguish or recognize clearly its shape or size, only a vague silhouette of a four-legged animal. Looking up, Andrew asked Simon, "Did you see that? Do you know what it was?" Simon did not respond.

Then both twins saw movement again near some small shrubs located just before the trail that started to the tigers' habitat.

"There they are!" exclaimed Andrew as both twins stopped and then walked slowly up to them. It was incredible, the kind of detail that the eyes and mind could absorb in crisis moments when they're focused and concentrated. Moving with exaggerated slowness, Mia circled them. "Just lower your voice and speak softly to them," Mia whispered, reminding herself of what Star had cautioned her to do. Slowly extending her hands in front of her, showing that she had nothing but good intentions, Mia gently approached the monkeys.

"We're not going to hurt you. We just want to help." Mia spoke softly, trying to explain. "We know that you're scared, but there is no reason to fear us," she continued, trying to imitate the gentleness in Star's voice.

Suddenly, as if the monkeys fully understood Mia and felt the kindness in the twins' hearts, they slowly walked over to Mia and Andrew, extending their hands like children reaching for their parent's safety and comfort.

Altogether, Mia, Andrew, and the two pairs of monkeys casually walked back toward the primate habitats, avoiding any of the zoo's officials. The twins had never felt such exhilaration and fulfillment. While on the way and upon further reflection, Mia and Andrew decided it best to just return all four monkeys to the clinic and place them into a vacant enclosure while no one was looking. While en route to the clinic, they came upon several other animals to which Mia and Andrew applied their gentle voices to also convince them to follow them back to the clinic. By the time they reached the rear door of the clinic, they had gathered quite a menagerie of wild animals.

"Okay, here is my idea," proposed Andrew. "I'll sneak in the main doors without being seen and work myself to the rear-side door and open it from the inside while you wait outside with the animals. That should give you enough time to explain to them that it's essential they remain silent when entering the clinic."

"That sounds like a good plan," approved Mia. "I'll do my best with the animals, but you know how animals will behave like animals!"

"Well, I'll tell you what," suggested Simon. "I'll go with Andrew and help him out, and Star will remain here with Mia and assist her, and I'm confident that among the four of us we'll have no problems."

"I just love it when a plan comes together," spoke Andrew. "Now that we have them inside undetected, what cages are we going to use?"

"I guess we can place the larger animals in that big holding cage in the back room of the clinic. The one that Dad said they use when they treat the larger animals," answered Andrew. "It's empty now. They should be safe in there."

"And we'll place all the others in the mid-sized cage," suggested Mia. "It's almost as big. It should be big enough to accommodate all the smaller animals."

"What about them fighting with one another?" questioned Andrew. "Shouldn't we be concerned? I don't think some of these animals should be left alone together. Some of these animals are natural enemies of one another."

"That shouldn't be a problem," interjected Star. "Mia, in your most beautiful voice, explain to them how important it is for them to cooperate with you. They'll understand and will follow your instructions."

Mia turned to the animals after placing them in the selected cages and spoke very gently to them. "I know how uncomfortable it has been all night for all of us. But tonight, we must all come together as a family and be tolerant with one another. It's imperative that we all get through this night without any further injuries. So I'm asking for all of you to cooperate because anything else will not be tolerated." No more was needed to be said. All the animals clearly understood Mia's orders, and there was no dissension among them.

"Before we go to see if we've been missed by Mom, we better go and find something to feed them," suggested Andrew. "I think it's going to take more than one trip to the storage room like it was for Rehab."

"Good idea!" replied Mia. "Let's see what we can find for them to eat. I overheard the staff say that most of the animals missed their normal evening meals and should really be hungry by now."

"What do you think they eat?" replied Andrew. "Every animal in the zoo has a specific diet. How are we going to know what each of them eat? Because I have no idea!"

"You remember when Cecilia gave us the tour earlier? While you were feeding the tiger cub, Cecilia took some of us into a storage room behind the nursery for food for some of the other babies. They store food there for almost any type of animal that they might have to treat. The room is very organized, and every type of food is plainly labeled, and what animal gets what is clearly listed."

"What about bananas for the monkeys?" Andrew answered. "All monkeys like bananas." He looked up to Simon for confirmation.

"If you're not sure," suggested Simon with a smile, "why don't you just ask them?"

"Oh yeah, I keep forgetting," replied Andrew.

Bananas are good, but grapes are my favorite was clearly heard.

"I saw a big crate of grapes in the walk-in refrigerator with an assortment of other fruits," replied Mia. "You get the grapes and anything labeled Monkeys, and I'll put our friends in the enclosure."

I like the green kind was heard distinctly.

Andrew was then taking requests from all the other animals.

"Mia, have you noticed that when the animals talk to us, they really don't make any sounds?" asked Andrew. "They don't even move their mouths."

"That's because when you hear them, they're not communicating by voice sounds," answered Star. "You're hearing their thoughts, not their voices."

"We're hearing their thoughts?" replied Andrew. "How's that possible?"

"How is talking to animals reasonably explained in the first place?" Simon responded, asking a rhetorical question. "It's a gift from God Himself, and it's done by what you would call mental telepathy. Have you ever heard that expression before?"

"Yes, we talked about it in school once. It's like reading someone else's mind, isn't it?" asked Andrew.

"Exactly!" responded Simon. "You were listening in class! Now, how would it look if you started talking to some animal and someone overheard your conversation and the animal replied verbally to you? It would not only prove to be embarrassing but unexplainable, right? Don't you think that mental telepathy eliminates those problems?"

"If the animals can talk to us by mental telepathy," asked Mia inquisitively, "does that mean that they can hear our thoughts as well?"

"That's right. It works both ways," answered Star. "That's the gift. It makes everything simple and convenient. In fact, you can do the same thing with Simon and me. You need not speak to us audibly, just by mental telepathy. We will all be able to hear each other. That way, when you feel the need to speak with us in a room with others in it, no one will be able to hear us communicating."

"Can Mia and I talk to each other in the same way?" asked Andrew.

"Yes," responded Star, "we can all communicate with each other in the same way."

"What a great trick," replied Andrew. "That way, Mia won't accidentally forget and give herself away."

Did someone forget about the grapes? You know, the green kind!

"No! Of course, we haven't forgotten, little guy," replied Andrew submissively. "Let's get going and sneak you guys into the clinic."

"And don't forget about Rehab," Mia suggested. "Find something for him. He's always hungry. He told me that he could eat a horse earlier and then jokingly started to look for one."

"Okay, I'll try to sneak in the front door while you stay near the rear-side door with the monkeys until I unlock it from the inside," instructed Andrew.

Turning slowly to Simon and with a large smile, Star stated, "Even by angel standards, I can see that this is going to be very interesting."

Andrew, now at the front door of the clinic, saw no opportunity to enter without being seen. That was until Simon told him, "Don't worry. I can help." Suddenly, while everyone in the clinic continued working, each one turned their backs to the door in unison, allowing Andrew to enter without being detected!

How did you do that? thought Andrew with a puzzled smile on his face, using his newly acquired ability of mental telepathy.

Oh, we angels have a bag full of tricks that we can use when needed.

As Andrew entered through the front door, he noticed that all the staff in the clinic changed their positions in unison so that their backs were always to Andrew's route to the rear-side door.

Upon opening the rear door, Star entered first, followed by Mia and the four monkeys. Again, using everyone's mental telepathy technique, Star cautioned everyone to be extremely quiet and not give their presence away. Even the monkeys were extremely cooperative. Again, Simon used his abilities to position everyone's back toward the group's entrance. With Mia leading the monkeys to the large lockup, Andrew headed straight to the food storage room.

Andrew returned with both hands full, causing Mia to start laughing, "Andrew! You have enough fruit there for twenty monkeys and ten horses!"

"Well, they said they liked fruit, so I'm giving them a choice!" rebutted Andrew. "Therefore, I brought a few other things that looked good, like oranges, apples, bananas, and some of these fuzzy green things. Besides, we're going back out there for more animals, aren't we?"

"They're called kiwis, you nut," replied Mia, laughing.

"They are? I've never seen them whole before," replied Andrew, looking dumbfounded. "I guess Mom has always peeled and sliced them for us."

After tending to their newly found friends' needs, Mia asked, "Now what? Should we go back to find other animals?" not expecting any opposition. It was meant to be a rhetorical question anyway. Obviously, she had an appetite for additional excitement.

"Well, like Mia just said, I guess we can always look for other lost runaways," suggested Star, not expecting a rebuttal. "Although I have never approved nor felt comfortable about anyone disobeying loving and reasonable parents looking after the best interests of their children. But these are very unusual circumstances. Besides, Simon and I will see to it that no harm will befall you. But we must have a clear understanding here. Simon and I are making an exception here tonight. This is not to indicate that we will approve any further deception of your parents in the future! Have I made myself perfectly clear?"

The twins together nodded in the affirmative and answered together, "Yes, crystal clear."

Turning to each other, smiles started to grow on the twins' faces, and without another word, as if by mental telepathy, the question was answered. Both twins dashed for the rear-side door as Star and Simon followed faithfully. Then they abruptly stopped.

"We should look in Dad's office to see how Kristin is doing," suggested Mia. "I can only imagine what will happen if she wakes up and finds that we are not there with her. She will probably go into the clinic, looking for us and then find Mom. She will ask Mom where we are. And how did you say it before? We will be grounded until White Dove graduates from college, gets married, and names her third child after me!"

They found Kristin still asleep on the sofa in their father's office, and apparently they were not yet missed by anyone. "Everything seems good, Andrew," Mia stated. "Let's get back and locate other animals."

But Andrew smelled food on a small table located in the corner in the main lobby that was set up by the Red Cross. "I need to get a bite to eat first," coaxed Andrew.

"Food? Seriously, Andrew," asked Mia, "is that the only thing you think about?"

"Well, a man has to eat constantly to maintain his strength, doesn't he?" responded Andrew.

"A man, yes. A boy, *no!*" replied Mia. "It wasn't that long ago that you ate a whole extra-large pizza with a mountain of toppings, plus a slew of other items on the table! Well, hurry up and stuff your pockets. There are many more scared animals out there to find. While you attend to your stomach, I'll let Mom know that we are behaving ourselves."

"Hi, Mia. I see that you are still awake." Mia turned to Cecilia's voice, and on cue, Cecilia appeared coming down the hall to the lobby. "Where is Kristin?"

"Oh! She is still sleeping on the sofa in Dad's office. I think that she is really tired from all the walking on the tour that you gave us."

"Good!" replied Cecilia. "It wasn't just the walking, but the running you all did from habitat to habitat. Kristin is an indoor girl like her mother, not like you and Andrew, loving the outdoors and physically fit from all the sports you two compete in all year. Kristin needs to recharge her batteries more often."

"Were you getting bored in Dad's office?" Mia's mother now approached her from Mia's other side. "And where is your brother?"

"Oh! Hi, Mom! Andrew just got a little something for Rehab as a night snack from the storeroom and now is getting a late snack for himself from the Red Cross food table in the front lobby."

"Okay, just don't get in anyone's way. We're already in a 'sea of trouble' out here."

"Oh! You're quoting Shakespeare! Is he out here too?" asked Mia humorously.

"Now a comedian, are you?" Rachel answered with a smile on her face. "After you and Andrew secure a snack for yourselves, why don't you go back to Dad's office and read up on all the animal books he has in his library and answer all your animal questions there instead of bothering the staff for them. Your father and I are always pleased to find you and Andrew inquisitive, but this isn't an appropriate time for Musketeer questions."

"Okay, we'll go back to Dad's office. But if Shakespeare does show up, let me know. I have some questions for him about *Romeo and Juliet*!"

"Is Kristin as sarcastic as Mia?" asked Rachel of Cecilia.

"No!" replied Cecilia. "She is not into the classics. She is more into Edith Head than Shakespeare. She knows all about Edith Head. That's why she wants to go to the University of California at Berkeley, because that's where Edith got her undergraduate degree. Kristin knows all about her history and how she won a record eight Academy Awards for Best Costume Design, starting with *The Heiress* and ending with *The Sting*. Oh, she is quite an aspiring sketch artist herself. You will always find her carrying her sketch pad with her. She has her eyes on Paramount and Universal. Edith started her career with Paramount Studios and ended at Universal Studios because of her successful partnership with Alfred Hitchcock. So I wouldn't bring up clothes designing, or she will talk your head off!"

"Very interesting," answered Rachel. "I didn't know about her interest. How wonderful and quite ambitious!"

*F*inally, with the relief in the weather, Dr. Steward worked his way back to David's location at Chester's exhibit and, without waiting for a break in David and Frank's conversation, politely interrupted.

"Well, looking at the expressions on both of your faces, I suppose you also have nothing but unwelcome news for me." He hoped that David and Frank would surprise him with the contrary.

"Like I was just explaining to David," replied Frank. "Right now, I only see three options, but none of them seems to be very workable."

"Why is it that I'm feeling a chill down my back?" asked Dr. Steward. "Okay, being that there is no chair here for me to sit down for this shocking news, I guess I'll have to take it standing up," he continued. "What are your suggestions?"

"Well, that bear is not going to cooperate in his state of mind and let anyone get close to him so we can talk him into letting us hook up some type of harness around his back and shoulders. If we could, then we would be able to pull him up with a crane," explained Frank. "That would be the simplest and quickest method, plus the least costly. But with this option, we would need his total cooperation, and at this stage, that is never going to happen. Not after someone tried to hose him down as if he were a high-rise fire! Even with Carol Lee's help—and she has been a tremendous help—there's no way he is going to let her place a harness on him."

"What does that mean?" asked Dr. Steward.

"I'll tell you all about it later, Patrick," responded David, "but the *Reader's Digest* version is that one of the employee's easy solution to our problem here was to wash down Chester's hot temper by using a fire hose on him."

"I think the better option is to anesthetize him," continued Frank. "But then again, if we do that, he's going to just collapse into dead weight, and he'll be even more tightly squeezed between the two retaining walls. We'll never be able to wrap a harness around and under him to gently lift him back to his landing."

"So what's your third suggestion?" inquired David.

"You're going to appreciate this idea even less." Frank continued with his dismal options. "We drill a large hole down this side of the retaining wall, then once we're about two or three feet below the bear, we break a large hole in the concrete. And all this is done while he's still anesthetized. The problem there is…the wall is eighteen inches of high-grade construction cement that is heavily reinforced with rebar. Then it would still be a big job to hook him up with a harness. That's a big bear down there."

"And how long is all this going to take?" asked Dr. Steward gloomily.

"Two, three days tops," responded Frank. "Then another five to seven days to repair the damage and let the cement set."

"Are you trying to tell me that this option may take up to two weeks to solve, and at what cost?" asked Dr. Steward as he started to shake his head in exasperation.

Raising his shoulders and eyebrows and making a squinting face to indicate that he was just making an educated guess, Frank replied hesitantly, "It's going to be somewhere between thirty to forty thousand dollars."

"Why don't you just shoot him and replace him with another bear? That would seem to be the most practical and cheapest course of action," a voice was heard from someone in the background.

As everyone turned in the direction of the voice, they identified Oscar as making the comment.

"Who is this guy?" asked David brusquely, recognizing him as the one with the hose who was watering down Chester earlier. "And where did he come from?"

"His name is Oscar Olson," replied Roger. "He's one of the new animal keepers we hired a few weeks ago."

"Well, will you please tell him to keep his opinions to himself?" David replied, not appreciating Oscar's suggestion. "How in the world did he ever qualify as a keeper in the first place? In fact, Roger, you can release him for tonight. We're not going to need any more suggestions like the ones he's offering."

Still unhappy with the options suggested to free Chester, David decided to postpone the idea to anesthetize him while searching for a more acceptable solution to rescue him. David suggested that the first thing they needed to do was to calm him down; otherwise, they would be forced to mildly sedate him with a dart gun.

"I thank God for all your help, Carol Lee," David told her with a slightly louder voice being that she was now standing on top of the enclosure's plateau.

Nothing they tried thus far seemed to work at all to calm Chester down, except for a few moments at a time by Carol Lee.

The more he tried to free himself, the more he became frustrated. Like a cornered and threatened animal, Chester lashed out at anything and anyone who was trying to help, except for Carol Lee. Every effort proved to be futile. If anything, he was getting angrier and more desperate by the minute. The only one he had any respect for was for Carol Lee, but she was limited on what she was able to do for him.

Benjamin had earlier excused himself to attend to other problems, and he returned now to the group with further updates.

"With the help of Carol Lee, we finally were able to coax a couple of the other bears from the plateau back to their lockups or their feeding grottos, but several others are still not accounted for. But I think that it's perfectly safe for the workmen to enter Chester's main habitat," reported Benjamin. "But we still have not been able to locate any of the other primates or birds that have escaped."

"Not one has been recaptured?" asked Dr. Steward disappointedly. "Not even after all the reported sightings that we had earlier?"

"Not one, Doc," replied Benjamin. "We did have so many sightings, but as we approached them, it was hopeless—as though they didn't recognize us at all. And you know that some of our staff have been working with these primates for years! You know how quick those primates can be. We couldn't keep up with them as they fled from us. Then suddenly, they would just disappear into the trees. And this weather isn't helping with our visibility. Although the moon has risen, it keeps darting behind the moving clouds."

"They're probably all terribly frightened and confused. We all know what great natural survivors they are," answered Roger. "And they all know how to avoid their predators. Their natural instincts are probably kicking in right now, and they know only too well how to make themselves invisible, especially when they have a dark night as their protector. And I don't think that the noise from the two helicopters is helping our cause. I fear that it might be another agitating factor for them. I also feel that they've probably all found shelter for the night and are so terrorized by everyone running after them that they probably won't come out until they're good and hungry."

"I agree," interjected David. "These primates are at a point where their instinctive reaction precedes rational thought and are following their own spontaneous sparking of the survival pattern."

"So you don't think that we have any realistic chance of capturing any of them tonight?" ask Dr. Steward.

"I don't think so, Doc," replied Roger. "I think it best to concentrate our time on preparing food traps and setting them out tonight. Hopefully, with any luck, by morning we may have captured a couple of them. This is such a large park, it may be weeks before they all are found. My biggest fear is that they may escape from the property and into the community."

Noticing that Security Chief Paul Chapin was approaching with his updates, Dr. Steward prayed for some words of encouragement.

"Any good news?" asked David.

"No! No good news… But if it's any consolation, there isn't any major bad news to report either. The park is sealed and secured as much as possible for its size. But we're still finding visitors all the time and escorting them off the property. There have been no new sightings of either monkeys or birds. But there is also no evidence that any of them have left the park, as far as the primates go. Who knows about the birds? It doesn't appear that the news media are aware of our problem. No mobile news trucks have shown up yet. But we may have to eventually inform them, especially if we must shut down the park. We're not going to be able to open for business tomorrow or any time soon, at least not until all the animals are accounted for. And I understand that this might not happen for weeks!

"Doc," Paul continued, "I'm afraid that you will eventually have to make a press statement. I'm very surprised that the press hasn't stormed our front doors yet. You know that some of the visitors have already left the park. Someone will eventually post a YouTube video or contact the news media. There are probably Facebook postings already. And you know how reporters are going to be all over this story! I'm sure that all the guests that have been hiding in the park have been taking pictures and videos on their cell phones galore. There is no way that we can maintain a media blackout, not on a problem of this magnitude. Neither I nor any of my staff, of course, has taken the liberty to inform the local media. As far as I know, only the hospital and the sheriff's department are aware of the magnitude of our problem. You know that when reporters do arrive, they will first be met by our security staff, who will not be permitting anyone access to the park. They are going to want information. They're going to see that the sheriff's department is on the scene with their mobile command post, and they will want to know what's up. Knowing the press, their imaginations will be in high gear, like someone was mauled by a lion or tiger or something equally outrageous. May I discuss this with you before they arrive in droves? I've instructed my men to follow normal protocol and to tell the press that they aren't at liberty to discuss the matter. That there will be a press conference soon, and all information will be coming from public relations or you personally."

"I don't see any need for alarming the public now," answered Dr. Steward. "If we feel that the animals are still all contained on the property, there shouldn't be any danger to the community. But should there be any signs that any of the primates has breached the park's perimeter, then of course, we have a responsibility to inform the public. What is your opinion, Sheriff Raphael? Do you disagree?"

"No, I agree with you, as long as all the animals are still contained on the grounds. I have assigned several of my deputies to patrol outside the park and around the community. None has reported any animals outside the park. If, of course, they breach the perimeter, they may revert to the call of the wild. Due to their newly found freedom, they may become a danger to anyone who tries to capture them on their own. Until there is a danger to the community, we should limit what's told to the public. Otherwise, everyone in town will want to come out and be the local hero. Until then, let's keep it limited, and I'll instruct my deputies to do the same."

"Well!" replied Dr. Steward despondently. "Let's do all that we can tonight and prepare for the worst while we pray for the best."

"I'm just receiving word that three zebras and two camels have been spotted roaming around the koala exhibit. Also, a hippo and his mate have been located at the reptile center," Michael informed the others.

160

"I can take care of those sightings," stated Benjamin and immediately left the area.

"As you all attend to your work," replied David, "I'll return to the clinic and prepare a fresh sedative for Chester in case one is needed. Hopefully, it will calm him down so that we can make him somewhat more comfortable until we can free him."

"And I better call in a crew to gather up the equipment we're going to need," suggested Frank. "We'll need to start as soon as we can because I see a whole lot of work in front of us!"

"Is it possible that we may get away with only making a small hole," asked Dr. Steward, addressing Frank, "sparing us a great deal of time and money?"

"How much do you think that bear weighs?" Frank asked David.

"I'm not sure. My educated guess would be about 1,700 pounds plus. But I can confirm that with our records back in the clinic from his last annual physical," responded David. "I believe that he was weighed last August with our large animal portable scale that we use in the field. For obvious reasons, we just can't weigh him in the clinic."

Frank, looking gravely at Dr. Steward while making a most gloomy and dispirited face, replied, "No, we're talking about a big hole, a very big hole."

"I can't see that we have a choice, so go ahead and do whatever David asks you to do," responded Dr. Steward. Then he turned to David with exhausted eyes. "Like I said earlier, I have total confidence in you. You're completely in charge. Just tell me what I can do to help."

"Well, if you like, you can come with me back to the office," answered David. "Maybe we should brainstorm a little longer. I feel that there is still a better option out there somewhere. I know that we can come up with a better alternate solution!"

*A*rriving back at the clinic, David was amazed to find the clinic full of people receiving medical treatment. His wife stood next to a gurney, giving instructions to several staff members while treating a patient herself. He was astounded to see how much she was in total control and obviously in an element for which she was well prepared and trained. He was so proud of her!

Placing his arm around Rachel's shoulders, David had only admiration in his eyes. "This clinic has never been so busy nor run so well!" complimented David. "I'm overwhelmed by how many people are here!"

"We have twenty-seven members of your staff, of which fourteen were called in from home to help by Julie," responded Rachel. "Thank God for them, because they know where all the supplies and equipment are located. We have eleven staff members from the hospital, all from the emergency ward, and nine paramedics from the fire department. Most of these people have never met each other before, yet they are all working together like a fine Swiss watch. I'm so envious of some of your high-tech equipment! Hospital staffs don't usually have access to such equipment nor are trained in some of your techniques. I'm so impressed! I'd like to steal some of your staff for myself."

"We are not just an animal hospital but an international veterinary teaching school. We have some of the best college professors in the nation on staff here. We also have researchers on staff working on state and national grants developing procedures and techniques. The reason that you're not familiar with some of our equipment is that developers come here so that we can evaluate it first before it is placed in any human hospitals. And don't think for a moment that I'm not going to count my staff members before you leave to make sure they are all accounted for," David said jokingly. "But seriously, why are there so many patients still here?"

"We have more than ninety victims present with multiple and varied injuries, male and female, and of all ages. Just to give you a small recap, we have treated a wide assortment of injuries, from minor to severe traumas to the face and head, to severe gouges to the face, neck, hands, arms, and abdomen. We've treated bruises and contusions from chasing loose animals in the rain and falling, from broken hips from being pushed to the ground by other guests in the park, from split lips and broken teeth to broken bones. As well as tending to animal bites from trying to grab onto a fleeing baboon or some other animal, etc., etc. In fact, we have several of your park employees in for treatment for a variety of reasons. It seems like for every patient we release, two others show up to replace them! We have had the fire department transport several individuals to the hospital after we have stabilized their injuries. Everyone has been logged in and out of the clinic and time-stamped. We know everyone's name and personal information. We have even initiated a separate log for all employees of the clinic, hospital staff, and fire department staff, and which patients each one has treated. Everything has been fully documented. I'm afraid that we all still have a long and busy night ahead of us."

"I'm so impressed!" acknowledged David gratefully. "I thank God you're here. I can't even begin to imagine what we would have done without you and your team."

"You should thank Cecilia for stepping in and taking the point in this hectic 'sea of troubles,' as Mia reminded me that Shakespeare said so well. It has been Cecilia who has been the overall coordinator," replied Rachel. "She was the one who divided the clinic into two parts to prevent cross contamination. There is a locked door between the two temporary clinics. The human patients are treated by hospital and fire department staffs in the front portion of the clinic, utilizing the double front doors to enter and egress while being admitted and released, and the animal patients are treated by your excellent staff and use the employee doors for admitting the animals. These animal patients after they are treated are either placed in individual cages and are frequently monitored to evaluate their condition and comfort or, if it is deemed appropriate, returned to their permanent personal habitat. All precautions of cross contaminations between human and animal treatments are safely eliminated, utilizing this protocol. For the number of patients that we are dealing with, I'm very pleased with our progress. Being that everyone on my side of the clinic is new here, Cecilia is here with me helping and answering all our questions. Your staff is all very familiar with the facility and requires very little coordination with your established procedures, therefore require very little supervision. If they have any questions, they just pick up a house phone and ask Cecilia or just talk through the window on the wall separating the two clinics. As you can imagine, we need her much more than they do."

"Well, I can see that you have given a great amount of thought into your protocols and have everything under control," expressed David. "I'm quite impressed. Only God knows how appreciative I am, and I will personally see to it that both teams' efforts are rewarded. But for now, I'm just here to get a sedative for Chester, our Alaskan brown bear. He got himself into a nasty predicament, and I need to get him settled down. By the way, where are the twins?" asked David. "Did my parents come for them?"

"No, they called and said that unexpected guests had arrived, so I told them that they didn't have to come. Besides, the kids really didn't want to leave and miss all the excitement. Mia was just here with me and said that Kristin was taking a nap in your office. She then went over to meet Andrew at Rehab's area where they were giving him some extra TLC and a late snack. You're not going to believe how smart that little red fox is and how he is milking his broken leg to the maximum. He has the kids wrapped around his little paw."

"And they haven't been in the way?" asked David.

"Not at all, David. The kids have been totally out of the way. In fact, they have hardly even been seen much," added Rachel.

David turned to Rehab's location and spotted the twins waving at him through the window separating the two clinics. He returned their wave and started to walk to meet them. Through the window, David asked, "Have you two been behaving yourselves and staying out of trouble? And are you implementing all the decontamination protocols that Cecilia taught you earlier today when you go from one treatment side to the other?"

"Of course, Dad. Both Andrew and I are being very careful. We've just been enjoying all the excitement and doing what our limited talents can do to help," replied Mia with a large grin on her face. "In fact, we have been constantly supervised by adults. You might even say some of them have been angels to us."

"Good, hopefully the three of you kids can be back home early enough to get some sleep before you need to get ready for church tomorrow. I, of course, will not be able to make it, nor your mother. It looks like it's going to be an all-nighter for most of us! Maybe after mass tomorrow we will have a better understanding of everything, and we can all go out for breakfast. Please tell Father Percarsic and Sister Mary Josephine that your mother and I are sorry for not attending. I'm sure they will understand under the circumstances. But for now, perhaps you two should get some sleep like Kristin is doing. I'll probably ask Rain Cloud and White Dove's father to drive you two to mass tomorrow. Your mother and I will have our hands full all morning."

"David, please come in," requested Mayor Yanez over the radio. "We have a wonderful surprise for you…well, I guess for all of us. Luigi and Maria from Dominic's are here with all their kids. They have arrived with their large catering truck, jam-packed with hot pizza and many of their Italian dishes. I'm sending them to the food court to unload. They can work out of there and set up their own area. Would you like for them to also drive over to the clinic and set up a table there too? They can work with the Red Cross. That way, Rachel's and your staff can eat at your pleasure in your lunch room."

"That's a great idea, Cynthia! Thank God for families like the Dominics! Our community is extremely blessed with their presence and generosity. But there is no need for them to deliver their dishes here. We are beginning to be cramped for space. The Red Cross has vans here, and they have been using them to pick up some food items from the food court and serve them in the break room. They can continue doing the same with the new dishes from Dominic's. Thank them for their thoughtfulness and also tell Luigi that his generosity is greatly appreciated, and we will be doing something special for him and his restaurant. The staff is already going crazy here for Dominic's pizza. In fact, earlier while we were having dinner at his restaurant, I was thinking about an idea that I wanted to explore with Luigi between his restaurant and the zoo. But then we were notified about all the turmoil here, and I didn't get the chance to talk to him about it. When I get the opportunity, I'll pop by the food court to propose it to him."

"I'll let him know. But now you have me intrigued what your idea is about. Whatever it is, if it is anything like all your other ideas, I'm sure it's a good one! In which case, you will undoubtedly have my support," responded the mayor.

Thank God for

CHAPTER 10

*A*s David returned with Dr. Steward to Michael's and Frank's location with the sedative, neither one of them could come up with a better alternative suggestion to Chester's predicament. "We may just have to go with Frank's third scenario, David," suggested Dr. Steward.

"You may be right, Patrick," David agreed reluctantly. "But among all of us, you would think that we could find another method without all the cost and time involved."

Just then, Benjamin ran up to them with anger in his eyes. "More animals are loose!" he shouted.

"What are you talking about, Benjamin?" asked Dr. Steward.

"There are many new animals loose! After we made our initial sweep, we went back to the beginning and found new habitant enclosures open that weren't originally opened the first time. We also found that those that were found opened the first time and closed and secured were reopened on the second run through. What I'm trying to say is that there is someone or several people out there still unlocking the enclosures! I'm not sure how many additional animals are out of their enclosures. We're still trying to get an accurate accounting, but I fear that it's going to be substantial."

"We need to locate this responsible individual or individuals quickly! This may be our new priority," replied Michael. "I'm getting on the radio and updating everyone working security. We're going to have to get much more aggressive in apprehending this suspect or suspects. We need to identify and capture this perpetrator, or it may motivate him or them so much that he or they will never want to stop and continue the releasing of animal after animal. We need to stop this hemorrhaging of escaped animals! But because this property is so enormous, this is going to be like the proverbial search for a needle in a haystack when the needle may not be a needle and the haystack may not be a haystack! We're going to need extra help. I'm going to get the PM watch commander to initiate an 'unusual occurrence event' and call in all off-duty personnel. I may also have to talk to the mayor so that we can call for mutual aid if needed from our adjacent law enforcement agencies."

"Sheriff, I'm beginning to think this could be a political statement by some kind of animal rights activist group?" proclaimed Dr. Stewart.

"Yes," Michael agreed, "the basic profile could be the work of a group or organization. If it is, they will certainly want to take credit, and quickly. They would crave the attention and the platform for whichever cause they believe in. The fact that it's been several hours now without any group claiming credit lowers that probability in my opinion. The longer without that contact being made, the higher the probability that this is the work of an individual or a small group with no specific agenda other than just being mischievous. But whatever the motive, we need to stop it now."

"I'm just receiving word via my Bluetooth that we have just hit the media," reported Michael. "There are too many visitors in the park to keep the lid tight on this incident. The media are not sure what's going on. They just know that something has seriously gone south. Everyone is following proper protocol. They're sticking to 'No comment' and telling the media to contact public relations or Dr. Steward. No one is saying anything out of turn. But there are now several reporters here with their mobile vans from a host of network TV stations. They are looking for answers. They know that the sheriff's mobile command center has been activated and deployed. And they can plainly see the department's helicopters circling above. What do you want me to tell them?"

"Tell them the truth: that I'm preparing a statement, and I'll meet with them shortly," responded Dr. Steward.

Dr. Steward, with his head lowered and shaking it slowly back and forth, was heard mumbling to himself, "What's going on? This is just getting crazier by the minute. I can't even imagine how much this is going to cost us in time and money, besides hurting our reputation. You have no idea how much I want to catch this guy and just strangle him!"

*M*eanwhile, Mia and Andrew slipped out the rear-side door again to continue their quest for additional animals loose in the park. They felt a sense of satisfaction and accomplishment in the rescue of all the animals that they had already found and were pleased with their decision to secure them in the holding cages in the clinic where the animals were enjoying their safety and security as well as being well fed.

"Where do you think we should start?" asked Andrew. "As you know, this facility is huge. With all the commotion going on and with the flashing lights on the police vehicles, animals must be scared to death."

"We have a few ideas," both Star and Simon said in unison. "Look what we just did!" Simon said. "We just did what the twins do. We spoke in unison. The twins must be influencing us!" All four of them laughed uncontrollably.

"Let us lead you in a few directions," suggested Star as she started to walk in a southerly direction. "I'm sure we'll find some loose creatures in this direction."

As the twins followed Star and Simon, they crossed the path of several loose animals hiding in the shrubs, trees, and behind small buildings on the grounds. And using the techniques that Star had taught the twins, they were successfully able to gain the trust and confidence of numerous additional animals, such as a clouded leopard, two wallabies, an armadillo, a tapir, an emu, a fennec fox, a wombat, two giant anteaters, an ocelot, two porcupines, a puma, and an assortment of other small animals. They not only were able to gather them up, but also convinced them to follow them. After a while, Mia suggested that they should return them to the clinic before searching for others. They had so many that it was almost impossible to remain unnoticed in their journey. In fact, the twins were surprised that they hadn't been spotted already.

"Now, how are we going to get these animals into the clinic without being noticed?" asked Mia.

"Why don't you leave that up to us, Mia?" suggested Simon. "Both Star and I have a few tricks that we can use to handle this little task."

And without any difficulty, both Star and Simon distracted everyone in different directions, so the twins were able to walk all their newly found friends into the clinic through the rear-side door and into the large holding area without being discovered.

"Now, we'll need to gather up some more food for them, Andrew," suggested Mia. "We promised them that we would. Don't forget that they all missed their evening feeding."

"I don't think that will be a problem. There is plenty of food in the storage room to accommodate them all. I'll be right back," replied Andrew.

*M*eanwhile, out at Chester's location, several of the workmen were getting tired and needed a break. Dr. Steward just received word that the food court was now in full operation with the help of Luigi. The good doctor suggested to David that maybe everyone could take alternate breaks and avail themselves of the food court, informing them that everything was on the house. That seemed to brighten up everyone's spirits.

"That's a good idea, Dr. Steward! We need to wait for additional help and equipment, so now is an appropriate time for my men to take a break," agreed Frank.

"Patrick, why don't we go back to the clinic and see if there is anything that we can do there to help. It looks like Frank has everything here under control," suggested David. "In fact, we should pass by the food court and propose my idea to Luigi. Hopefully, he will agree with me and work with us on this new project that I have in mind."

"Good idea, David. I would like to tag along and thank him myself. In fact, there is a whole lot of thanking that needs to be done! Without the staff from the hospital, fire department, police department, and of course, your clinic's staff, I don't know how we would have survived this far, and all in extension to their regular duties. I want to see if Rachel has any further needs that I can assist with from my end. They're all going way beyond the call of duty."

Upon reaching the food court, the two men found that the zoo's personnel had stepped aside and let Luigi run the kitchen, being that he had more experience than all of them put together, and they were honored just to be working with this famous chef. Entering the food court, David immediately was able to spot Luigi in the kitchen. As he approached him, Luigi walked even faster over to David and gave him the second Italian bear hug of the day.

Luigi spoke first, "My friend, what can I do to help? Me and my family are here to serve you and your staff. Whatever we can do, count us in."

"Luigi, you're doing so much already! I would be embarrassed to ask for anything else. But there is this idea I have. What do you think about opening another restaurant here at the park? I'm thinking about what a terrific opportunity for Andrea to utilize his enormous creativity. Nothing that would interfere with his school work, of course. That will always have first precedence. But he could test market his great ideas here in a new restaurant before you incorporate them in your existing restaurant in the city. With your and Maria's management and public relations expertise, you will have two outstanding restaurants for our community to enjoy."

"But what about your food court? You want us to compete against you? No, my friend, I could never do that! Your friendship is worth more to me than money," responded Luigi.

"No, not compete! I want you to take over the food court. We have a captive audience here. Our guests come here for an all-day experience, most staying from six to ten hours. They need to eat, and they don't want to leave the park and come back through the main gate, so they need to have at least one meal here. With your presence here, we know that their dining experience with you would make a great match with their entertaining educational experience with us. It's a win-win for both of us! It's what we scientists call a symbiotic relationship. We are both better off being together. Our guests will have a choice between fast food, like an Italian deli, which would be a vast improvement over our food court menu or a great Italian sit-down dinner. You will run both. And we should continue offering our famous Italian sausage dogs and lemonade through our popular kiosks throughout the park. What do you think?" asked David as Dr. Steward nodded in approval.

"You humble the Dominic family, Dr. David, but I, too, think it's a great idea! And I, too, enjoy the zoo's Italian sausage dogs and lemonade and would never discontinue serving such a signature item. I've also been thinking about opening a new restaurant for more than a year, for Andrea," Luigi replied. "He has come up with so many great ideas already. He wants to spread his wings and fly like an American eagle. Andrea has made the Dominic family very proud. I would love to sit down and discuss how to start such a brilliant concept later. May I suggest calling the restaurant Andrea's Italian Cuisine? What do you think?"

"I couldn't come up with a better name myself." David laughed. "Andrea's Italian Cuisine it is! But now I must return to the clinic. We will talk at length about this later. But first I must step over and personally thank Maria, Andrea, Anna, and Katarina for being here."

"And I must return to feeding your hungry employees. They eat like unemployed Italians!" Luigi laughed. "But nothing pleases a chef more than seeing someone enjoying their food."

And before David left the food court, hugs were passed around freely.

*R*eturning to the clinic and entering through the front door, David was approached by Rachel. "You look so tired, David," sympathized Rachel.

"Not any more than you should be," replied David, as he closed his eyes. "I hope the twins haven't gotten themselves into any mischief since I was here last. I'm quite aware how much they love to get involved in things that should be left to adults. I'm sure they feel that they can do things equally as well as adults, if not better! They always seem unaware of their limitations and get themselves into unnecessary trouble. With so many of our staff out searching for the escaped animals, no telling what they've been doing without someone looking over them, and that goes double for Mia!"

"Oh! Come now, what kind of trouble could those two adorable, intelligent, and innocent children possibly get themselves into?" interjected Dr. Steward.

"Adorable and intelligent, yes! Innocent? Yeah right, fat chance!" Rachel laughed. "Knowing how easily Mia gets bored, she probably has all the animals dressed up for a St. Patrick's Day Parade."

"Oh! You have something against St. Patrick, do you?" replied Dr. Steward in his best Gaelic accent.

"I'm sorry. I meant no offense," Rachel quickly replied. "I forgot you're his namesake."

"Well, you should be ashamed of yourself!" replied Dr. Steward. "Not only for making jest of St. Patrick but also for disparaging those beautiful young wee bairns of yours. You'll see, when you find out what they've been doing, you'll be proud of them."

"We'll see who's right," David acknowledged skeptically, looking around the clinic for them. "By the way, Rachel, have you or any of your staff looked at Roger's hand?"

"Oh! Not that I'm aware of. What happened to his hand?" asked Rachel.

"He scraped it on a nail while opening a crate of fruit. Even though he had it bandaged, I could see that it was swollen, and I'm concerned that it might be infected," replied David. "I'll suggest it again when I see him."

"Please do," agreed Rachel. "I've seen where something minor has turned into something very serious because they thought it was so innocuous it didn't require any medical attention. So tell him to get his caboose in here, because it might not be as harmless as he thinks."

"I'll do that," responded David. "He thinks like our kids and is oblivious that he could succumb to disease or injury."

Turning to the window separating the human and animal clinics, David was met by Mia on the animal side speaking through the glass window. "Hi, Dad, what's up?" Mia asked with her usual playful, teasing smile, feeling that she and Andrew had just been caught with their hands in the cookie jar.

"What's with all the fruit?" David asked. "There is no way you can be hungry again after gorging yourselves at Dominic's!"

Without thinking, while both Andrew's and Mia's arms were filled with fruits and vegetables, Mia responded. "It's not for us, it's for Rehab."

"Do you think that Rehab will be able to eat all that food?" asked their father.

Trying to think fast on her feet, Mia responded, "Of course not. We were just going to give him a selection to choose from. And I overheard that some of the loose animals have been hurt and would require medical attention here at the clinic. So Andrew and I were getting prepared to help feed them. You know I only have so many cookies left."

Suddenly a voice came over David's radio. "David, come in, please," asked Roger.

"I'm here, Roger. What's up?" replied David.

"Can you please come back to Chester's habitat? The sedative you gave him isn't calming him down any longer. I'd like you to reevaluate him if you can," answered Roger.

"I'll be back in five," answered David. Then he said to Rachel, "I have to go back after I prepare another sedative for Chester." Then he turned to the twins. "As for you two, just keep staying out of trouble and out of the way unless your help is asked for, okay?"

"We'll stay out of the way and only do what we can to help," answered Mia. "We will be so far out of the way that nobody will even know that we are here!"

*A*s soon as their father left the clinic, Mia and Andrew fed the animals that they had rescued, and then exited the rear-side door of the clinic and paused just outside the rear exit. "Okay, what do you want to do next?" asked Mia.

"Well, let's see if we can find some additional animals," replied Andrew with a smile on his face as wide as the Grand Canyon.

They had gone no farther than a hundred yards, however, when Deputy Foster and his partner spotted them and stopped them. "So it's you two again! And where do you think you two are going?" asked the senior deputy. "What in the world are you doing outside the clinic again?"

"We're just out for a little fresh air and some peace and quiet," responded Andrew. "It's hectic inside there!"

"You two are perfectly aware how dangerous it is out here with all the loose animals. Now follow us because we need to escort you back to your mother. Oh, I know about you two very well! My two kids also go to Holy Family. Do you know Aaron and Irene Foster?"

"Yes, Deputy Foster," responded Mia. "Irene is in our class, and Aaron is a grade ahead of us. Do they belong to you?"

"Yes, they belong to me, and I'm aware of your vocation of looking for sick and injured animals. But this isn't a meadow where there are small local animals. This is a zoo with large wild animals from all over the world. That's way beyond your ability to help. So come on with us. We're taking you back to Dr. Brooks."

As Mia and Andrew entered the main entrance of the clinic, Rachel looked up and noticed the twins followed by the two deputies.

"I'm sorry to inform you, Dr. Brooks, that my partner and I found your children about a football field away outside the rear of the clinic. I'm quite sure that you were probably unaware of their whereabouts," spoke Deputy Foster.

"I had no idea that they were outside the clinic, Deputy Foster! They were supposed to be in their father's office. Thank you so much for bringing them back," replied Rachel. Now turning to face the twins, she went on to say, "So you two went back outside again without permission? You have no idea how much trouble you're in this time! But fortunately for you, I'm busy right now suturing Mr. Desmond's leg, so this issue will have to wait. But either your father or I will attend to this matter later! Now go over there and sit down in those two chairs until one of us can get back to you. I'm so disappointed in both of you!"

All she heard back in response was "Yes, Mother" in unison.

Now as Mia and Andrew sat at the far side of the clinic, Andrew started to look around for Simon and Star; but not seeing them, he started to whisper their names. As they appeared, Andrew asked, "Why didn't you use your little trick so we wouldn't be caught? You intentionally let us be caught! Why?"

"Andrew," Simon responded, "there is a reason for what we do, and there is a reason for what we don't do. You're just going to have to wait to see the reason why. So are you ready to start again?"

"Start what again?" asked Mia.

"I thought that we were looking for additional animals," Simon explained patiently.

"What!" asked Mia. "Didn't you hear what our mother said? We are in serious trouble! There is no way that our butts can leave these chairs. Simon, I love you more than you realize. But if we're caught again outside this clinic…" She turned to Andrew. "How did you put it so well before, Andrew? It went something like this: 'We will be grounded until White Dove graduates from college, gets married, and names her third child after me.'"

"I can assure you, Mia, this time no one will realize that you are missing. I guarantee it!" Simon responded.

"You promise that you will do one of your tricks?" asked Mia.

"I do, and it will be one of my best!" assured Simon.

"Okay. I'm satisfied," answered Mia energetically. "Then let's rock and roll!"

"Oh, Doc! I'm glad you're back!" Roger shouted in exasperation. "Chester is going ballistic down there again. His sedatives have not been that effective. Carol Lee has been trying to calm him down by feeding him but with no success. He refuses to eat."

"Well, I have something here a little stronger this time that should help," replied David. "It's not going to put him to sleep, but it will calm him down and make him a little better-natured. What I need to do is find a suitable location where I can get a clear shot at him with this dart gun."

"I think down inside the habitat would give you the best angle, Doc," suggested Roger. "From there, you would only be about fifteen feet away. Even a shot as terrible as yourself should be able to hit a sitting duck from there!"

"Oh, is that right?" David replied as he flashed him a surprised look. "I must admit, I'm not very experienced at shooting defenseless animals. But let me inform you of a well-known fact: When I was at vet school, I had the nickname of Deadeye Dave, and I still have the school record for hitting a moving zoologist at a thousand yards."

"I was only joking, Doc," replied Roger, laughing as he raised both hands in a soothing, pacifying gesture of surrender. "Okay, remember that you only have one shot with you, and Chester needs it a lot more than I do."

"Speaking of needs," David continued, "I understand that you have still failed to report to the clinic to have that hand looked at. So I'm telling you again, the first chance you get, march down to the clinic and have that hand looked at, or I'm going to place the hotdog carts off limits to you. Then let's see where you are going to get those chili-cheese dogs that you are so fond of!"

"Doc, you wouldn't cut off a man's lifeline, would you?" Roger pleaded. "Those little dogs are my epicurean delights, and my body will go into withdrawal if denied."

"Then you know what you must do, as much as I know what I must do about Chester," answered David. "Or I'll sedate both of you and have you carried down to the clinic while we continue to work on Chester."

Once in place, David was trying to get a clear shot of Chester's rump. But it was difficult because while he was standing upright, his back was against the cement retaining wall. As Carol Lee was keeping him distracted, David took careful aim and fired. Confirming that the dart hit exactly where he intended, right in the middle of Chester's right buttock, David shouted, "Bull's eye!"

"Bull's eye!" repeated Roger. "Doc, you hit the rear end of a 1,700-pound bear at fifteen feet. The only bigger target would be to hit the Goodyear blimp at five feet."

"Roger, you don't think by any chance that this was the last of my supply of sleep-inducing drugs, do you?" asked David with a devilish smile. "For your information, I have sufficient quantities left at the dispensary to put someone like you into hibernation until well after next Christmas."

"Doc, I don't know what came over me," replied Roger again, laughing with his hands high in the air. "It must be all the stress. It must be making me say what someone else is thinking. That's it! Someone else must be putting these thoughts into my head and forcing me to say all these disrespectful things."

"Yeah, sure!" replied David jokingly. "Like someone else made Cain stab Abel in the back."

"*I* don't know where to start. There are so many loose animals now! Maybe we should start with some more monkeys? There are still missing chimps," Andrew reminded Mia.

"That's right!" Mia responded, with the same look that Sherlock Holmes must have had when he was engaged in hot pursuit of one of his hideous criminals. "But how are we going to find them?"

"The same way we found all the others," Andrew quickly replied.

Both twins started to turn in all directions, searching for Star and Simon. And no sooner had they softly whispered their names than they appeared right at their sides.

"Do you know where we can locate some of the other missing animals?" Mia was the first to ask. "We know that there are other missing chimps for sure. Do you know where we can find them?"

"Are there saints in heaven?" replied Simon, demonstrating that even angels have a sense of humor.

"We'll need to take a little walk over to the African elephant sanctuary," replied Star to Mia's question. "But I'm afraid that they may not cooperate as easily as the others."

"Why not?" answered Mia, mystified. "I don't understand. Why wouldn't they want to return to their friends and be where they're safe, fed their favorite foods, and well taken care of by their zookeepers?"

"It may be best if we discuss this when we find them," replied Star with an obvious look of concern.

As the twins and their guardians walked the distance to the elephant sanctuary, the sun had set long ago, and the rain had subsided to a light sprinkle, but the skies in the horizon still had a charcoal gray to them due to the moon darting in and out between the clouds. And even though the park was well lit in most areas, there were still other small pockets that were dark and uninviting. Normally, Mia and Andrew would have been very conscious of this fact, but since they were in the company of their now-visible guardian angels, it was of no concern to them at all.

"You may find it difficult to believe why these two primates that we are about to find are reluctant to come forward," stated Star in her most motherly voice. "But with your intervention, I believe we will be able to resolve the problem and relieve a great deal of their pain and suffering."

"Were they injured by some other animal?" asked Mia.

"Kind of!" answered Star. "Sometimes psychological injuries can be more painful than physical ones. But you are going to have to see for yourselves and let them describe their injuries in their own words."

Upon reaching the sanctuary, Mia and Andrew could see a couple of elephant cows with their calves bathing in one of the deep-water ponds. Elephants like baths every evening, so in the wild they never wander far from the availability of a pool or stream. And after bathing, they normally coat their skin in dirt or mud for protection from insects. Nearby, the twins were also able to see that these elephants were under the leadership and protection of a large mature female, to whom every other member of the group was related.

Although the African elephant is the largest and most powerful of all living land mammals, it is also among the gentlest, living in peaceful family units with strong family ties. Normally, the male elephants didn't socialize with the females until it was mating time, but for now, they were in close proximity to each other. They would even drink and bath in separate ponds in this vast sanctuary. There were several ponds throughout the sanctuary, all connected by a slow-moving stream designed to simulate the waters in the rural district of their native country. The flowing stream was made possible by an elaborate system of huge water pumps and filters to maintain the fresh water circulating throughout the sanctuary.

But this sanctuary was an enclosure of dozens of acres in which many different types of animals could mingle together as they would normally do in the wild. In this compound, there was enough room for not only the elephants but also other compatible species such as giraffes, zebras, and white rhinoceroses—to name only a few that live in pairs or up to herds of several dozens.

Andrew and Mia took several minutes to scan the terrain but were unsuccessful in locating the chimps. Looking up to Star, Mia asked, "I can't see them, but this habitat is so large they could be hiding anywhere."

Star pointed to an area above and to the right of the bathing calves. "There, do you see that cluster of trees?" pointing to the right at about a hundred yards from their location.

"Yes," replied Mia. "Is that where they are?"

"Yes," answered Star, nodding.

Calling several times for the chimps to respond to their summons, and being unsuccessful, Andrew turned to Simon. "Maybe they're gone? Maybe they're hiding somewhere else now?"

"No!" replied Simon. "They're still there."

"Then why won't they come to us?" stated Mia. "Maybe they can't understand us like the other animals?"

"No, they understand you!" replied Star. "And they want to come to you, but they're exceptionally afraid."

"Afraid! Why would they be afraid of us?" replied Mia confused. "We would never hurt them."

"Oh, they're not afraid of you," answered Simon. "They're afraid of what might happen to them once you return them back to their habitat. That's what they're afraid of, and appropriately so."

"I still don't understand," responded Mia with a puzzled look on her face. "What do you mean 'appropriately so'?"

"Seeing that they won't come to us"—Simon sighed—"then we'll just have to go to them."

"What?" answered Andrew. "Oh, I don't know about that! Do you know how many wild animals there are in there with big teeth? Dad would go ballistic. No! Dad would go Super Thermonuclear!"

"Normally, I would be the first to agree with you, Andrew," replied Simon. "I would never allow you to do anything dangerous, but in this case, it appears to be the only solution. Besides, all precautions have been taken by Star and myself to ensure your safety."

"What kind of precautions?" replied Andrew, wanting to know the details.

"Andrew, for crying out loud!" cried Mia. "Stop and think! You're talking with Simon. Do you think for a moment that he would let anything happen to you or me after he's guaranteed our safety?"

"Oh, I guess I forgot!" Andrew paused for a moment. "I'm sorry, Simon, I guess I wasn't thinking. But how are we going to get in?"

"Not a problem," answered Star. "I just happen to see a gate over there by the side of the road."

"But they're always kept locked," replied Andrew.

"Well, I just happen to know that this particular gate is unlocked now," answered Star with a smile, a smile that spoke volumes. "You can trust me. The gate is unlocked."

Everyone entered through the unlocked gate, and shortly before reaching the cluster of trees, Mia called out, "I can see them! They are over there! By those small bushes on the left side of those three tall trees! It's Brigitte and Dennis! Can you see them now, Andrew?"

"I can," replied Andrew. "Let's go over and talk to them."

As the twins started to move forward, they noticed that many of the animals started to crowd around them, preventing them from moving forward. "Simon, I see a problem here," Andrew said, looking to his right where Simon was standing. "What should we do?"

"Just talk to them," replied Simon. "They're just feeling anxious, so don't keep them in suspense. Just tell them what your intentions are. They'll understand you, and then they will escort you through."

After Andrew in his most soothing and gentle voice explained his and Mia's purpose for their intrusion into their sanctuary, the animals opened a hole so that the twins could move forward and escorted them in the direction where the two chimpanzees were located.

"Remember," warned Star, "you need to be extremely cautious with them. They both have suffered a traumatic experience. They both are exceptionally suspicious of a human presence."

"What type of a traumatic experience?" asked Andrew.

"It might be best to ask them yourselves," responded Simon. "I think it would be best for you to hear it in their own words."

Mia and Andrew stood quietly facing the chimps, concentrating on the two, waiting, watching. The twins were trying to work through the problem thoughtfully and with compassion. Mia and Andrew could sense their pain, yet both chimps were revealing an incredible amount of strength and perseverance but without a successful response to the twins.

"They're still not responding to us, Simon. What else can we do to get them to cooperate?" pleaded Mia.

"I suggest that we let them talk it over between themselves," responded Simon. "They now know who you are but are still extremely scared. Let's concentrate on capturing a few more of the other animals, and then we'll come back and see if they are more trusting, okay?"

CHAPTER 11

$\mathcal{U}$nder the direction of Star and Simon, Mia and Andrew traversed a couple of new areas of the property, and they were again successful throughout the night in rescuing many more newly found animals using Star's method of talking slowly and calmly to them. However, Mia's curiosity was aroused. "Andrew, have you noticed how we seldom run across any of the zoo's staff or guests?" she asked. "There have to be a couple hundred of the zoo's staff out searching for the animals in their cars and trucks. And what about the sheriff deputies also roaming in their vehicles looking for animals as well? Although I presume they are mostly concentrating on finding guests and escorting them out of the park. And yet we still haven't been discovered, although we have this large animal entourage following behind us. Don't you find that strange?"

"You're right," responded Andrew. "I've been so concentrated on us finding the animals that I hadn't thought about it. But now that you mention it, it is strange. In fact, very strange! It feels like someone is directing them in one direction and us in another so that our paths don't bump into each other."

Both Mia and Andrew turned simultaneously to Star and Simon. "You are using one of your tricks again, aren't you?" asked Andrew.

"Tricks can be very convenient when you have a serious and important job to do," responded Simon. "This way, we can accomplish so much in just hours that would normally take days, if not weeks, to complete. So to answer your question, yes, Star and I, through the help from above, have been granted special abilities to assist us in completing our missions. So let's continue, but first, I suggest that all of you take cover over there behind those trees and shrubs and try to remain motionless and without making a sound."

"Why?" quested Andrew. "I don't see or hear anything." But they and the animals with them promptly did what they were told with no further comments whatsoever, leaving the walkway to go into the trees and shrubs, crouching to lower their silhouettes and merging with the shadows.

Within a minute or two, the group started to hear a small truck and then could see headlights coming around the corner from the giraffes' area. "Great call," whispered Mia with the thrill of adventure.

As the truck started to pass their location, Mia recognized the passengers to be the zookeepers and caregivers from the zebra, rhinoceros, and hippopotamus areas led by Dr. Albert Harrison, Dr. Julie Harrison's husband. And as soon as Mia felt it safe enough, she slid out of the shadows, edging around a tree trunk. "Okay, it's safe to come out now," Mia said, addressing the others.

"Whew! That was a close call!" breathed Andrew. "And the animals were so cooperative! They did exactly what we told them to do. There was no pushing and shoving. They didn't make any sounds and hid behind the bushes and trees just like we did." He focused on Simon. "That was another little trick of yours, wasn't it?"

"Little tricks can come in handy," responded Simon. "A large majority of these animals are natural enemies of each other in their native environments. But not tonight. There will be no hostility tolerated among them this evening. Cooperation is essential and absolutely necessary for us to be successful. So until this unusual occurrence is over with, all the animals that you come in contact with tonight will follow your orders perfectly."

After they had a troop of animals following them, they again decided to return to the clinic and place them into appropriate lockups. "I wish that I had a key to the back door so that I didn't have to sneak in the main door without being detected," Andrew commented.

Then the twins turned to face both Star and Simon, nodding, signifying yes, that would be a great idea, hoping that their angels would get the hint and provide them with one.

"Angels don't need keys," remarked Simon. "All we need is the power of thought."

"You mean that all you have to do is think what you want done and it automatically happens, even doors that are self-locking when the door is closed?" asked Andrew.

"Yes! That's all it takes," confirmed Simon.

"Why didn't you mention that before?" asked Andrew. "That would have made so many things much easier!"

"You will find that the rear door is now unlocked," declared Simon. "So let's get the animals inside where they will be safe and warm!"

After all the animals were safely inside and divided among the cages and cautioned by Mia about the no tolerance for fighting rules, she suggested, "Well, Andrew, I guess we better return to the storage room for more food. Thank God that there is so much food on hand!"

"You know, Mia, I don't understand that either," Andrew stated. "Every time I go to the storage room for more food, it seems like there is more food than ever before. And the food that we need for each new animal is always easy to find up front and clearly labeled. I didn't notice some of these food items there before. It kind of reminds me of the miracle about the two fish and five loaves of bread. These food items seem to be multiplying by themselves," mused Andrew thoughtfully.

Looking at their angels, both Star and Simon just had large, bright smiles on their faces—no words needed.

*M*eanwhile, at the front of the clinic, Rachel looked up from her patient as the front door opened. She was hoping that it was not a newly found injured person or animal. They had more than they could handle now. She was relieved that it was David and Dr. Steward returning from the field.

"Is everything okay, David?" Rachel asked.

"I'm sorry to say no!" David replied. "I had to administer an additional sedative to Chester. The poor guy is hysterical and extremely uncomfortable. But for the moment, there isn't anything else I can do for him. We're trying to find a solution for his predicament, but even after putting all our heads together, we've come up empty. It's kind of like the nursery rhyme of Humpty Dumpty, where all the king's men couldn't put him back together again. Only in this case, it's all the zookeepers can't get Chester free again!"

"Well, I'm glad that you're back. One of us needs to have a stern talk with the twins," answered Rachel.

"What did they do now?" sighed David tiredly.

"Deputy Foster found them outside the clinic! Only God knows where they were going! I told them to sit on those two chairs over there, oh my god! They're gone again!"

"No, they're not," replied David. "I see them over there, again with armfuls of food. What in the world are they doing?"

Moving over to the animal side of the clinic, followed by Rachel, Dr. Steward and Cecilia, because now their curiosity had also been aroused, and of course going through the decontamination protocol, David approached the twins, "Okay, you two. Don't tell me you're using all the food to feed Rehab again. No one animal can eat that amount of food, so what's up?" queried David.

"Oh! It's not for Rehab," answered Mia. "It's for the monkeys, birds, and other animals that Andrew and I found."

With total bewilderment on his face, their father asked, "What monkeys and birds and other animals? We're not treating so many animals or birds in the clinic now to require that much food."

As Andrew and Mia led the way carrying their delectable fruits and vegetables, their parents, Dr. Steward and Cecilia, followed closely behind. The twins led them to the rear of the clinic, to the location that was described to them earlier as a large recovery rooms after treatment, where animals were kept before they were returned to their respective habitats.

"These monkeys and birds and other animals!" answered Mia triumphantly. "We found them running and hiding from everyone, and they were really scared!"

Speechless, with their eyebrows raised and their mouths fully opened, the four adults just stood there thunderstruck.

Finally regaining his composure, David slowly and almost in a whisper asked, "How in the world did you find them? And how did you manage to capture them and bring them here without anyone knowing about it?"

"Oh! It was easy, Dad," replied Andrew proudly and with an enthusiastic sense of achievement. But when he received no quick response from his father, Andrew's face turned from exultation to consternation. "You're not mad at us, are you, Dad?"

"No, son!" replied David with tenderness in his voice and still in a state of shock. "I'm not mad at you." As David slowly stepped over to the twins, he placed an arm around each one of them, unable to take his eyes off the evidence of their accomplishment. "If anything, I'm extremely proud of both of you! But I'm still in shock that you were able to find them, especially after we asked you not to leave the clinic. Also, what I find amazing is how you were able to get them through the clinic without being detected."

"Oh! That was because we brought them in through the rear-side door and told them to be very, very quiet," explained Andrew.

"And they all understood you and did exactly what you told them to do?" replied David with a smirk on his face. "Do you realize how many trained staff members it would have taken to get all these animals into these cages? Not to mention all the commotion that the animals would have made in doing so? It's impossible that you were able to gather up all these animals without making a sound!"

"Well, you didn't hear us, did you?" returned Andrew.

"No, we didn't. And how did you avoid setting off the rear door alarm when exiting and reentering through it with the well-behaved animals?" asked their father.

"There's an alarm on the door?" the dumbfounded Andrew responded. "I guess it's not working properly!"

"No! It should be working fine," answered David. "For safety concerns, the alarms are checked daily by our security staff. Cecilia, would you please open that rear door? Now I'm concerned!"

As Cecilia walked over to the door in question, she opened it, and the audio alarm was activated as was expected, as well as several lights flashing on and off throughout the clinic. Both Mia and

Andrew stood there in amazement. Searching the room for Simon and finding him, Andrew was thinking, another one of Simon's little tricks! Simon just looked directly into Andrew's eyes and smiled.

As one of the staff members finished resetting the alarm, Andrew walked over and reopened the door. This time the alarm failed to activate. "See what I mean, Dad!" He had one of his own smiles. "No alarm!"

"I'll call maintenance in the morning to come over and take a look at it," suggested Cecilia. "Apparently, it's malfunctioning!"

"That might explain the alarm issue," conceded David, "but here is another mystery to me. Some of these animals that you put in the same lockup should never be placed together because they are natural enemies and in the natural order of things should be fighting with one another."

"Oh no, Dad," Mia spoke up. "We told them that fighting would not be tolerated. Until this dilemma is resolved their full cooperation is demanded, and no exceptions would be permitted."

"And they just listened to you?" asked David. "And like Andrew said earlier about telling the animals not to make any noise when entering the clinic, the animals agreed to resist fighting among themselves even though that contradicts their natural instincts and patterns of behavior? The faulty alarm system explains how you got the animals in the clinic, but how are you going to explain the logic of them not fighting among themselves? What makes you think that they understood you? Princess, it's contrary to all reason to believe that they can! We don't speak the languages of the animal world, so it's not feasible that they would understand you about not fighting."

"Are you sure, Dad? You really think that it's not feasible? Just look around—you don't see any of them fighting, do you?" replied Mia.

"No, I don't see any of them fighting," replied David, totally bewildered. "In fact, they seem very comfortable with each other, and that really baffles me. As I said before, we would never even consider placing all these diverse types of animals in the same enclosure. At the same time, how can I say that it can't be done? My eyes can't lie to me! I can see for myself that they are very serene with each other. You know, I'm not even going to ask how you got them to agree with that demand," remarked David. "Seeing this for myself is answer enough. But that doesn't mean that we are not going to revisit this at a later time."

Patrick interrupted, "If you call this getting into mischief," directing his comment to Rachel, "I'll take a dozen of them any time! All I know is that I have a combination of over 320 employees, including the police officers and firefighters, throughout the park looking for escaped animals, and these two young twins bamboozled all of us!"

Noticing that the twins were struggling to balance the food in their arms, Cecilia stepped forward to help.

"Here, let me give you a hand!" she said as tears were starting to grow in the corners of her eyes.

"How in the world did you catch them?" asked David. "You have no idea how hard we've been trying to find them. We have team after team out there looking for them and have been unable to locate them because of their natural ability to hide in the trees and in the shadows of the park. You must have some unexplainable methods that obviously we don't have of finding them. And then the toughest part is being able to catch them."

"Well!" Mia explained meekly. "We really didn't catch them. We saw them running from everyone who was trying to capture them, but like Star said, you must walk up to them slowly so that you won't frighten them, then just lower your tone and speak softly to them. Then they will be able to understand you and not be frightened."

"Star? Who is Star?" asked Rachel.

"Worms! Maybe the birds would like some worms!" Andrew interrupted, gritting his teeth as he clenched his fist at his side. "The quiet kind that birds take back to their nests to eat. Do you have any?"

"Oh! Did I say Star?" Mia's voice started to stumble and stammer, and she looked defensively over to Andrew. "We were outside looking at the stars. I meant Andrew, Andrew told me that. He wanted me to talk to them like I talk to Noah when I want him to do something."

"But you said that they would understand you?" asked Rachel. "What do you mean that they would understand you?"

Andrew, thinking quickly on his feet, jumped in and answered. "You know, Mom, the way we talk to Noah. If you speak gently to him, he'll understand you. In fact, you and Dad talk to Noah all the time yourselves. Now, don't you think he understands you? You tell him to come here, and he comes to you. You tell him to sit up and bark, and he'll do that too. You see, it's the same principle."

"Yeah, but that's a lot different," answered Rachel. "Noah is our pet. We've had him since he was a pup. He's been trained over the years. All these tricks were developed by teaching him to respond to certain commands."

"So you don't think that Noah understands us?" asked Andrew.

"No," Rachel replied reluctantly, "I'm not saying that he doesn't understand us. Noah is an intelligent animal. I'm sure he can understand you to a point."

"You see!" answered Andrew smugly, feeling that he had made his point. "Dad has always said that next to man, monkeys and apes are some of the most intelligent animals on earth. So if a dog can understand you, it makes a lot of sense that a monkey can understand you even better. I rest my case!"

Not being able to control their laughter and although Star and Simon would never condone deceiving one's parents, they couldn't resist in enjoying how Mia and Andrew were trying to squeeze themselves out of their predicament. Besides, there was a great deal of truth in what they were saying. Animals do understand if you have enough patience with them.

"I'm so flabbergasted about all this. I don't know what to think!" stated Rachel. "All I know is that whatever you two did, it worked, and I couldn't be more thrilled."

"I think they may be on to something here," arbitrated Dr. Steward. "Perhaps, because of their youth and innocence, the animals could sense their good intentions and felt comfortable with them. This may only be a theory, but I think it's something worth pursuing."

"Well, I'm most certainly not going to argue with you, Dr. Steward. You're the resident expert on animal behavior," interjected Cecilia. "But I think the twins are right. All these animals look hungry to me. Due to all the ruckus, they did miss their evening meal."

As they all helped in feeding the twins' newly found acquaintances, David was the first to ask, "How many did you see outside? Because there are many more missing."

"Because you told us not to leave the clinic, Andrew and I just stepped outside close to the back door for some fresh air and to get away from all the noise. We didn't see any others, and we didn't know how many were missing. We just talked to the ones we could see and placed them in the huge cage and told them to behave and that fighting with each other would not be tolerated. So here they are, and they are not fighting each other either. So how many are still missing?"

"I'm unable to answer that question, Princess," replied her father. "We're not sure. We can't get an accurate count. We keep discovering that more and more are being released."

"You mean that someone is releasing them on purpose?" Mia gasped. "Why and who?"

"Those are good questions that we keep asking ourselves," admitted David. "We don't know who or why, but someone is releasing them on purpose. But I can see a total of eight monkeys in the recovery enclosures, and so many other animals in the large enclosure, plus twelve birds in our large aviary that weren't there earlier. So that is a tremendous help," reported the twins' father. "I'm just so amazed."

"Do you see now why Andrew and I said earlier that we felt that we could help you with Chester?" suggested Mia. "All Andrew and I do is speak slowly and softly to them, and they seem to understand us, and they trust us. You saw how Rehab responded to us earlier. We talked to him, and he just lay down and cooperated with you and Mom while you were fixing his leg. I don't understand why you don't let us help you with Chester."

"She has a point, David. I have never witnessed or heard about anything as remarkable as what happened while we were treating Rehab," intervened Rachel. "How can it hurt?"

"I only heard about your treatment with Rehab, because I wasn't here then. But I see all these animals that you said weren't there earlier. And like you also said, that's a tremendous help! And like Rachel just said, what can it hurt?" Dr. Stewart agreed enthusiastically. "Just let them try. I'm in favor of the idea! Besides, I'm eager to see what other talents they might have developed. You must admit, these children of yours have a gift that defies all reason. But they are your children, and as always, I will respect your final decision."

"I don't know," replied David. "It sounds a little crazy and dangerous to me." Then addressing the twins, "I think it best for the both of you to remain here with your new friends where you can stay warm and dry while we take care of Chester... Wait a minute... You know, on second thought, okay, you talked me into it! All that can happen is we lose a little time, and it's worth the delay," consented David. "Let's do it!"

"Oh my god! I almost forgot the reason why we're here!" David smacked his forehead and raised his voice so his staff could hear him. "I wanted to make sure that all the employees and guests got the word that the food court has been fully reopened and that Luigi and his family from Dominic's are the backbone for running things there. And that includes some of his signature dishes from his restaurant! I know that not all the employees were issued a radio so that we could issue additional radios to the sheriff's department. So if you see one of those employees, please pass the word to them. Furthermore, everything is on the house! So maybe everyone can stagger their breaks and go to the food court and help themselves? The Red Cross is also going to bring a variety of the dishes here and serve them in the break room. It's your choice where you want to take your break, here or at the food court."

All that was heard were loud applause, cheers, and whistles throughout the clinic.

"Now that that's done," continued David briskly, "I also need to prepare a fresh sedative for Chester, just in case we need it." He was talking to no one in particular. "We all got so caught up in Mia and Andrew's outstanding rescues, I almost forgot all about him. I better prepare it and take it back with us, because I'm sure that we're going to need it at some point. He is so agitated, and I'm sure he is so uncomfortable being in that same position for as long as he has been. So we better get back there before he bursts a blood vessel."

"So we can go back there with you to try to help?" Mia asked. "I know we can do it!"

"My first instinct was to say no. I would prefer if you two would remain here with your new friends while we adults take care of Chester," replied David. "But it looks like I'm outvoted, and besides, you've earned the right to come. I just don't want you to get hurt. Just promise that you won't get in anyone's way! And if an adult asks you to do something, you do it without complaining, okay?" requested David.

"If an adult asks us to do something, we will obey without an argument or challenge their reasons why," answered Mia. *But our guardian angels are adults*, Mia was thinking to herself. *And we will always follow their directions as well.*

"That's all I ask," responded Davis, thinking to himself, *This is way too easy, and I smell a rat here someplace. I'm not going to be that gullible. But for now, I'm going to take them at their word.*

As the group started to return to the bears' habitat with Chester's sedative, Cecilia turned to Mia and said to her, "You know, it's ironic. This morning, you were my helpers in feeding and caring for the babies, and then suddenly the situation has reversed itself, and I end up helping you and Andrew feed and care for the larger animals that you captured. And now I'm maybe helping you with Chester. You have to admit it's been a pretty exceptional day!"

"You know, Cecilia," Mia confided in her. "If Dad would listen and let us help, I know that Andrew and I could come up with some way to get Chester out of that drainage ditch or whatever you call it. I just know that we can! In fact, I think I just came up with an idea."

"After seeing for myself what you and Andrew did today, nothing that you two are determined to do would surprise me," replied Cecilia. "I saw the way you two can completely bond with each animal you touched today. It's nothing short of amazing! Nothing would surprise me! But you must admit, Chester is in no mood where he's going to be cooperative. I don't think it's going to matter how soothing your voice is. He's not going to listen because he's not only mad, but he's scared about being stuck between two walls of cement. But like Dr. Stewart said, it's certainly worth a try. All in all, it's been a pretty exciting day for all of us. But come on, let's catch up with the others!"

CHAPTER 12

"Oh, thank God you're back, Doc! I'm so glad to see you! Boy, have we been having problems again!" Roger exclaimed in exasperation. "Chester is going ballistic yet again down there, and he's about to blow a fuse. Nothing that we have done has given him any relief for more than for short periods of time. Carol Lee again has been an immense help. She's been very patient with him. It sounds like she might even have been singing to him. I must admit, she has been creative in trying to bring down his anxiety level. But like I said, even for her, he only responds for short periods of time. Then when he recollects how uncomfortable he is stuck in that position, he goes back into a rage."

"Well, I have something here that's a little different," replied David. "I'm going to give him enough to make him a little more serene. Hopefully, it will reduce his anxiety a little. What I'm fearing is that I'm overmedicating him. I've only been giving him small dosages at a time. Again, it's not going to put him to sleep, but it will calm him down just for a brief time and make him a little more of a gentleman. As we know, the real solution is to get him back on his plateau as quickly as possible. So I think that I better get down to the location where I was the last time. That was a good vantage point for getting a clear shot at him."

"It's not going to hurt him, is it, Dad?" asked Mia with concern in her voice.

"No, not at all, Princess," reassured David. "If I do it right, he shouldn't feel anything at all. At worst, it will feel like a minor tingling of the skin."

"Can I go with you, Dad?" asked Mia.

"Absolutely not!" was David's quick response. "And it's not open for debate. I told you that you could come, but you must do what you're told. Do you remember when I told you that?"

"Yes, Dad," Mia responded, "I remember," as she rolled her eyes.

"Good! Mia, there are other bears in that enclosure, and it's not a safe place for children. Not even for you. So just wait here until I get back, okay?" Not even waiting for her nod of agreement, he continued, "Good! But on the other hand, Carole Lee, would you please accompany me again? The other bears are very familiar with you, and you have established such a good relationship with them that your help will be much appreciated."

"Of course, Doctor, I would be more than happy to accompany you. Anything I can do to help, all you have to do is tell me what you need me to do," replied Carol Lee with a wide smile on her face, pleased that Dr. Brooks had such confidence in her. Then they both left for the plateau just above where Chester was wedged directly below them.

"Dad!" Mia shouted from the viewers' railing to her father and Carol Lee below in the enclosure. "I know how we can get Chester out of the ditch!" Mia was eyeing the equipment assembled nearby by Frank and his team. "I have a great idea!" Even though David clearly heard Mia, he ignored her as he was preparing his shot to sedate Chester for the second time.

"If you don't mind, Dr. Brooks," Carol Lee was saying, "I'd like to stay here for a little longer to see if I can further calm down Chester."

"That's fine, Carol Lee. Meanwhile, I will return to my daughter to see if I can calm her down," David responded, laughing a little. "She has such compassion for animals in pain, it sometimes takes her to the razor-edge of hysteria!"

"Sweetheart," Cecilia was addressing Mia, "there's not much that you or your brother will be able to do here now. It's in your father's and Carol Lee's capable hands. So why don't you, Andrew, and I take advantage of the situation and go over and visit some of the other bear exhibits? We can even go back again and see the great panda exhibit next door. Maybe if we're lucky, we might even get to see one of her babies. We'll take one of the deputies with us just in case we come across another loose animal or two. We'll always stay in eyesight of your mother, okay?"

"But, Cecilia," Mia pleaded. "We want to help! And you know that I love the other bears, but we've already seen the bears today when you gave the Musketeers the tour this morning. And you gave a great explanation about each and every bear that we have here at the zoo. I listened to you and enjoyed everything you told us. But have you ever experienced the feeling when you know that you can help and no one will listen to you? Well, that's how I feel right now! Why can't anyone give me the same courtesy that I gave you and listen to what I have to say?"

"Sweetheart, please!" Cecilia continued emphatically. "I know that you feel frustrated and unappreciated right now. And God only knows how much respect and love I have for you. What you and Andrew showed us today was nothing short of amazing! But your father oversees everything tonight, and we must all follow his instructions. This is very serious. And none of us wants to be in the way, right?"

"Come on, Mia," Andrew said with an unusual smile on his face, pulling her by the arm. "Let's go over and see the black bears, okay? We promised Dad that we would stay out of trouble and do what the adults told us. That was the condition we agreed to for letting us tag along."

"Andrew, I don't want to see the black bears," Mia replied, trying to free herself from Andrew's grasp. "I want to stay here and help Dad free Chester. Andrew and I won't be in the way," cried Mia enthusiastically to Cecilia, with rekindled adventure in her eyes. "There is a lot more that we can do. We can even capture more of the outstanding animals. We just didn't realize how many more were still at large."

Upon his return to the viewers' railing, David overheard Mia's plea to Cecilia and stepped into the conversation.

"Thank you, Princess," replied her father. "You've already done more than your share of the work, and we really appreciate it. But now that Chester has been tranquilized again, I think he will be okay for a while. It's best if we adults do the rest."

"But, Dad, we still want to help," insisted Mia. "Do you really appreciate what we did? Do you really?"

"Of course we do, Princess," replied David as he bent over and put both hands on her waist and touched her forehead with his, showing affection. "More than you'll ever know."

"Then prove it!" replied Mia spiritedly.

"Prove it?" asked David, grinning. "And how do you suggest that I do that?"

Taking full advantage of her beautiful blue eyes and in her newly developed soft and gentle voice that made it almost impossible to say no, Mia responded, "By letting Andrew and me continue to help. You must admit by now that we know how to find the animals, and besides, they trust us."

"Is this the same soft voice you use when you talk to the animals?" asked David.

In an even softer and gentler voice, Mia responded, "Yes, just like this. This is my animal voice. I try to soothe the animals into trusting me. I speak very slowly and softly to them, and they listen to me."

"Well, it works for me. Besides, I'm embarrassed to say that you've been more successful tonight than all of us put together. Who was it who said something like 'And a little child shall lead them'? For some reason, it seems very applicable to me now, especially since it referred to unlikely animals getting along with each other when nature dictates otherwise."

Rachel spoke up, "Actually, it was Isaiah in 11:6, 'The wolf shall dwell with the lamb, and the leopard shall lie down with the young goat, and the calf and the young lion and the fattened calf together, and a little child shall lead them.' And then it goes on in Isaiah 11:7, 'The cow will feed with the bear, their young will lie down together, and the lion will eat straw like the ox.'"

"How can I say no now after something like that?" surrendered David. "Somehow, I feel that we adults still have a lot to learn tonight."

"Okay," Mia suggested. "Let's all go back to the clinic."

"OH MY GOD!" Roger screamed at the top of his lungs, as many of the workers also shouted.

"What? What just happened?" David asked, fearing the worst.

"It's Carol Lee!" Rachel yelled. "She fell in with Chester!"

"What!" David reacted as everyone ran to the viewer's railing. "How did that happen?"

As everyone reached the railing, they could all see Carol Lee lying flat on her stomach next to Chester's feet.

She seemed to be unconscious. "Carol Lee, Carol Lee, can you hear me?" David shouted. There was no response.

"Carol Lee, move your hand or your foot if you can hear me!" There was still no response.

"You don't think that Chester will hurt her, do you, David?" asked Rachel.

"I don't know," answered David. "I'm sure he recognizes her to be his friend. He's been acknowledging that all evening. But he is not in a good mood. In fact, he's fighting mad even though he's drugged. And he remains extremely strong. There is no way that his reactions can be predicted at this time, and obviously, the situation has just grown more complex. Cecilia, put on your animal behavior hat. What do you think?"

"That's a tough question! If he recognizes her as his friend, he may not try to harm her. But if he doesn't, in his stage of rage, there is no telling what he may do. I wish I could be more decisive and more encouraging. Unfortunately, it could go either way."

"Look, Dad," Mia interrupted, "Chester is picking her up with one arm. He's holding her close to his neck on top of his shoulder. He knows who she is! I think that he's trying to protect her. But he's having a tough time with it because he is so stuck himself."

"He does seem to recognize her as a friend," responded David. "Let's see what he plans to do now."

"Dad, I need to talk to him. Please, dad, let me talk to him!" urged Mia.

"Mia, this is no time to try to play hero. This is a life-threatening situation. Please stay out of the way!"

"David," Rachel tried to get her husband's attention, "do you have a better solution?"

"Not now, no!" was David's response.

"Then let Mia try," Rachel spoke again. "She may be unorthodox sometimes, but she has her own way of working through a problem thoughtfully and successfully. Meanwhile, radio the clinic and tell them to send us a gurney, with a backboard and neck brace."

As David radioed the clinic, Mia stepped forward as close as she could to the railing. She turned her eyes skyward, searching for answers. Then suddenly with dancing eyes, she had a solution. Using her mental telepathy abilities, Mia directed, *Chester, look at me! I want you to see my eyes.*

Chester immediately looked up and made eye contact with Mia. *Don't harm Carol Lee. She's your best friend. She is already hurt, and we need to help her.* Now she talked to him vocally, softly and slowly, "Chester, we need to help Carol Lee. We need to have my mother look after her. Can you please help your friend? Now we have a double problem. We need to find a solution to get both of you out of that ditch. But maybe you can help us get her out first, okay?"

I'll do whatever I can to help her. She takes loving care of me and feeds me my favorite foods. Yes! I want to help her was Chester's response as he held her tenderly, now thinking of Carol Lee before himself.

Mia swallowed hard and addressed her dad, "Okay, Dad, you need to get some people down there where Chester lives. He is going to help. You need to get three ropes with loops at one end and have two people at the other end of each rope, okay?"

"I can get the ropes, and I'll meet you down on Chester's plateau," volunteered Benjamin as he ran off.

Soon everyone was in place on the plateau: David and Benjamin on one rope, Frank and one of his men on another, and Roger and a sheriff deputy on the last rope. Mia instructed the men on the middle rope to lower their loop end first. Chester was still holding Carol Lee tenderly against his chest, rubbing his forehead lovingly against her cheek. Mia again gave Chester some commands using her mental telepathy powers, and he did what he was told without hesitation and with no vocal commands whatsoever. He assisted the men above in placing one loop around Carol Lee's waist, then an additional loop around and under her shoulders, and finally the last loop around both her knees. Chester then raised Carol Lee over his head as far up as his arms permitted and stretched his body as much as he could. The men then pulled Carol Lee up as carefully as they could to the waiting backboard and gurney, and Rachel carefully placed a neck brace on Carol Lee. The viewers at the railing started to cheer and whistle in pandemonium, and swiftly Carol Lee was wheeled to the clinic so that Rachel could examine her.

David then turned to Mia. "How in the world did you know what to do, and how did you get Chester to cooperate with us?"

"It's just a gift, Dad. 'It's just a gift' is all I can say," responded Mia. "But let's get to the clinic to see how bad Carol Lee's injuries are."

"Okay, let's all go," her father responded. "She is in excellent hands under your mother's care."

"*H*ow is she doing?" David asked.

"Better than one might think," replied Rachel. "How convenient for her that there was a state-of-the-art clinic and staff here for her! With such a crack team and equipment, she is going to be fine. She regained consciousness between the plateau and the clinic. She has an assortment of abrasions and contusions, hairline fractures on a couple of ribs, but no internal injuries, thank God. She also dislocated three fingers on her left hand when she tried to protect herself when she fell. But she will be fine in a week or two. She needs to take a few days off work to rest properly."

"What happened to you, Carol Lee?" David asked. "How did you fall in with Chester?"

"It was just carelessness on my part, Dr. Brooks," answered Carol Lee. "I was lying on my stomach at the edge, trying to give Chester some fruit to see if that would calm him down. Between the wet edge and my wet clothes, I slipped and fell in. All that I can remember is that I stuck out my hands to help brace my fall, and I guess I hit my head on the side as I was going down." She turned to Mia. "I guess you and Chester are my heroes. If there is anything I can ever do for you, all you need to do is ask."

"I didn't help because I wanted something in return. I did it because you needed help. And it was a team effort by a group of people, but on second thought, I know how you can help a group of people," answered Mia. "We are starting a Musketeer Program, where we kids can come to the zoo and not only volunteer to help the staff, but the staff can teach us how important animals are and how to care for them. My dad calls it a symbiotic relationship, meaning in this case that it's a mutually beneficial relationship between staff and student members. We need more staff members to join the program. Do you think you might be interested?"

"I heard about that program on my lunch break this afternoon, and of course, I'm interested! That's how I first got hooked on zoology myself. My aunt and uncle in the state of Washington would invite me to spend my summer vacations with them. My uncle was a lab technician at their local zoo and would take me to work with him. That's when I fell in love with zoo animals. He passed away a couple of years ago, and now my aunt lives with me. I love working with kids, and it would be a great tribute to my Uncle William. Thank you for inviting me. Count me in, and I suppose that you will probably be interested in feeding the four bear cubs that I care for."

"Are you kidding? Of course, we do!" confirmed Mia.

"Well, I guess I should be getting back out to Chester," Carol Lee said, addressing no one in particular, as she was trying to get up on her feet.

"No way! I haven't released you yet. I said you will be fine in a week or two, but you are not yet ready to go back to work," Rachel reminded her.

"But Chester needs to see that I'm all right. He needs to know that we are still trying to get him out, and he needs to know that we haven't given up on him," Carol Lee said with a few tears starting to run down her cheeks. "You can't send me home now! Dr. Brooks, your husband said earlier that he could use me in helping Chester. Well, things haven't changed much. Chester is still stuck, and I can still help. Please, Dr. Brooks, don't send me home!"

"Rachel," David interrupted, "there are a couple of wheelchairs in one of our storage rooms. Would it be all right with you if we wheel her back out there so that Chester can at least see her?"

202

"If you promise that you won't let her get near the edge again," replied Rachel. "The last thing we need is for her to fall in again."

"That's another one of your rhetorical questions that you don't expect me to answer, right?" asked David.

Before Rachel could respond, Mia asked, "Dad, do you remember what we were talking about before Carol Lee fell in with Chester? Remember I asked whether you appreciated Andrew and me? You said yes, and I told you to prove it. Well, are you ready now?"

"I think that this is an excellent time," replied David, "to show us your idea."

After Mia and Andrew saw for themselves that all the animals that were collected earlier were resting comfortably for the night, with an extra dollop of attention to Rehab, Andrew and Mia returned to the outer offices of the clinic and retrieved a couple of white towels that they had left there earlier. Without saying a word, the adults observed the twins each wrap a towel around their forearm several times.

Looking up at their parents, Mia directed, "Follow us, and we'll show you how we caught the birds."

Burning with curiosity, everyone eagerly followed the twins outside to one of the smaller amphitheaters with anticipation of learning their techniques.

"Would you please stay here by the wooden benches?" cautioned Andrew. "We don't want anyone to unduly frighten the birds. I think it would work better if we talk to them first."

"Talk to them?" repeated David brightly. "You can talk to the birds? And I'm sure they talk back to you too, right?"

"Just a bad choice of words, Dad. What I meant was, until the birds respond to us," replied Andrew. "It should only take a couple of minutes."

"Okay!" answered David. "We'll trust in your good judgment. So go do your thing. And we'll all wait right here on the benches."

Although everyone carefully watched the twins walk out only about a hundred feet into a lighted clearing, no one could observe their very special invisible friends who were accompanying them. Friends who could guarantee that no harm would befall them.

Friends that had a special love for them while taking seriously their role in their guidance and protection.

Suddenly, while the twins were apparently talking to one another, Andrew and Mia slowly raised their arms, and two multi-colored Brazilian tropical parrots appeared from the darkness, each of them perching on one of the twins' arms. Then several of the stork-billed kingfishers appeared in the air, circling the twins before they landed at their feet. Soon after, several other birds appeared as well and landed on the ground next to them. Afraid to say a word and spoil the moment, the adults just turned slowly to face one another in total astonishment.

As the twins returned to their parents, Andrew asked, "Cecilia, do you know if we have enough seeds and nuts? They said that… I mean, I couldn't find that much before in the storage area, and I think they're awfully hungry, especially the parrots, and they all probably would like extra seeds and nuts with some fruit."

Still unable to comprehend what they had just witnessed, David replied dazedly, "Yes, I'm sure that we do. If not in our clinic store-room, the zoo maintains a large warehouse on the grounds from which we replenish our stores. But I'm sure that Cecilia knows exactly where we store everything and how to request additional inventory when needed."

"Well, if she doesn't have enough of something—and why should she under these unforeseen events?" interrupted Dr. Steward, equally in shock as the others. "I'll find someone at the warehouse who will be able to get you all you need or want. Because of the size of the property and the number of animals in our charge, our ware-house is in operation 24-7."

As Cecilia led the way to the clinic, David, Rachel, and Dr. Steward fell behind the group as the birds followed them from the air.

Reaching for David's elbow to get his attention, Dr. Steward, still in awe, whispered, "I don't believe my eyes. How in the world were they able to do what we just witnessed? How did they develop such skills? No! David, this is far beyond amazing!"

"I have no idea," responded David humbly. "Like you, I've been around animals my entire life, but I've never seen or heard about anything like this before. Somehow, they've developed a talent that they most certainly didn't learn from me! It must be a special gift. And I was watching very closely to everything that they were doing, and without speaking a word, they were communicating with them somehow. There are a lot of questions that need to be answered."

"Well, they've earned my respect," interjected Rachel. "I think that maybe we should pay a little more attention to them from now on."

"I agree," mused David. "I think that it's something that we should explore and encourage—not that it looks like they need any encouragement! It seems like they already have all the self-motivation that they'll ever need. You know, Pat, for them being so young, they've always had not only this burning desire to learn as much as they could about nature and its many different life-forms but also to preserve and protect it. It's like they developed this natural talent to be nature's parents. I guess what I really mean is that we should try to make available to them as many opportunities as we can. This only shows that Mia and Andrew were born older than their years, capable of a degree of personal commitment and dedication unmatched within their age group—or any age group!"

"Well, you most certainly have my support," replied Dr. Steward. "I'm more than willing to open as many doors as I can for them. I can't even envision where this may all lead. But I am looking forward to the journey and watching how it's going to progress!"

As the twins entered the clinic through the rear-side door, the flying birds, without any verbal commands, landed as close as possible to the same rear-side door and followed them inside.

While petting them softly, the twins continued to speak to two of the parrots ever so gently and slowly. David quickly opened the door to one of the small walk-in aviaries so that the twins could add these newly found flying animals to the birds that they had recovered earlier. Although it would be considered small in aviary terms, it was much larger than the typical parrot cage. It was only used when the infirmary occasionally treated large birds, normally birds of prey. But it was ideal for this occasion when they had such a host of birds to house.

"This should make them all happy," Cecilia said as she entered the room carrying a plentiful supply of a variety of seeds and nuts.

"Oh yes, that should make them really happy!" answered Mia. "Can I help?"

The twins distributed the seeds and nuts into individual containers next to the assortment of fruits that had already been placed in the aviary. Andrew asked, "Dad, maybe we should return to free Chester? I feel sure that he's going to need our help."

"That's a good idea," replied his father. "I'd sort of forgotten all about Chester. We better get back to see how he's doing. We still need to come up with a workable solution on how to free him. We all got so caught up with your and Mia's outstanding talents, I got distracted and momentarily forgot all about him. We better get back there before he goes berserk."

"Then we can go back again?" begged Mia. "Because now I'm sure you feel that we can help!"

"I don't see why or how I would want to stop you now," replied David. "Let's go."

"Dad," Andrew asked, "can we join you in a few minutes? I think Mia and I should stop at the food court first to thank Andrea, Anna, and Katarina. They showed us such hospitality when we were at their restaurant, and I think it would be rude not to reciprocate their warmth and cordiality by not welcoming them ourselves personally when they are in our extended home here at the zoo."

"Sweetie, that's such a lovely thing to say," responded his mother. "I think that's a beautiful idea! I'm glad that you haven't forgotten your manners during all this commotion."

"Okay," their father agreed. "We can walk you over there on our way to the bears' habitat. But you must wait there until someone escorts you to meet us again. I'm sure that we can get one of the deputies or even a Red Cross van to transport you safely."

"Andrew," Mia said sternly, "finally Dad said we can go back without an argument, and now you want to go to the food court? I want to go and help Chester first! Then we can go and see the Dominic family!"

"Come on, Mia," Andrew said with a strange smile on his face as he was pulling her by the arm. "Let's go over to the food court first."

"All you're interested in is feeding your face!" Mia retorted, trying to free herself from Andrew's grasp. "I want to go and help Chester! You go alone and play ambassador if you like to say hi to them for me."

"Mia, we need to go to the food court together," repeated Andrew, gritting his teeth and shaking his head, as if he had ulterior motives in mind.

Finally, he succeeded in getting Mia to one side. "Mia, have you forgotten? There are still two chimpanzees who need our help at the elephant sanctuary!"

"Oh, that's right!" Mia responded quietly. "I forgot all about the other two chimpanzees! This is an excellent time to see if we can now get them to trust us and maybe to tell us why they are so afraid. So let's do it!"

Turning to her mother and blinking her blue eyes, Mia said, "You know, Mother, on second thought, Andrew is finally right for the first time all day! It would be rude not to stop and thank the Dominic family. I'll go with Andrew if that's okay with you."

"That's fine, but make sure you notify us when you want to rejoin us. The staff at the food court has a radio so they can contact us, okay?" her mother responded. "Tell them for me that I will also be there shortly."

As soon as they entered the food court, no more than three steps inside, they made an about-face and realized that both Star and Simon were at their sides. "Let's go," Mia was heard to say. "Time is a-wasting!"

Thank God
for

CHAPTER 13

*T*he twins entered the African elephant sanctuary as before and again negotiated the same route with the same full escort of the animals that lived within the compound. When they reached the last known location, they were able to find the pair of chimps just a few feet deeper into the low-growing shrubs. Sitting on the ground directly in front of the chimps and with their eyes riveted on them, Mia and Andrew started negotiating with them again but received no response. For several minutes, everyone just waited for each other to start the conversation. "This is a very delicate situation," Star advised the twins. "You need to take your time to establish their trust. As I said earlier, they both have had a very traumatic experience."

"What kind of traumatic experience? You never said," asked Mia.

"I still think it would be best if they told you in their own words. That way, you will fully understand their hesitation in trusting anyone," replied Simon.

Looking upward toward the heavens then closing his eyes, Andrew searched for divine inspiration. Drawing a deep breath of air into his lungs and then exhaling slowly, Andrew returned his attention to the two chimps before him.

For several minutes, the chimps and the twins just sat across from one another without saying a word. It was difficult to see clearly due to the shadows of the night, but when Mia squinted her eyes and bobbed her head, using the limited moonlight available, she noticed that both chimps had dried blood around their mouths and ears that she hadn't noticed before. Mia now considered this not only an animal rescue but also an intelligence gathering mission. When Mia asked them about their injuries, the twins noticed that the female chimp started to make soft crying sounds. It was obvious that she was in a great deal of pain and was physically suffering, but "from what" was Mia's concern. Was it caused by some kind of injury from another animal or a current illness? With the help of Star and Simon, the chimps hesitantly started to speak. Soon the chimps realized that the twins were empathetic and sincere in their efforts to help. As the conversation continued, the chimps started to feel more comfortable and trusted the twins more and more. As the chimps let down their guard, the conversation proceeded more smoothly in depth. Then Mia started to choke on the female chimp's pain, and tears started to flow freely, falling over her high cheekbones until she couldn't prevent herself from sobbing. Suddenly Mia, with a great deal of pain in her heart, shouted, "I need to find Dad! We need to find Dad, Andrew! He needs to know about all this!"

Mia and Andrew jumped to their feet and raced across the sanctuary. They were followed by their escort of animals toward the unlocked gates. As Andrew secured the gates behind them, the twins were running as fast as humanly possible to Chester's habitat, where they thought for sure they would be able to locate their father and inform him of the chimpanzees' situation, for he needed to sort out and solve this state of affairs immediately.

"*W*hatever it was that you gave him this time, it sure did the trick, Doc," remarked Roger. "It looks like Chester isn't sure if he's getting up or going to bed. I wouldn't mind having a little of that around the house for when the wife and kids get out of control."

The peacefulness of the night was suddenly split by a mélange of voices in the distance, polluting its tranquility. A group of men became visible on the pathway leading from the zoo's entrance. They sounded more like a riot out of control than a team of engineers and workmen assembled to free Chester!

"Here comes my crew now," announced Frank. "We'll start as soon as we gather the equipment and put it in place. We still need to calculate all the materials that we're going to need."

"Exactly what do you think we're going to need?" asked Dr. Steward, hoping for as little as possible but anticipating the worst.

"Well, to start with," replied Frank, "we'll need an aesthetic designer and draftsman, an architectural engineer, a structural engineer, and a master builder. But don't worry, Doc. All those people are in one: me! But we will also need a couple of operating engineers, construction and carpenter crews, artistic masons, stonecutters, etc. As far as equipment goes, we'll need at the very least a couple of concrete jackhammers, a medium-sized drilling rig, a backhoe, a truck-mounted crane, a forklift, a man lift, generators, compressors, a skip loader, and a dump truck. For supplies and materials, we'll need shorting timber, steel I-beams, plywood, hydraulic jacks, scaffolding material, high-grade construction concrete, and plenty of rebar, plus an assortment of small power and hand tools, and undetermined other small items. And that's only what immediately comes to mind. Oh, and in this weather, plenty of hot coffee!"

"Frank!" replied Dr. Steward overwhelmed. "For crying out loud, we're just trying to free a bear, not build a skyscraper!"

"Rachel, has Andrew or Mia radioed for us to send someone to escort them here yet?" asked David.

"Not that I know of," replied Rachel. "Maybe they are having a good time with the Dominic kids, and decided to stay a little longer?"

"I'm getting concerned. It's not like Mia to delay getting here, especially after she made a big deal that she had an idea to share with us. Right now, I'm ready to listen to anything, no matter how strange it may sound. I can sense that something is wrong," David said with a shaky voice. "Food court, come in. This is Dr. Brooks," he spoke into his radio.

"Yes, Dr. Brooks, this is Tracy O'Leary from the food court. How may I help you?"

"Yes, can you see if my children Mia and Andrew are there with the Dominic children?" David replied.

"The Dominic children are just a few feet from me helping to serve our employees and guests," radioed Tracy. "If they were here I would be able to identify them. Everyone at the zoo knows your children. I'm sorry to say that no one here has seen them, including the Dominic family."

"Now where did they disappear to? What can they be up to this time?" asked David, not expecting an answer. "The last thing I told them was to stay at the food court until someone could escort them here! It was made perfectly clear that I didn't want them to venture off without an adult escort."

After looking around the immediate area, which proved to be fruitless, Rachel suggested to Paul Chapin to radio his security force to see if any of them had noticed them wandering somewhere in the park.

"Not a problem, Dr. Brooks," Paul responded. "We have a spotless record of never losing a child in the park."

"That's reassuring," answered Rachel. "But you never had to deal with our twins before. I hope that they won't blemish your sterling record."

"Security 1, to all units," Paul announced to his security force. "Has anyone noticed the location of Dr. Brooks's twins, Andrew and Mia? If so, please report in."

"Security 1, this is Security 7. I saw them just a couple of minutes ago near the jaguar habitat. They seemed to be running as fast as they could to your location."

"Security 1, this is Security 9, I have them in view now. They're just passing the Siberian tiger exhibit heading toward the bears' habitat. I'll tell them that you're looking for them. If I can catch them, that is! They have a good head start on me, and I understand that they are quite good athletes, so that seems unlikely."

"Thank you, Security 9. If you can, ask them not to stop for coffee and doughnuts."

"There they are!" shouted David. "But what's wrong with Mia? She looks like she may be crying."

As everyone dashed toward the twins, David was the first to reach her and asked, "Princess, what's wrong? Are you hurt?"

Trying to catch her breath and swallowing, "No! Yes!" replied Mia, still in tears. "We found two chimpanzees. They're both hurt, but one of them is really hurt, hurt badly! Dad, they need your help!"

"What happened?" asked David with a genuine concern and gentleness in his voice. "Did one of the other animals attack them?"

"No! Yes!" answered Mia.

"Sweetheart!" Rachel interjected. "You're not making any sense. What do you mean? No, yes, make up your mind!"

"I mean, yes, they're hurt. But no, not by a wild kind of animal but by a supposedly friendly kind of animal."

"I'm still confused, Princess," started David. "You have to do better than this for us to understand you. Try to calm down and catch your breath, then tell us the problem!"

"We better show you, Dad," declared Andrew. "You're going to have to see for yourself, like we had to."

"I told them that you were an animal doctor and that you will make them better, but they still wouldn't come with us," added Mia. "They're too scared and not very trusting right now."

"Okay, show us where they are!" answered David. Then he looked over to Paul. "Paul, would you mind if we borrowed your security cart for a few minutes?"

"Not a problem," replied Paul. "Take it for as long as you need it. Besides, I can use the exercise."

As David, Rachel, the twins, Cecilia, and Dr. Steward jumped into the three-bench security cart, Andrew directed his father to the section of the African elephant compound where the chimps were located.

As they stopped in front of the sanctuary, David asked, "What in the world were you two doing out here by yourselves? You were supposed to stay at the food court until you asked for an escort. Can't you totally understand that these are trying circumstances and it's dangerous to be out here alone?"

"Dad, we get it!" answered Andrew. "But we too have things to do. Trust me, you will eventually understand."

The group stepped out of the cart and walked over to the fencing. Andrew pointed inside the sanctuary. "They're over there, in the trees."

"Inside the compound?" bellowed David. "You were inside the compound on foot? What in the world were you thinking? Do you know how dangerous that was? Not only on the far side of the park by yourselves, but inside with wild animals in the dark. I may expect something like this from Mia, but not from you, Andrew! You have always been the sensible twin. I'm extremely disappointed in you! In both of you!"

"It's all my fault, Dad," exclaimed Mia, now with uncontrollable tears. "I convinced Andrew to go in with me. He didn't want to, but when I told him that I would go in by myself, he wouldn't let me go in alone. But can we please be punished later? Can we please help the chimps first, and then we can deal with the other part later? Okay? Please!"

"We'll have to go back and secure an open-air safari vehicle," replied David, obviously still irritated. "There is no way that this security cart will be able to maneuver inside the compound and give us the safety that we would need."

"We don't need a truck, Dad," replied Andrew. "We can just walk in. I can guarantee you that we will not only be safe, but we'll be protected. I'm pretty sure you will see that it's now one of the safest of all places to be in the zoo."

"Andrew, there are wild animals inside there," returned David, still unable to regain his composure.

"Not any wilder than some animals outside the fence," interjected Mia.

"You're still not making any sense to me, Mia," replied David. "You're still talking in riddles."

"Mia," asked Rachel, standing directly in front of her and placing both hands on Mia's shoulders to get her total attention. "Weren't you afraid to just walk inside there? Weren't you concerned for your safety?"

"No, the animals won't hurt us!" answered Mia. "Like Andrew told Dad, if anything, the animals will protect us from the dangerous animals outside their compound."

"But, Princess!" David was beginning to calm down as his heartbeat started to return to normal and he realized that Mia was in emotional pain. "How did you ever manage to get inside in the first place?"

"That wasn't a problem," answered Mia. "We just walked in through those gates over there by the road."

"Those gates are always locked," replied David. "Only security and certain designated employees have access to the keys."

"No, there're actually unlocked right now," answered Andrew. "Trust me, Dad, they're unlocked."

"And you can trust me when I tell you again that the animals won't do us any harm," added Mia.

Looking at them carefully and seeing some sort of a special aura about them that she had never noticed before, Rachel interjected, "I trust them. And you know that I'm not known to be a very trusting person. But I have a very strong feeling about this, David, and I'm willing to follow them on foot."

"You can count me in," replied Cecilia. "After what I have seen tonight, I believe that they could make a blind man see. I'll follow them anywhere."

"I'm in," stated Dr. Steward. "And if they told me that they could fly, I wouldn't dispute it."

David looked at the twins very carefully and noticed that their white tennis shoes were perfectly clean. Considering the compound and observing that the area the twins had pointed out was surrounded by thick mud, David surmised that it would have been totally impossible for them to have entered the compound, managed to negotiate to that cluster of trees, and then return without a trace of mud on them. And even more disconcerting was that both their shoes and their clothes seemed to be perfectly dry—this was totally impossible to believe! No, not a chance. It would have to be beyond the bounds of possibility or reason.

"Let me see the bottoms of your shoes," requested David of the twins. The twins, as well as the others, were confused, but Mia and Andrew did as they were asked. And after David inspected them, he not only found them to be spotless but completely dry. Baffled, he continued, "Okay, I tell you what. If we find that those gates are unlocked, of which I entirely rule out its plausibility, I will agree. We'll walk in."

Noticing how easily Andrew opened the gate, which in fact was unlocked, David raised his hands and held his head while he quickly started to shake it back and forth.

"I don't believe it," David softly said. "I just don't believe it."

"Well!" asked Rachel. "You did say that if the gates were unlocked, we would walk in, didn't you?"

"Are you sure you don't want to reconsider this idea?" responded David. "Why don't you just let Patrick and me enter alone? That would make more sense."

"Not on your life, mister," was Rachel's retort. "You don't think for a minute that you're going to talk us out of this adventure now, do you?"

"Dad," Mia spoke up, "you and Dr. Steward can't do this alone. The other animals won't let you in without Andrew and me. Trust me, Dad. You will be much safer with us than without us."

"Okay, let's go!" Dr. Steward said. "Time's a-wasting." He and Cecilia grabbed some flashlights that were always stored in each security cart and led the way through the gates.

"Don't forget to latch the gate," Andrew reminded his father as David was the last to enter the compound.

CHAPTER 14

$\mathcal{A}$fter entering the sanctuary, there was a clear and obvious sense of intrusion transmitted throughout the compound because of the human presence. All the animals were aware of the abuse of the chimpanzees, and all were committed to their protection. The alarm was sounded to the inhabitants of the compound; every animal was called to participate in the chimpanzees' protection, and everyone responded.

As the small group made their way toward the identified area of the injured primates, keeping their flashlight beams on the treacherous ground, the adults grew increasingly uneasy as they noticed that several of the animals simultaneously started to wander to their location. And as they proceeded deeper into the compound, even more of the animals came forward.

"Is it just my imagination or is there a crowd gathering around us?" asked Rachel with concern in her voice. "Mia, are you absolutely sure that we're safe?"

Mia turned and looked up to Star and thought, *We are, aren't we?*

Star, with a large smile on her face, just nodded in the affirmative.

"Yes, Mother, we're perfectly safe," responded Mia. "The animals just want to thank us for attending to the injured chimpanzees. They're not interested in doing us any harm."

"I think that we better start moving slowly back to the gate," replied David. "This was never a promising idea in the first place."

"Don't worry, Dad," responded Mia. "They're not going to hurt anyone. Andrew and I won't let them. If anything, like I told Mom, most of them just want to protect the chimpanzees. Others want to protect Andrew and me, and the rest of them are just curious."

"Why would they be concerned about your and Andrew's safety?" asked Rachel. "Just who do they think is going to harm you?"

"Animals," answered Mia. "The two-legged kind."

"You're still talking in riddles, Mia," replied David, still confused.

"You'll see!" said Mia. "Just follow us."

"I trust Mia." Rachel tried to placate David's fears for everyone. "The animals don't seem to be aggressive toward us, just a little anxious. But I have a great deal of interest on what you, Cecilia, and Patrick think since you three are the real experts here."

The closer the group came to the location of the chimps, the tighter the circle of animals closed around them, until they were surrounded by the animals of the compound. Although none of the animals tried to charge or harm them, they did make it obvious that they did not want them to progress any farther and obstructed their forward movement.

"Now what?" asked David. "They obviously are not going to allow us to reach the chimps, and they are now blocking our way back to the gate. Mia, what do you and Andrew have to say now? Didn't I say this wasn't a good idea? Now look at the precarious position we are in!"

From the center of the group, Andrew and Mia stepped forward. After a couple of moments of what appeared to be concerted efforts of serene meditation by the twins, suddenly several of the animals stepped aside, creating an opening to the trees that harbored the injured chimps.

"It's okay now," announced Mia. "We have their permission to help the hurt chimps."

"This is amazing," mumbled Dr. Steward to no one in particular. "This is beyond my dreams. I could never imagine this could ever happen. These events are way more than phenomenal. We definitely have a lot to think about and discuss."

The twins moved forward, leading the small cadre of medical experts to their first of many wonderful adventures. Adventures that they most certainly would never forget!

"There they are!" Mia declared as she pointed her flashlight to an area near the middle of a group of trees. "You can see them up there on the large branch near the center of the tree. The last time Andrew and I were here, they were on the ground. Somehow they got back up in the tree, probably with help."

"I see them, Princess," David acknowledged, shining his flashlight over them quickly. "But I don't see how we're going to get them down to examine them."

"We already tried," responded Mia, "the first time we were here. Even though they want to, they're so scared of humans, they're extremely hesitant to trust any of us. But after talking to them for a lengthy period, they were willing for us to bring Dad. We made it clear that Dad could help them with their injuries. And they really want to be able to trust humans again. So, Dad, it's very important that you use your very best bedside manners. The kind you and Mom use on Andrew and me when we're sick or injured. Okay?"

"You can count on it," responded her Dad. "So you are telling me that this is the third time you have been here tonight? We are going to talk about this later, but why would they be afraid of humans? They've been around humans all their lives. They've been fed, housed, and cared for by humans since they were babies. They were born at the zoo, not in the wilds of the jungles."

"We'll tell you all we know about it later, okay?" pleaded Mia. "Right now, I think it best to help them as quickly as you can. Can you see Jennifer on the right?" asked Mia. "Do you see how her left arm just hangs straight down? It hurts her so much that she can't use it."

"Yes! I can see that," exclaimed David. "But I don't think that it's her arm that's injured. It looks more like it's her shoulder that's probably causing the pain. She probably had a serious fall. What I don't understand is how she was able to climb that tree with her injured shoulder. She must be in a great deal of pain. And I believe that her name is really Sarah."

"She must have had someone help her, probably Barnard. And she didn't get hurt in a fall," replied Mia, as tears started to form once again in the corners of her eyes. "It was a human who mistreated her. That's why she's hurt. And you may call her Sarah, but she prefers Jennifer."

"I don't understand, Mia," asked Dr. Steward. "What do you mean it was a human? Who? Who was it who hurt her? How and why did they hurt her? And who is Barnard?"

"I don't know!" answered Mia. "That's not clear right now. All I know is that it was someone they used to trust. Someone who would bring them food and clean their enclosure. And then he started to hit them with a stick! Oh, I'll introduce you to Barnard later."

"Mia, how do you know all this happened?" asked Rachel. "That seems so inconceivable to me." She was now embracing her daughter. It was so obvious that Mia was in anguish over the mistreatment of both chimps. "Who told you?" continued Rachel. "Was it another zookeeper?"

"I just know! I just know this to be true," replied Mia. "You're just going to have to believe me."

"Of course, we all believe you," replied her mother. "Everything that you and Andrew have said and shown us has been remarkably true. Trust in us now to believe in you."

"Well, the first thing that we're going to have to do is get Sarah to come down out of that tree so that we can examine her," declared David. "And if she won't trust us, it's going to be very difficult to coax her down."

"Jennifer, David," said Dr. Steward. "She prefers Jennifer."

"Yes, of course, Jennifer," repeated David, trying to bring a little levity to the situation. "How do you suggest we get Jennifer down, Mia? And cause her as little pain as we can in the process?"

"Well!" said Andrew. "I may have an idea." He casually walked over to an enormous bull African elephant. "If she won't come to us, then we'll go to her." As he walked back to the group's location, the massive male elephant was at his side.

As both Andrew and the elephant stood beneath the tree, to the astonishment of everyone except Mia, the elephant knelt to the ground, permitting Andrew to climb up onto his back. As soon as he was securely sitting on his back, Andrew reached down and assisted his sister so that she could also safely mount. Then upon command, the eleven-foot elephant slowly rose to his full standing position. Standing on his back, Andrew and Mia could almost meet the chimps at equal eye level. After a short visit with the primates, they were again returned to the adults' location.

"Okay, Dad," Mia said triumphantly from the elephant's back. "She'll let you examine her, but please don't shine your light in her face. And you'll have to do it while she remains in the tree."

"In the tree!" exclaimed David. "How am I going to examine her in the tree?"

As the twins started to giggle, Mia responded first. "Dad, let me introduce you to Barnard. He'll be more than happy to assist you."

As Mia patted the bull elephant on the top of his head, again the elephant lowered himself to all four knees. "All you have to do is step up on his knee, then grab on to his ear, and pull yourself up on his back," suggested Mia. "It's easy! You've seen how they do it at the circus."

"You do know that he's not a circus elephant, don't you, Mia?" responded her father. "And you know that he's not trained to give rides."

"Dad, it's going to be okay," answered Mia with a smile. "Why do you think he got down on his knees? He's not interested in taking a nap."

"Don't be such a chicken," Rachel teased. "If you don't want to do it, I will!"

"I'll do it," replied David, not appreciating Rachel's challenge. "She has an injured shoulder, not having a heart attack, so she needs a veterinarian, not a cardiologist."

David then complied with Mia's instructions and mounted the elephant in the same manner as Andrew and Mia. With David sitting in front and Mia just behind him, Barnard stood up with his precious cargo of David, Mia, and Andrew on his back. Mia took her father's shoulders and whispered into her father's ear, "Dad, may I remind you again about making use of your best bedside manner? She's still not quite thrilled about humans, especially those that are supposed to be friends."

"I'll be as kind and gentle with her as a loving parent," responded her father. "I'm always very conscious of it with all my patients, but thank you for reminding me that this is a very sensitive case."

David stood up and started his cursory examination while standing on Barnard's back. But to complete his examination, it was necessary for him to softly touch Jennifer's shoulder. As he did, she immediately flinched and started to whimper. The other animals on the ground immediately reacted and paid attention even more closely. The mere touch on Jennifer's shoulder caused her a great deal of pain. "She certainly has a broken clavicle, in my opinion," stated David. "But it needs to be confirmed by an x-ray. Trying to get her down to the ground is going to be our greatest problem. If she refuses to cooperate and we try to force her down, that will compound her injury. And I'm not sure how the other animals will respond when she starts to scream in pain," David said with concern in his voice. "But it's imperative that we get her back to the clinic so that we can get her x-rayed and properly treat her. My other concern is if the other animals will understand why we need to take these two chimps with us, so we can help them." He turned and addressed his children. "Do you have any suggestions?"

"Let me try talking to her again, Dad," requested Mia. "I'll do what I can."

This time, David made up his mind to study very carefully Mia's communication techniques and not miss anything. At this point, he was positive that his children were somehow able to effectively communicate with the animals, no matter how ridiculous it sounded, which is why he kept his opinion to himself.

Now it was time for Star and Simon to come to Mia's aid. Calling upon their guardian angels though her telepathic ability, Mia instantly saw Star and Simon appear on the ground next to their mother. *Is there anything you can do to help?* asked Mia.

We can always try, responded Simon. After Simon's common-sense intervention with Jennifer, he turned to Mia. *She wants your father's help now, but she also wants you to help her down from the tree and be at her side at all times, okay?*

Mia repositioned herself closer to Jennifer while still standing on Barnard's back and gently placed her hand on Jennifer's foot, staring motionless into her eyes without even blinking an eye. After approximately three long minutes, Jennifer reached out with her only healthy arm, wrapping it tightly around Mia's neck and shoulders. Mia carefully lifted her free of the tree and then sat down securely on Barnard's back. Mia was confused. Jennifer seemed not to be as heavy as she was expecting her to be. In fact, Mia picked her up quite easily and thought that was bizarre.

Andrew then stepped forward and around Mia and his father and reached for Jennifer's companion, tenderly asking, "Come on, Kevin, let me help you down." Andrew had no idea how much to expect Kevin to weigh and braced himself for a much heavier primate. He, too, was surprised at how easily he lifted Kevin off the branch and held him to his chest while Kevin wrapped his arms around Andrews's neck. But this was not the time to question Star or Simon about it; he decided to wait for a more opportune time.

Sitting security on Barnard's back and without attempting to say anything, David casually turned to Rachel, then to Cecilia, and finally to Dr. Steward with bewilderment in his eyes. Two female elephants came forward and, without any vocal command, knelt in front of Rachel, Cecilia, and Dr. Steward.

"They're offering you a ride back to the gate," explained Mia. "There's no reason to be frightened. Just climb up like we did."

"You don't have to ask me twice," replied Rachel. Then she looked over to David. "Yeah! And you wanted us to stay back where it was nice and safe," Rachel said with a shrug. "I wouldn't have missed this miraculous experience for anything in the world!"

"Mia, I have to ask," Dr. Steward pleaded as they were riding the elephants. "How did you come up with the names of Jennifer, Barnard, and Kevin? You know those aren't their real names. Why did you want to change them?"

"I didn't make up any names," responded Mia. "Those are their real names. The only name that Andrew and I made up was Rehab. And that's because he didn't know his parents and had no real name."

"Rehab? Who is Rehab?" asked Dr. Steward.

"Oh, you haven't met Rehab yet!" interrupted Cecilia. "We'll have to introduce you to him when we return to the clinic. Oh, he's a real charmer! He'll win your heart over in seconds."

"Yes, he sounds like an interesting character. I would like that very much," replied Dr. Steward. "And I would also like to hear more about this individual with the stick."

"I would like to know more as well," concurred David. "If it's true what Mia told us—and everything inside me tells me that it is—we need to identify who it is and take appropriate action."

"Whatever happened to 'Be as quiet as a worm'?" mumbled Andrew. "No one ever keeps their word anymore."

*J*ennifer was still very apprehensive of everyone and only allowed Mia to carry her. As the rescue group entered the clinic, the entire staff turned to see what all the commotion was about, for the other primates that were captured earlier started to raise a tremendous commotion. Apparently, they were celebrating the safe return of their separated comrades. Cecilia quickly walked ahead of everyone, and she promptly prepared an examination table and wheeled a stainless steel surgical cart next to the table containing all the medical supplies and equipment that would be needed.

As Mia placed Jennifer on the examination table and backed away, allowing full access for her father and Cecilia to conduct a thorough examination, Jennifer quickly leaped from the table and scampered to Mia's side, hugging Mia with her good arm. Even though it caused her a great deal of pain as she did so, it showed that she didn't want Mia to leave her side and wanted to reach for Mia's hand.

"It's obvious that she isn't going to let us examine her without you next to her side," acknowledged David. "So, Mia, why don't you please place Jennifer back on the table, but this time I want you to remain and assist us, okay?"

"Okay," replied Mia. "But what do you want me to do?"

"For now, I just want you to hold her hand and utilize that miraculous soothing quality of yours," directed David. "It's obvious that she has total trust and confidence only in you."

Mia easily picked up Jennifer and returned her to the examining table. As she placed her on the table, Mia, while gently holding both of Jennifer's hands, gazed directly into her eyes with total concentration and started a dialog with Jennifer using her recently acquired mental telepathy gift. After a minute or so, Kevin jumped up on the table, sitting next to Jennifer, and he also wanted to hold Jennifer's good hand.

"Okay, Dad!" exclaimed Mia. "You can start your examination. Just be as tender as you can. She's in a lot of pain, okay?"

As David and Cecilia conducted their examination of Jennifer, it was obvious from all the chatter that Kevin and the other primates were conducting a conversation all their own.

"Patrick, let's make ourselves useful," suggested Rachel, "and see if Andrew's little friend has any medical concerns resulting from today's adventures."

"I'd love to!" declared Dr. Steward. "I've been so involved in administrative affairs that I've become far too removed from the real pleasures of working for a zoo, which is the daily contact with the wildlife that has been entrusted to our care."

"Oh! Let me prepare a table for you, Doctors," suggested Cecilia.

"That's okay, I can do it!" Dr. Steward eagerly offered. "I'll enjoy making my hands useful again. It will be refreshing to do something useful for a change."

"What was it that you called this chimp, Andrew?" asked his mother.

"Kevin, his name is Kevin," Andrew quickly replied.

"Okay! Would you please place Kevin up on the table so that we can have a look at him?" requested his mother.

Reluctantly, after a few intense moments, Andrew was able to talk Kevin into separating himself from Jennifer, but not before Andrew convinced Kevin that he, too, needed to be examined by his mother. Andrew assured Kevin that Jennifer would always be in full view during his examination. After placing him on the table, he then sat next to him for reassurance. Kevin quickly spun himself around so that he would not lose eye contact with his companion.

"I see that they are quite devoted to each other," remarked Rachel. "Do you know if they're mates?"

"Yes, they are!" answered Cecilia. "Sarah and Charlie have been together for the past four years. We've been trying to breed them for the last three, but so far we've been totally unsuccessful."

"Their names are Jennifer and Kevin," replied Mia, slightly raising her voice, not in disrespect but wanting to emphasize that their names weren't Sarah and Charlie.

"Again, that's interesting, Mia," interjected Dr. Steward. "You said earlier that Jennifer and Kevin are their real names and you didn't just make them up. How is it that you know that these are their true names?"

"I didn't rename them," answered Mia. "Those are their real names. I guess that's what their parents named them! I'm not sure. It was the zoo that named them incorrectly."

This only convinced David that his children were truly communicating with the animals. How else to explain their confidence that the chimps' true names were Jennifer and Kevin? David decided that this wasn't the time to confront his children on this issue. But after digesting further facts that he hoped to collect, he intended to revisit this point.

"Okay, if you say it's true, your word is good enough for me. Among your father, Cecilia, and my administrative staff, we'll now correct the mistake!" replied Dr. Steward, enjoying the frivolity. "From henceforth, they will only be addressed as Jennifer and Kevin."

"Sounds good to me, Dr. Steward," interjected Cecilia. "I'll direct Julie to officially change their names when she's free after all this commotion and we're back to a regular schedule."

"Oh my god!" Rachel gasped. "He has a large area on his back that is badly bruised and really tender to the touch. In fact, I'm finding several other bruises on his arms and back."

"And look here on his legs, Rachel," Dr. Steward remarked in shock. "I can see many others."

As she and Dr. Steward conducted a more thorough examination, Rachel continued, "David, when you have a minute, could you please come over here and take a look?"

"Mia, please keep an eye on Jennifer for just a moment while Cecilia and I look at Kevin," requested her father. "We'll be right back."

As David walked over to Kevin's location, Rachel pushed aside some of Kevin's hair so that David could gain a better view of Kevin's injuries.

"You say that you and Patrick found several other bruises?" asked David.

"Yes, as a matter of fact, there are tender spots and swelling all over his body, including his legs," answered Rachel. "These bruises are not from a single incident. This evidence shows a pattern of abuse over several days, if not several weeks. No wonder they were so apprehensive about being around humans. Who could blame them? They were being abused systematically. He has a bad split lip that I'm going to have to suture. I have no idea how Mia and Andrew knew about this prior to our examination and came up with their conclusions in the dark. But they were both absolutely correct in their assessment."

"I found the same evidence of abuse on Jennifer," replied David. "Just that in her case, it appears to be a little more severe. I won't know for sure until we x-ray her, but it looks like she sustained a broken collarbone. I think we better carefully examine all the primates with the help of our staff, to include x-rays, and see if any of them have also sustained the same abuse."

"Now that returns us to Mia's earlier statements about someone with a stick," replied Dr. Steward. "Mia, can you tell us anything more about this man who you said hit them with a stick?"

"All I know is that he's supposed to be someone that is in a position of trust," responded Mia. "He pushes a cart with food on it, and he keeps a wooden stick in one of its drawers. That's the stick that he uses to hit them with." And again, Mia's eyes started to tear, and she hesitated again, choking on her words. "I'm sorry, Dr. Steward, I just don't know anymore." She stopped, speechless, trying to regain control of herself. She clenched her fists at her sides, her eyes bulging, her complexion turning red in anger. She started to count to twenty-seven—this was her method to regain her composure. Twenty-seven was her lucky number, the date in July of Andrew's and her birthday.

Dr. Steward immediately stepped over and placed his arm around Mia's shoulders. "Mia, don't worry. We're going to find out who this person is, and we're going to stop him. We will absolutely not tolerate any abuse of any of our animals." Worried frowns and questing glances were furtively exchanged. Mia regained control of herself with an obvious effort, unclenched her fists, and her face relaxed, the color fading.

Now David was totally convinced that his children were somehow communicating with the animals. How else could Mia know that it was a stick in one of the zookeeper's food wagon that was the cause of the chimpanzees' injuries? And also know that their true names were Jennifer and Kevin? It was obvious to him that his children were keeping their gifts a secret from Rachel and himself. But why? Both Rachel and he had always been available to them to speak on any topic among themselves. Knowing how emotional Mia and Andrew were at the moment, he decided again this was not the time to push the issue. He was convinced that nothing was quite what it appeared to be. Nothing could be taken at face value.

"It sounds like it may be a food service wagon that each zookeeper uses to feed and care for his assigned habitat," replied Dr. Steward. "But that also sounds preposterous! It couldn't be a zookeeper! The animals in their charge love them all. Maybe they got into some kind of a fight with one another?"

"It wasn't a fight, Dr. Steward," answered Andrew respectfully. "Unless you call someone hitting a defenseless animal with a stick a fight!"

"I have to agree with them, Patrick," responded David, supporting Andrew's and Mia's accusations. "Their injuries aren't from scratches and bites, which would be indicative of a fight with another primate. These injuries clearly support abuse by some sort of a blunt instrument over a prolonged period of time."

"Mia, I don't want you to think for a moment that I don't believe you," reassured Dr. Steward. "After what we all witnessed today, I can't see how anyone would question your word. Just that it is so hard to believe! I guess I'm just thinking out loud, trying to make some sense of their injuries. I hate the idea that an employee of the park would commit such an abomination."

"I know, Dr. Steward," answered Mia. "I wish that I knew more, but I don't. But you do promise me that you and Dad will stop him or her and make sure that no other animals are injured?"

"You have our word on it," Dr. Steward replied sincerely. "We will find out who is responsible for these acts of violence. You have no idea how much all of us appreciate you! How in the world you found Jennifer and Kevin up in that tree is beyond me! We would never have looked for them in the African sanctuary. But you did! How did you know?"

"Maybe they had guardian angels looking after them?" answered Mia. "Maybe God was looking after them? All I can say is that some-one must have whispered in our ears. You do believe in guardian angels, don't you?"

"Mia, I'm an Irishman from the old country. If I can believe in little bearded solitary creatures called leprechauns who wear green coats and hats, who partake in mischief, who make and mend shoes, and who have a pot of gold at the end of a rainbow, how in the world would I not believe in guardian angels?"

"That's the funniest thing I've ever heard, Dr. Steward." Mia giggled. "You really know how to make me laugh."

"Well, on a day like this, we certainly can use a little frivolity while we still give due respect to such a serious matter of abuse to our animals. Humor is an important part of our humanity, a part that we can't live without. Unfortunately, I must now try to get this issue resolved, David. May I use your radio?" requested Dr. Steward. "I must have left mine outside in the security cart."

"Of course! You'll find it on top of the table next to Cecilia behind the bandages," answered David.

"Admin 1 to Mammals 1! Please respond."

"This is Mammals 1," replied Roger after a short delay.

"Roger, can you please pick up a landline and call me at Veterinarians 1's office?" requested Dr. Steward as he headed to David's office.

*P*icking up the ringing phone in David's office, Dr. Steward recognized Roger Richardson's voice immediately.

"Roger, thanks for calling so quickly," answered Dr. Steward. "I didn't want to make our conversation public over the radio airways. But we have a situation. There is conclusive evidence that there was substantial abuse sustained by two of the escaped primates. We suspect that it was committed by utilizing some sort of a stick or club. As illogical as it seems, we also suspect one of the zookeepers of committing the abuse. What I need you to do is to play detective and inspect all food service wagons of the zookeepers who work in the primate habitats. And then get back to me ASAP, okay?"

"You can't be entertaining the notion that one of our zookeepers would abuse an animal in their care!" replied Roger. "It's not possible! All our zookeepers are devoted to their animals. There must be some sort of mistake."

"I wish that there were," answered Dr. Steward. "But all the evidence indicates deliberate abuse. Would you please inspect each wagon carefully? I need the results of your findings as soon as possible. I can't see how we'll be able to return any of the primates back into their habitats until we discover the individual or individuals responsible."

"I'll get a-hopping, Chief," responded Roger. "But I can assure you that there won't be any stick or instrument resembling anything like that. There would be absolutely no reason for anyone to carry a stick or a club in their service wagon. But if it will make you feel any better, I'll check it out for you and get back to you immediately."

"*D*ad, is Jennifer going to be okay?" asked Mia, as her father worked methodically on the female chimp.

"She's going to be fine," replied her father. "Thanks to your help, we have several very clear x-rays showing that she indeed has a broken collarbone. What we call the clavicle. That's what caused all the swelling and pain and why her shoulder flattened, and she had to let her arm hang close to her body. She may feel a little uncomfortable wearing a cast for the next few weeks. She will require some medication for both her broken clavicle and her bruises and abrasions. But with a lot of tender loving care—which I can assure you she will receive from our staff—there is no reason why she won't heal rapidly without any other problems. And being that she has full trust and confidence in you and Andrew, it looks like you two have another couple of patients to care for besides Rehab!"

"Is the baby going to be okay too?" asked Mia with a concerned look on her face. "It would be an additional tragedy if she lost her baby!"

"What are you talking about?" inquired David. "What baby?"

"Jennifer is going to have a baby," insisted Mia.

"No, Princess, Jennifer is not going to have a baby," her father contradicted gently. "We tried to mate her for three years with Kevin, but nothing happened. So we gave Jennifer a test, and we found out that she was infertile, which means that she can't conceive a baby. It's impossible."

"That's right, Mia," confirmed Cecilia. "It's impossible. In fact, we started looking for a new partner for Kevin to mate with about four weeks ago, and we were successful. In about two weeks, we will receive a new girlfriend for Kevin from another zoo."

"I don't know what kind of test it is to see if you're going to have a baby or not," persisted Mia. "All I know is that Jennifer and Kevin are going to have a baby girl!"

David started to smile and was about to explain even further how it was impossible for the chimps to conceive. Then suddenly he remembered about the twins' shoes. They were still spotless. Then he anxiously looked at everyone else's shoes, and they were covered in mud. In fact, they had tracked mud all over the clinic's pristine floor. How could that be? They all walked the identical path. They all walked across several feet of thick mud due to the rain. It was totally impossible to avoid it. Yet although everyone's shoes where covered with mud, as would be expected, Andrew's and Mia's white tennis shoes remained spotless as if they were brand new, straight out of the shoe box!

"Cecilia," David called, getting her attention. "Would you please draw blood from Jennifer and give her a pregnancy test?"

"Okay, David," responded Cecilia. "If that would make Mia feel more comfortable, I'll gladly do it. But I don't think we will find the results different than before."

"Maybe she wasn't pregnant before, but she is now. In fact, it's going to be a baby girl!" Mia responded with a large smile on her face.

Mia then started to look for Star to confirm her prediction. Unable to do so, she tried to contact her by using her mental telepathy abilities. *Star, where are you?*

I'm right behind you! replied Star.

I'm right about Jennifer having a baby? Right? I don't want to look foolish! questioned Mia.

No! You are not being foolish, answered Star, nodding with exuberance. *I can assure you, Jennifer is going to have a healthy baby girl as I said before. I have another question for you,* Mia asked. *I'm curious to know why it was so easy for Andrew and me to be able to lift and carry Jennifer and Kevin. It seemed like they weighed only as much as marshmallows or a pillow stuffed with feathers. They are fully grown, and I know that it should have been much more difficult than it was? So what gives?*

Well, Star replied with a full smile, *you should be well aware by now that Simon and I can perform little tricks now and then when the situation calls for it. We needed you to have the strength for this little task, so we made it possible.*

Are you saying that Andrew and I are going to have superhuman strength from now on? queried Mia.

Not at all! answered Star. *Simon and I will be able to give you each certain abilities but only when needed to complete a task and for only short periods of time.*

Why only for short periods of times? Mia wanted to know. *It would be so cool! I would really be able to put the O'Connor brothers in their proper place.*

"Sweetheart! Sweetheart! Where is your mind? Your father is asking you a question! It seems like you are riding an asteroid in outer space."

"I'm sorry, Mother. I was just thinking about Jennifer and her baby. I wasn't daydreaming. I was in deep contemplation." She looked at Andrew steeling his explanation from before as Mia was caught off guard.

"Mia, your dad and I are asking how in the world are you so convinced that Jennifer is pregnant. I'm perplexed, and I for one would like to know why you feel so confident!" her mother exclaimed. "It seems that you feel that you are more accurate than a blood test. So give us a hint on your method."

"I just look into their eyes and listen to what they have to say," responded Mia with her smiling eyes.

"I see," Mia's father had to weigh in, "you listened to Jennifer's eyes and they told you that she was pregnant?"

"That's my trick," answered Mia. "It's foolproof!"

"Well then, in the future when we need to pay for a costly pregnancy test, we'll just call you in to consult. Does this work equally well for hippos, rhinoceros, and elephants, or are you limited to just chimps?" asked her father with a large grin on his face.

"No! I would say it works well for all animals," Mia responded, knowing perfectly well that her father was teasing her now. "In fact, Blanca, your female Siberian tiger, is also having a baby."

David was now more confused than ever! *How could Mia know that Jennifer was pregnant without any tangible proof? Even if she could communicate with Jennifer, that wouldn't explain the paradox. How would Jennifer know herself? Even women see their doctors to confirm if they are pregnant or not. No, science provides reliable proof, not eye contact. If Mia is right and Jennifer's test comes back positive, not only are the scientific lab results contradicted, but the twins must be able to do more than speak with animals and understand them. What else can they do? And how can they do these things? And do I really want to know the answers to those questions?*

CHAPTER 15

"*O*kay, Mia, now that your mother and I are finished treating Kevin, you mentioned earlier that you knew how to get Chester out of that ditch," remembered Dr. Steward. "May I now ask what exactly did you have in mind?"

"Oh, yes!" replied Mia. "Andrew and I have a great idea that we know will work, and it will only take a few minutes to do it."

"Well, I'm certainly ready for an easy solution," replied Dr. Steward. "Please, I'm all excited to hear exactly what you have in mind, and what is it that you will need?"

"I think that it will be easier if Andrew and I showed you," responded Mia, bursting with self-confidence. Finally, she and Andrew were being recognized for having an idea worth considering!

"If you can just wait for a few more minutes?" requested David. "Now that your mother and Dr. Steward have finished working on Kevin, Cecilia and I will be finished shortly with Jennifer. And by the way, Rachel, we're both aware that many doctors use their own style of suturing, but I couldn't help but notice that you used a technique on Kevin's lip that I have never seen used before. It looks very ingenious!"

"Oh," responded Rachel, "it's a method I developed when I suture young children, so they don't accidentally remove them. You know how difficult it is when you must replace them if the originals have been torn out."

"Fascinating to say the least," responded David. "I hope you won't be offended if I steal that method and apply it to some of my patients. I have the same problems when I need to work with my excessively active animals. Our solution is we either just bandage their paws, or when possible, we tape mittens on the primates' hands so they don't scratch them out."

"I say go for it." Rachel chuckled. "Imitation is the sincerest form of flattery!"

Still working on Jennifer, David continued, "With some prescribed meds and extra tender loving care from the clinic's staff, Kevin will be fine in no time. On the other hand, for Jennifer with her broken clavicle, she's going to need a little more care than Kevin, but she also will eventually make a full recovery. But as I was saying, we should be through treating Jennifer here shortly, and then we can all go and listen to the kids' solution for Chester. I must admit they now definitely have my attention. And I don't think any of us want to miss it."

Meanwhile, the twins continued to watch every procedure performed by their most capable father with intense scrutiny. Even Kevin was very attentive, watching everything that David was doing for Jennifer, the love of his life. Although they had always been an extremely tight-knit family, the twins had never been so proud of their parents as they were this day. They were now cognizant, perhaps for the first time in their short lives, that they, too, wanted to devote the rest of their lives to helping sick and injured animals. And after observing the professional skills of their parents, they realized how very much there was still left for them to learn. But also, in the back of their minds, with the help of their guardian angels, perhaps there were also a couple of things that they, too, had to offer for the common good.

As soon as Jennifer's medical needs had been met, Mia asked, "Are you through with her now, Dad? Can Andrew and I place them together in a separate lockup so that no other animal might accidentally bump into them and aggravate their injuries? And we also need to feed them. I know that they must be hungry—especially Jennifer since she is now eating for two."

"And I think that Kevin is going to need a little extra food, too, because he's having sympathy pains for Jennifer," suggested Andrew as everyone in the room erupted into laughter.

"Okay, you can place them into that empty lockup next to their friends," answered their father. "I have a feeling that they will want to share the entire events of their day with them." Mia and Andrew tenderly lifted the two chimps off their examination tables, gently placed them together into the designated enclosure, and oversaw that they had plenty to eat.

"Please don't leave without me!" pleaded Cecilia. "I don't want to miss a thing, but I need to document everything the good doctors did for Jennifer and Kevin in their medical files first."

Although most of the veterinary staff had to continue with their other assigned patients, they all were very interested in how the twins were going to solve Chester's predicament. One by one, the veterinary staff asked Dr. Brooks to please get back to them with the solution without omitting a single detail. Rachel also gave her staff some additional directions before she felt comfortable leaving the clinic.

"Being that our very capable staffs have everything under control," declared David, "it looks like now is the time we've all been waiting for. So why don't all of us go out to the bears' habitat and see what we can do for Chester? Now, Princess"—David leaned down to Mia's eye level—"I want to advise you in advance. We've consulted with several experts in trying to free Chester, and we were not comfortable with any of their ideas. So if we feel that your and Andrew's suggestion is not logical and we choose not to implement it, don't be embarrassed or disappointed. We have eliminated several promising ideas. We just felt that something better was needed for Chester. It's the adults that must make the final decisions though, okay?"

"I'm not worried," answered Mia. "I know that you're going to approve our idea. It's going to be very easy and very quick."

"It's hard for me to believe that if it's so easy and quick," wondered David, "why hasn't an adult discovered it first?"

"I think it's because adults are too complex," responded Mia. "Kids think in much simpler terms. But there is something that Andrew and I must do first."

While Cecilia was finishing up her paperwork, the twins went throughout the clinic and rapidly checked on each animal that had been treated that night, including Rehab. And as they went to each area, they reassured all the animals that they would return to say good night for the evening and to make sure that they were all satisfied with their care and last meal of the day. When Cecilia's and the twins' tasks were completed, they became over-energized. The twins were the first out the doors of the clinic and first in the lead to Chester's habitat. It was after midnight by this time, and the chill of the night air was quite apparent. The rain had subsided to a mere intermittent sprinkle, the moon was high and full among scattered clouds, and a gentle breeze circulated the fragrance of the flowers in bloom throughout the park.

As Andrew and Mia led their parents, Dr. Steward, Cecilia, and Carol Lee, who was being pushed in a wheelchair by David to the bears' habitat, they were met halfway up the hill by the huffing and puffing Roger Richardson. He was holding a half-eaten extra-large chili dog loaded with all the extra fixings.

"Roger! Where in the heck were you able to find a chili dog at this time of night?" asked Dr. Steward. "The concession stands for hotdogs have been closed for hours, and they don't sell them in the food court."

"Oh, I had bought three of them earlier from the hotdog stand near the cheetah and jaguar exhibit," replied Roger. "But since we were so busy with Chester and all the other pandemonium going on, I only had time to eat two of them. So I kept this one in my locker for a snack."

Cecilia, known always to be polite and diplomatic, couldn't help but interject a couple of her out-of-character but well-meant disapproving remarks. "Roger! Just listen to yourself. You can't be thirty-five years old, and you can hardly breathe from walking halfway down a little hill! You should throw that hotdog away and take better care of yourself before you become diabetic! All you need to do is watch your diet and start a moderate exercise program. Before you know it, you will be able run in both the Boston and New York marathons!"

"Easy for you to say!" retorted Roger. "I'm sure you probably haven't gained a pound since you were a cute, adorable little cheerleader in high school. But for us metabolism-deficient, Monopoly-playing athletes, all we have to do is watch someone else eat and we gain the pounds for them!"

As everyone found the humor in Roger's comments, Cecilia fired back, "I'll have you know I was never a high school cheerleader! I played softball and was on the swim team. And I'll challenge you to a game of Monopoly anytime, and the loser has to buy the both of us a healthy spring garden salad!"

"I may have to buy the salads, but you'll never make me eat one! Lettuce is for rabbits and tortoises!" declared Roger. "But that's not why I was on my way down to see you. I have terrible news to report. I searched all the service wagons as you asked, Dr. Steward, and I'm ashamed and shocked to report that you were right!" As Roger reached for the rear pocket of his rain pants under his rain jacket, he retrieved a wooden stick about eighteen inches long and one and a half inches in diameter.

"Where did you find that?" asked Dr. Steward.

"In one of the zookeepers' service wagons," responded Roger reluctantly. "It looks like it may be a cutoff piece of a broom or mop handle. I can't imagine why anyone would need to carry such a stick in his or her food service wagon. But I still can't believe any of our zookeepers would use it to abuse an animal! There must be some logical reason why he would carry it. And I will defend everyone under my supervision that they would never use such a device against any animal entrusted to their care. I'm sure that it must be intended for some practical use. We need to give the person a chance to explain why it was in the wagon. We don't want to jump to conclusions."

But nothing that Roger said could improve Dr. Steward's temper. "I'm asking again, where did you find it?" Patrick was determined for the answer.

"Let me look at it, Roger," requested David. And after examining it under one of the walkway's overhanging lamps, he continued, "Look at these little splinters on its side. Do you see where several strands of hair are caught under them? I'm no detective, but I would say that it's safe to assume that we're looking at the guilty weapon.

These hairs appear to contain their roots, indicating they were pulled off the victims by the force of the blows with it."

"Whose cart was it, Roger?" demanded Dr. Steward.

"I still think we shouldn't jump to conclusions," replied Roger, still trying to defend a possibly innocent employee. "We should all take a deep breath and listen to his story, and if there is any uncertainty whatsoever, we must give him the benefit of the doubt."

"Oh, we'll listen to his story all right!" insisted Dr. Steward. "But right now, I want to know in whose cart you found this club!"

"Oscar's, I found it in Oscar's service wagon," admitted Roger reluctantly and swallowing hard.

"Oscar's!" exclaimed Dr. Steward. "You mean the guy who was found squirting Chester with that high-power water hose and who later suggested that we should just shoot him because it would prove to be a cheaper solution than trying to rescue him? You mean that same Oscar?"

"Yes, the one and the same person!" replied Roger. "But like I said, let's not jump to any conclusions. He may have an innocent reason to have it."

"I want him!" insisted Dr. Steward. "Please find him and send him to me. What he really deserves is to be beaten with that club in the same manner that the chimpanzees were beaten! Then we'll listen to his excuses!"

"Listen to yourself, Pat," objected David. "I've never heard you to be unreasonable, so don't start now. You have an impeccable reputation of always treating people fairly, so let's keep it unsoiled."

"But, David, we're talking about brutally beating defenseless animals!" replied Dr. Steward. "Animals that we have a responsibility to protect and care for at all times."

"Wouldn't it be best if we waited until Monday?" suggested Roger. "That way, we would have a little more time to think about what course of action we should take and give us the extra time to cool off."

"No! I would prefer to handle this matter now! So please find him and have him report to me! Please!" commanded Dr. Steward.

"We're going up to Chester's habitat, so Oscar can easily find me there."

"Okay, you're the boss!" answered Roger meekly, realizing that Dr. Steward was adamant.

*R*eaching the habitat, they were met by Benjamin, who immediately updated them on Chester's condition.

"He's not completely out of control like before," reported Benjamin. "But it's obvious that his sedative is wearing off. Are we about ready to begin with the drilling?"

"We don't think that it will be necessary after all," responded Dr. Steward. "We may have an alternate solution, something that will be quick and easy."

"Great!" answered Frank, walking up from behind the group. "I'm always open to a workable plan. So what do you have in mind that's going to be quick and easy?"

"Andrew and Mia here think that they have a less invasive idea," replied Dr. Steward.

"Excuse me!" exclaimed Frank. "Are you trying to tell me that these two kids came up with a better solution than we proposed?"

"We believe so," replied Dr. Steward. "Just hear them out."

"I don't need to," responded Frank. "For hours, I've been trying to come up with alternate solutions to solve Chester's situation but keep coming up blank. Therefore, for the last several hours, my crew and I have been gathering all the equipment and supplies we'll need to start. The rest should arrive by the first thing in the morning, and then we can start the drilling."

"After seeing what these two incredible children have accomplished today, well, we're going to try their idea first," stated Dr. Steward. "And if it doesn't prove to have the merit that we think it should, then we'll try it your way. But for some reason, I don't think that it will be necessary."

"I'll tell you what, Patrick. Even after witnessing what they did for Carol Lee—and I acknowledge that it was incredible!" Frank continued with an obviously sarcastic grin on his face, "If you're so confident that their little plan is workable, how about proving it with a little act of faith?"

"Act of faith?" asked Dr. Steward. "What exactly do you have in mind?"

"If you're so confident, let's say that if it works, you will not have to pay everyone here time and a half, which you would normally owe us for coming in after hours," responded Frank. "But if it doesn't work, then you pay everyone double time."

Turning to the rest of his crew, Frank continued, "Does everyone concur with this proposal? If not, speak up now!" Hearing no objections from anyone, Frank returned to Dr. Steward. "Now do you really want us to stop and listen to their plan?"

Frank's crew was heard laughing and cheering in the background for Dr. Steward to take up the challenge and agree to the wager. Oh, the crew noisily discussed how they were going to spend this extra unexpected cash and not even tell their wives about it so they wouldn't run out and buy new shoes!

Turning to Mia, Dr. Steward saw her look of total confidence, bobbing her head in the affirmative. "Uh-huh! I'd take that bet," she said without any hesitation in her voice, and nodded firmly.

"You're on!" answered Dr. Steward with a smile growing to the size of Texas. "I have total confidence in her."

"Oh, this is too easy!" exulted Frank. "I'll tell you what I'll do, just to make this a little more interesting. If this little plan of theirs works—and I'm confident that it won't—I'll also buy everyone here Sunday brunch tomorrow morning."

"Whatever we want? And at a restaurant of our choice?" asked Dr. Steward.

"Anything you want! And at any restaurant you want," confirmed Frank. And now turning to the twins, he stated, "So let's hear your plan."

"First, we'll need to get all this equipment out of the way," began Mia. "The only thing that we'll need is that truck with the little crane on it. At the end of the cable, we need a bar like the ones that we use for chin-ups at school, and maybe some extra lighting like those lights you have on that trailer. Some to be placed on this side and maybe some extra lighting on the plateau side. Then all we'll need to do is lower the cable over the side so Chester can grab hold of it. Then we raise the cable, pulling up Chester, carefully swing it over to his side of the ditch, and lower him so that he can touch the ground. Problem solved!"

Frank and his crew simultaneously burst out laughing. "This is you plan?" guffawed Frank. "This is the best you can do? You think that if we lower a cable with a monkey bar on the end of it, the bear would understand exactly what to do and grab onto it so that we can pull him up? Please tell me that you're not so naive! That's never going to work! All he is going to do is slap at it. If anything, it's going to irritate him even more than he already is. This idea is just going to be a complete waste of time!"

"That's the plan," answered Mia, showing no signs of intimidation. Then she began turning in all directions, trying to locate Star and Simon. She first observed Simon standing next to Andrew, then realized that Star was standing directly behind her. She found both were smiling and nodding gently up and down, confirming Mia's suggestion as workable.

"Patrick, are you sure that you want to gamble on double time?" David interjected, a little skeptical himself. "You realize that Chester has no hands to grip the bar. All he has are paws. He has no thumbs, which are needed to grasp onto something. This plan is not going to work. It's impossible for Chester to hold on! Pat, this isn't just playing for marbles at a local park when you were a kid. The difference between time and a half to double time will be in the thousands. No! Call it off!"

Dr. Steward gazed deeply into Mia's big beautiful eyes and saw them dancing with confidence and, without any hesitation in his voice, declared, "Absolutely! It's on!"

"Okay, let's do it!" shouted Frank to his crew, still confident that this proposed endeavor would prove fruitless.

"Now what do you need for us to do?" asked Dr. Steward, directing his question to Mia and Andrew.

"I need to get as close as I can to the bear," replied Mia. "I need to make complete eye contact with Chester."

"Well, you can get as close as you want from the viewers' railing here," David answered. "Wouldn't that be close enough? It worked when you spoke to Chester when he was helping Carol Lee."

"I don't think so, Dad," replied Mia. "I don't think that I will be able to make total eye contact with Chester from here. I need to have his absolute attention, without any distractions. When I spoke to him before he wasn't roaring like he is now. He was trying to comfort his friend. This time, he's alone and crying out because he's scared and uncomfortable. It's going to be hard to get his attention. Can't I go down into his habitat like you did when you sedated him?" requested Mia. "You were real close to him from there."

"Princess! You're not suggesting that you go down into his living area? He's extremely wild," replied David as tenderly as possible. "Especially now after being trapped at the bottom of that safety zone for the last six or so hours. He'll be starting to recover shortly from that sedative I gave him earlier, and he'll probably be screaming at the top of his lungs and fighting mad again."

"But, Dad, I'm sure that I'll need to be closer," persisted Mia, trying to show the necessity of it by the inflection of her voice. "It can't be any more dangerous than being in the sanctuary with all those elephants, rhinos, and hippos."

"Princess, it's completely out of the question!" David responded firmly, indicating that there would be no compromise in this matter. "I know that you and Andrew have done some miraculous work today. Work that I will never be able to fully understand how you accomplished it, but this request of yours is impossible for me to grant. Please try to understand my logic and concerns for your safety. Look what happened to Carol Lee! She is an adult and was being careful, and she still fell in. A loving parent would never allow his child to be placed in such a position of danger!"

"I have to agree with your father, sweetheart," interrupted Rachel. "As much as I believe that you and your brother possess this incredible aptitude to bond with animals that you both displayed today, we cannot permit you to put yourself at any further risk."

"This may be in direct conflict of our overtime incentive," interjected Frank, "but I have a suggestion. I'm kind of hoping that your little girl can come through with her plan. I have a daughter about her age, and she surprises me all the time. And I still think that this plan of hers is totally crazy. But I have an idea, if she needs to make full eye contact with the bear."

"Feel free." David sighed. "We're all in this together."

"We have a cherry picker back in the parking lot," replied Frank. "We can place her in the basket and lower her over the side. She will be completely out of harm's way yet close enough to see the whites of his eyes, if that's what she has in mind."

"She would be completely and absolutely out of danger of any kind?" inquired David.

"I wouldn't have suggested it if I thought I couldn't place my own daughter in it safely," replied Frank. "I'll have my best operating engineer at the controls. She would never be in proximity of his paws. If you like, you can even go with her."

"It can hold two?" quizzed David, a little more interested now.

"It's a two-man basket," answered Frank. "It's designed to handle two large men with all their equipment. Should I have it brought out?"

David turned to Rachel for her opinion as she declared, "I have no problem with it, if you go with her."

"Bring it out," announced David boldly.

"Yes!" shouted Mia, extending her right hand up in the air. "Give it to me, Dad!" She accepted a high-five from her dad.

As they waited for the arrival of the cherry picker, the group observed Roger walking up the hill, still huffing and puffing.

"Roger! You're still completely out of breath!" This time, it was Rachel making the comments. "I don't think it's just a matter of being a little overweight and out of shape any more. I feel it may be much more serious! You aren't a smoker too, are you?"

"He smokes more than a fleet of steam locomotives back in the western days," responded Dr. Steward.

"Oh, it's not that bad! Maybe a pack or two a day," replied Roger.

"A typical smoker's response," answered Dr. Steward, "always understating the extent of their habit. I bet that it's closer to three or four packs a day!"

"Well, I don't care if it's one or two cigarettes a day. As you know, Roger, I'm a cardio-surgeon. Every cigarette shortens your life expectancy. I want you to come and see me in my office first thing Monday morning—don't worry about an appointment. And, Roger, I'll expect you to be there!"

"Okay, Doc," replied Roger. "At this point, I'm inclined to agree with you. I think I may need some help. But I'm basically here to report that I couldn't find Oscar. I've been all over the park. I'm sure that he's probably halfway home by now. When you announced, David, that you wanted him sent home for his unacceptable remarks and actions, I released him. Of course, I took the liberty of keeping all the necessary personnel under my control that you suggested, especially those who worked with Chester, like Carol Lee here." Carol Lee was sitting quietly at Rachel's side in a wheelchair.

"I guess that makes sense," responded Dr. Steward. "But I really wanted to confront him and get some answers tonight."

"Security 3 to Security 1."

"This is Security 1. Go ahead Security 3."

"Chief, are you still looking for that zookeeper Oscar?"

"That's an affirmative, Security 3. Do you know of his whereabouts?"

"That's a roger. He's here in the employees' parking lot in a light-blue van. What are your instructions?"

"Security 3, have him immediately report to Dr. Steward at the bears' habitat!"

"That's a roger, Security 1. Will do. Security 3 out!"

"Why am I not surprised to find that the light-blue van in my parking space belonged to him?" remarked David as he made a disgusted face.

"Here's the cherry picker," announced Frank as he directed the driver to the exact spot that he felt would be the most advantageous.

"Just climb in, and we'll hook you up to the safety belts, put these around your waists, then we'll need to set the safety bar in place," instructed Frank. David and Mia did everything exactly as he directed. "Do you feel comfortable and secure now?" asked Frank.

"Yes, totally!" declared David. "Oh, this is much better than I expected!"

"Okay!" continued Frank. "Let's put them in place." He was addressing his operating engineer.

Suddenly, the basket began to rise, and as soon as it cleared the viewers' railing, the arm of the basket started to pivot. Slowly the basket was lowered over the viewers' railing and down to a safe level far above Chester's reach, but still close enough so that Mia could have direct eye contact with him.

Chester was not in the least appreciative of the incoming basket. In fact, he raised himself on his hind feet, stretched as high as he possibly could, and started to slash out at the basket, not realizing that it was much too far away. And apparently not recognizing Mia as the same person that he was working with earlier in helping to get Carol Lee back to safety. Mia turned to her mother and received a warm supportive smile, and then Mia realized that Star was standing right beside her unsuspecting mother. Mia had such regrets that her parents couldn't share in the joy of being able to see and talk with her and Andrew's angels. Mia had always considered holding high moral and ethical standards to be two of her strengths, and it wounded her that she was unable to tell her parents of God's gifts to her and Andrew. She would need to find a way to solve this dilemma. If she and Andrew could come to an agreement over this issue, she would feel so relieved and wouldn't need to hide the facts from her mom and dad. It would also reassure her parents that she and Andrew would always be protected from any danger while carrying out missions, if those missions were approved by Star and Simon first.

Mia was able to hear Star's familiar voice repeating, *"Just lower your tone and speak to him slowly. He'll understand you."*

Chester switched from a warning growl to a roar, obviously now fully free of the effects of the sedative and apparently seeing the basket as a threat to his domain. Enraged, he continued to slash out at the basket. He was in no mood to listen to any form of reason. He was uncomfortable, mad, humiliated, and wanted everyone to know about it!

Mia started to speak slowly and gently to him as Star had instructed but was unable to be heard over the roars and screams of Chester.

"Mia," shouted her father, "he's not listening to you! You're going to have to speak much louder for him to hear you."

"He's not going to hear me with his ears," replied Mia. "He's going to hear me with his mind."

"What are you talking about, Mia?" replied her father. "This is not going to work. Chester is just getting more frustrated and out of control. I'm going to have to signal for them to swing us back up to the viewer's railing area."

"No, Dad!" pleaded Mia. "I can do this!"

Mia lowered her head and stared directly into Chester's eyes. Without her saying a word out loud, Chester lowered his arms and stopped his angry cries.

After a few moments of silence, Mia requested that the bar attached to the end of the cable be lowered by the truck-mounted crane. Slowly it came down until Mia asked it to be halted approximately at the level of Chester's shoulders. Without any verbal instructions, Chester reached up and tightly wrapped his elbows around the bar.

"Okay!" Mia instructed. "Pick him up slowly."

The operating engineer complied with Mia's instructions and slowly started to raise the bar. The cable became taut, and the shock absorbers on the truck felt the strain of Chester's enormous 1,700-pounds of weight. As Chester was being lifted, the operator of the cherry picker also raised the basket to correspond with Chester's height so that Mia would not lose direct eye contact with him.

Once Chester cleared the height of his living plateau, the operator carefully swung him over so that he would be able to touch solid ground. As soon as Chester felt the ground beneath him, he quickly released his grasp of the bar. Everyone, without exception, started to scream and jump for joy, as if it were the stroke of midnight on New Year's Eve!

As soon as Chester realized that his ordeal was over, he sat in the middle of his habitat, staring directly at Mia, his eyes speaking a thousand thanks.

Meanwhile, Carol Lee started blowing kisses to Mia and sharing Chester's relief and jubilance from his plateau. Mia could see Carol Lee's moving lips, which appeared to repeat a plain thank-you over the roar of the people at the viewers' railing.

No one could contain their euphoria, all expressing their astonishment at Mia's remarkable ability to solve a problem that highly educated engineers were unable to solve as simply and easily. Frank, who was patiently waiting at the side of the viewers' railing, walked over to the basket to help Mia and her father unbuckle from their safety belts and climb out of the basket. Finally, when the opportunity arose, he stepped forward and addressed Mia with a big smile on his face. "I have never been so delighted to eat crow for being such a foolish nonbeliever in all my life—and from such a beautiful opponent! But I must admit publicly that you were right and I was wrong. After seeing what you did for Carol Lee, what was I thinking? I should have known better!" Frank maintained that great smile and continued, "I have never been so happy to lose a bet! Breakfast is on me!" And after conferring with his crew, they decided unanimously not to charge the zoo at all for assembling the crew and equipment. The opportunity to see Mia at work was payment in full.

"Oh, I never considered you as an opponent, Mr. Hartman," Mia replied humbly. "Just another team player with a difference of opinion. Besides, it was you who thought of using the cherry picker."

"Not only beautiful and smart, but now diplomatic," Frank grinned. "Is there no end to your talents? I expect also that you're expensive. You probably will want steak and lobster for breakfast?"

"No," Mia laughed. "My favorite breakfast is pancakes with fresh strawberries on top!"

"A woman after my own heart!" Frank declared. "Why couldn't I find someone like you when I was looking for a wife?" And he asked for permission to give her a hug and a kiss on the top of her head.

Carol Lee, now back at the viewers' railing, rolled herself forward in her wheelchair and asked if it was okay to also give Mia a big hug. "Of course!" answered Mia. "I never turn down hugs from friends!"

And as Carol Lee embraced Mia, she whispered in Mia's ear, "Thank you so much from Chester and me." Then she said loudly, "Do you think that it's okay to give a little extra food to Chester? I was feeding him earlier while he was trapped, but maybe a little extra fruit as a treat would be in order."

"Oh yes! He's very hungry now, so be prepared to give him a lot extra tonight! Is that okay with you, Dad?" queried Mia.

"I agree," spoke up David. "He burned up a lot of energy trying to fight his way to freedom. Something extra is well called for."

"You should stay and watch. After I feed him his favorite foods, he thanks me by doing a little dance," invited Carol Lee. "He's not only very good at it, but it warms your heart to see him so happy."

"Can we, Dad? Can we watch Chester dance?" pleaded Mia.

"Of course, we can! I'd like to watch him dance myself," responded David. "I understand that he was once a circus bear."

"He was?" Carol Lee laughed. "I didn't even know that."

As everyone was still enjoying the dancing bear and the success of the day, Dr. Steward noticed Oscar coming in their direction, riding in the front seat of a security cart.

Oh yes, it was now going to get really interesting!

CHAPTER 16

"Did you want to see me, Dr. Steward?" asked Oscar innocently.

"I most certainly do!" replied Dr. Steward, glaring at him with a stern expression on his face. "What on earth were you thinking? Or were you thinking at all?"

"I don't know what you're talking about," responded Oscar with a confused look on his face.

"Don't give me that innocent look!" exclaimed Dr. Steward angrily, raising his voice and shaking his finger directly in Oscar's face.

"I still don't know what you're talking about," answered Oscar, frightened by Dr. Steward's tone of voice.

"You know perfectly well what I'm referring to!" shouted Dr. Steward, rolling his eyes in exasperation. "I'm talking about your method of mishandling and mistreating the animals in your charge."

"Are you talking about squirting Chester with the water hose?" replied Oscar with a trembling voice as his heart started to pound with trepidation.

"As stupid as that idea was, it's still not what I'm furious about!" snapped Dr. Steward, knowing that he was losing control but didn't care.

"Are you talking about my comment about shooting Chester?" replied Oscar, his eyes searching frantically for the reason why Dr. Steward would be so angry with him. "I wasn't serious about that. I was only trying to make a joke to release the tension in the air."

"Well, if that was supposed to be a joke, it was tasteless and inappropriate!" cried Dr. Steward. "But I'm still not referring to that disgusting and barbaric comment. But I am talking about your treatment of the primates. You should be taken out and horsewhipped for your abuse of them."

"What! Abuse of the primates?" bellowed Oscar in protest. "You're accusing me of abusing the primates? Not true! I have nothing but love and respect for them! No one is more devoted to their animals than I am to my primates. I don't have a family, so I consider each and every one of them as my child. I even come in on my days off to see them and to make sure that they're okay. No! I never abused any of them. And I don't appreciate your accusations."

"Then what is this used for?" roared Dr. Steward as he showed Oscar the discovered club. "To conduct a symphony orchestra?"

"I have no idea," acknowledged Oscar. "I've never seen it before in my life!"

"That's a predictable excuse. But I don't see how you can deny it. It was found in your service wagon!" exclaimed Dr. Steward. "And it explains perfectly well all the injuries sustained by the primates."

"My god, I swear to you, I have no idea what you're talking about. Please tell me who was hurt!" Oscar asked with instant concern.

"They have all been abused," explained David. "But it was Jennifer who suffered the most significant injury. She sustained a broken clavicle."

"Jennifer? I don't recognize any primate by the name of Jennifer," declared Oscar. "I know all the primates, but we have no Jennifer."

"Oh yeah, I forgot. That's another thing. You know her as Sarah. Sarah has the broken clavicle," explained David.

"Sarah was injured?" cried Oscar, his expression grim, frightened. But not for himself—frightened for the welfare of the primates that he considered members of his family. "Where is she? Please, Dr. Brooks, please let me see her!"

"She's at the clinic," declared David. "Let me take you to her. It may be best anyway for us to sort this out in the privacy of my office."

As the group walked down the hill to the clinic, Oscar was in the lead, walking more briskly than the others, anxious to reunite with his adopted family.

As they entered the clinic, David escorted Oscar to the back recovery room where the primates were temporarily housed.

Oscar was stunned for a moment when he first observed Sarah, the only name that he knew for her, wearing a cast. As soon as he reached the enclosure, he opened the door, entered, and walked directly to Sarah. He placed his arms around her and kissed her tenderly on the nose. Sarah in response wrapped her uninjured arm around Oscar's neck and placed her head affectionately on his shoulder.

Oscar and Sarah held each other for several minutes, then Oscar went personally to each primate, carefully examining for himself every injury pointed out to him by the veterinary staff.

As Mia and Andrew walked over to the enclosure, Kevin reached through the bars and held Andrew's hand.

Both twins knelt and gazed into Kevin's eyes. Andrew then stood and addressed his father.

"Dad, it wasn't Oscar who injured them!" declared Andrew. "It was someone else."

"Yes, I totally agree," responded David. "Jennifer's and Kevin's actions more than vindicate Oscar. It is obvious that they are very fond of each other."

"I also agree," entered Dr. Steward with his opinion. "It's crystal clear that there are no ill sentiments between Oscar and the chimps. I was so sure that it was Oscar! The club was found in his service cart. But who else? That would mean that someone intentionally placed that stick in Oscar's food wagon to falsely blame him. I can't express strongly enough how serious and important this matter is to us! Other than Oscar, I can't imagine anyone else. After how Oscar squirted Chester and said about shooting him today and finding the club in his food wagon, you can see how I unjustly jumped to conclusions. Now that we have eliminated Oscar as a suspect, you two don't have any other ideas of who could be to blame? Because I don't know where to go from here! It's not like we have surveillance cameras in all the areas of the park, including the employees-only areas of the animal enclosures. There are blind spots not covered. We never felt that it was needed—it would be like spying on our employees. Not to mention the enormous cost! Do any of you have any ideas or suggestions about how we can find this scoundrel, this beast among us? Please, any one at all!" Patrick searched the room, looking at everyone and ending up at Mia.

Mia paused, and there was pain in her voice. "Believe me, Dr. Steward, Andrew and I take this matter as seriously as you do! No one wants to find out who is responsible more than we do, but we want to identify the right person, don't we?" Mia hesitated again and then shook her head, a firm negative. "We just don't know any more than what we have already said."

"Of course, we believe that you told us everything you know, and we would never want to punish an innocent person," declared Dr. Steward. "But now that we know that it's not Oscar, then who? And I want you and Andrew to know how very proud your parents and I are of you. We would never have found these two beautiful chimps out in the sanctuary, never had known how badly they needed medical attention, and never would have known that they were beaten by a stick if it weren't for you two. It's not fair of me to continue asking for additional help. You have done more than your share. I've known you since the day you two were born, and I think of both of you as grandchildren. It's our job to find this rapscallion."

"I don't know who, but I still plan on finding out," declared Mia. "And what is a rapscallion?"

"Oh, it's a word we Irish use to describe a scoundrel. It's an old English word I believe we stole from them in the early fifteenth century. And it's from the word *rascal*, what the English used to call pirates."

Turning to Oscar, Dr. Steward apologized. "I'm so sorry for jumping to conclusions, Oscar. I really don't have any excuse for my behavior. But I must confess that I'm totally stressed out over this incident. Please forgive me for my false accusations."

"Not a problem!" Oscar replied, softening his expression. "If I were in your shoes, I would have jumped to the same conclusions. Now I'm as frustrated as you are. I want to find the culprit too. Only I feel partly responsible for all of this. I work with them every day. Like I said earlier, I even come in on my days off just to see them. And I had no idea that they had been abused. I should have been the first one to notice it!"

"Don't beat yourself up, Oscar," remarked David. "It would have been difficult to see their bruises with all their hair and having dark skin. Kevin didn't receive his split lip until today on your day off. We were able to find the injuries because we were looking for them."

"Dr. Brooks," interrupted Cecilia, "I guess that I should start knitting booties when I get home."

"What are you talking about?" asked David. "Are you going to start talking in riddles like Mia?"

"No, I'm just trying to say that Mia was right on target again," Cecilia happily announced. "It's been confirmed. The pregnancy test corroborated Mia's suspicions. Jennifer is with child. She is probably about four weeks along."

"Excellent!" Mia exclaimed, enjoying the announcement, and flashing everyone her notorious half-grin, bursting with joy over the good news. "I told you Jennifer is going to have a healthy baby girl!"

Mia couldn't wait any longer. She rushed over, entered the enclosure, and sat on the floor. Jennifer walked over and sat on her lap, draping her good arm around Mia's shoulder and leaning her head so that they were touching forehead to forehead.

"Jennifer, you're going to have a baby!" Mia crooned excitedly. "That makes me an aunt and Andrew an uncle." Then she looked up at Oscar. "And I guess that makes you a grandfather!"

"A grandfather!" exclaimed Oscar. "I've always wanted to be a grandfather. Does that mean that I need to learn how to change diapers? But why do you keep calling her Jennifer?"

"She prefers Jennifer. She doesn't like being called Sarah," Mia explained.

Then Jennifer turned and looked directly into Mia's eyes, and everyone in the room felt the atmosphere turn tense. It was obvious to everyone that Mia and Jennifer had blocked out everything around them and were concentrating solely on each other. After a few minutes, Mia turned to no one in particular and announced, "I know who it was. I know who abused them! It was someone younger than Oscar. Someone overweight and who constantly ate hotdogs."

In unison, everyone in the room all said out loud, "Roger!"

Suddenly the front door of the clinic flew opened. It was Benjamin.

"Dr. Brooks, it's Roger!" shouted Benjamin. "He just grabbed his chest and fell to the ground. We think he's having a heart attack!"

"Don!" directed Rachel. "Get one of your ambulances prepared to transport Roger to the hospital as soon as we can get him stabilized! Then I'll have my team at the hospital notify the emergency room that we have a cardio patient en route. They will clear an OR in anticipation of Roger's arrival."

Turning to Benjamin, Rachel asked, "Where is he now?"

"He's just a few yards outside the front door of the clinic. He was on his way down here to see Dr. Steward. He said that he had to confess something to him. That's when we saw him grab his chest and fall to the ground."

Rachel didn't wait for the full explanation; she was already out the door and attending to Roger. She knew perfectly well that every moment counted. She found him unconscious and not breathing. Her training jumped into overdrive—she knew exactly what to do. She immediately started CPR. After a few short minutes, Roger opened his eyes and started to cough. Soon after, he began to breathe on his own.

"I see that you didn't want to wait until Monday to see me," Rachel quipped playfully, trying to calm Roger.

As Roger looked up, he first recognized Rachel and then Dr. Steward at her side. "It was me. It wasn't Oscar who hit them. I did it. I didn't realize that I hit them so hard. Every time I would enter their habitat, they would storm my service wagon, trying to get at the food. They overturned it several times on me. I used the club to keep them back. But I didn't mean to really hurt them, just to keep them away from my wagon. They wanted more and more food every day. Way more than their normal diet called for. But it was worse today. The real story on how I injured my hand was that Sarah wanted extra food again today, so I hit her to keep her away. Then she bit me on the hand, so I guess I hit her harder. Then Charlie jumped in to help Sarah, so I hit him too. That's when they escaped from their enclosure."

"Well, I can tell you now why Jennifer, who you refer to as Sarah, wanted the extra food. She's with child and needed the extra nourishment," Patrick explained.

"Sarah is pregnant?" asked Roger. "I had no idea!"

"There is no need to worry about that now," replied Rachel. "You can talk to Patrick about it later. Now I just want you to relax and remain calm. Everything seems to be under control. But as you know, we doctor types never take any chances."

Almost the entire clinic emptied to watch the paramedics prepare to transport Roger, lifting him onto a gurney and into the ambulance. Roger wanted to continue to apologize, but Rachel interrupted, "Now I'm going to have to insist! No more talking until after I make a full examination at the hospital. You will have plenty of time to talk later."

"Are you coming with me?" asked Roger.

"Of course, I am! I'll be right behind you," Rachel replied as he entered the ambulance. "I'm your doctor, aren't I? Where else would I be? I've already talked to my colleagues, and they are ready to receive you. I'll be a few minutes behind you. But don't worry, my cardio team is there now waiting for you."

"Do everything that Rachel tells you to do," agreed Dr. Steward with a soothing tone in his voice. "We'll talk later. We'll work everything out later."

"Well, it appears that the mystery has been solved," David addressed the clinic's staff. "Chester is no longer unhappy, and a great many of the animals have been recovered and medically treated, thanks to Mia's and Andrew's ability to locate a great many of the animals. But I think for now we should put in place several food traps and hope for the best. We'll be back tomorrow and continue the recovery of the remaining outstanding animals. All that remains is a little discussion among us to determine a plan forward."

After the clinic employees got back to work, David sat down with Mia and Andrew. He solemnly addressed them, "You can communicate with the animals, can't you? And they can somehow communicate back with you? Am I right, or am I just imagining things?"

"Dad, we're awfully tired. It's been a long day! And it's very complex. Can't we just talk about this later? Okay?" Mia asked. "Why don't you go and set up your tactical plan? I would like to go into your office now and get a little sleep next to Kristin. That sounds so good to me!"

"Yeah, Dad, that sounds so good to me now too," echoed Andrew. "Let's talk about this later? We'll have plenty of time to talk tomorrow, okay?" pleaded Andrew, hoping that he could come up with a plausible explanation by morning but realizing that it would take another miracle. And after all of today's miracles, he didn't think that they would be eligible for another one so soon. One thing for sure, he most certainly couldn't count on any help from Mia. All he had asked was for her to remain as quiet as a worm hiding in a bird's nest, but could she do that? Noooo!

"Okay! I guess that tomorrow will be soon enough," as David capitulated to their request. "We still have a lot of work and ground to cover tonight. Go ahead and take a nap in my office."

As the twins entered their father's office, they found Kristin still asleep on one of the two sofas located across from their father's desk. "Who can sleep so long?" asked Mia. "Do you realize that Kristin slept through all this excitement? Boy, is she going to be sorry in the morning that she missed everything!"

"I know," answered Andrew as puzzled as Mia. "It's as though someone gave her a couple of sleeping pills."

Then both Mia and Andrew immediately turned around, looking for Star and Simon. Not finding them, they softly called their names as they suddenly appeared sitting on the empty sofa. "Did you give Kristin a sleeping pill?" asked Mia.

"Of course not," answered Simon. "It's not necessary for angels to administer pills to induce sleep. You know that Star and I have a few tricks up our sleeves that are extremely safe. We couldn't afford for Kristin to wake up and find you missing and alert everyone to your disappearance, could we?"

"No! So that's one of the ways that you kept our leaving the clinic a secret! Nice trick," acknowledged Mia. "What should we do now?" she continued. "I know that it's late, but I'm still not sleepy. Is that another one of your little tricks? You can either make someone sleepy or wide awake?"

All that Star and Simon did was to beam the twins a bright smile.

"We still need to find the culprit or culprits and stop them from releasing the animals," David commented in a small meeting located in the lunch room.

"We also need to come up with a plan to prevent the animals from breaching the perimeter of the property," Dr. Steward pointed out with great concern in his voice.

"And we still need to retain a medical team here in the clinic all night to treat guests still hiding in the park and any employees as well as sheriff deputies who may sustain additional injuries," added Rachel.

"And how are we going to stop the animals from fighting among themselves when they run into each other inside the park?" Cecilia was heard saying.

"We may have solved many of our problems tonight thanks to a team effort that included Mia and Andrew, but we still have a host of issues ahead to resolve," concluded David. "Our night is far from being over!"

"Richard, shut off your flashlight and step into the shadows," directed Deputy Gorman of his partner. The moon was playing peekaboo with scudding clouds, lighting the scene with pale illumination just long enough to provide quick fixes on two figures roaming unsystematically around the mountain goat enclosure. "It doesn't look right, Rich. They are either guests hiding from us or the culprits releasing the animals. Let's keep an eye on them and see what they're doing."

"It looks like they are trying to open the doors to the mountain goats," replied Richard. "Now they are taking pictures as one of them is trying to coax the animals out. One of them is talking on his cell phone. Can you hear what he is saying? I think we need to get a little closer. I think he is telling someone else to go ahead and let them out. I think I can hear him say to be sure to take plenty of photos as they let the gazelles out! Okay, we've seen and heard enough. Let's nab them before the animals escape their pen. And contact the command post with what we've found. They will coordinate and radio whoever is patrolling the gazelle area and alert them to pick up the co-conspirators before those animals escape."

The staff meeting was starting to wind down when the doors flew opened and Sheriff Raphael entered along with four suspects in handcuffs followed by four of his deputies.

"What's this?" asked David.

"Well, we finally caught a break on the culprits who've been releasing the animals. Meet John Pickford, Jean-Paul Toulouse, Harry Gilfoyle, and Sandra Sistine. They are all freelance photo journalists. Apparently, they witnessed a couple of chimpanzees escape from their enclosure and were able to capture it on their digital cameras. Then they noticed that the chimps started to open up some of the other primate habitats. Again, they captured the events on their cameras. So they thought that to make it an even bigger scoop, they would get involved and release a few more animals on their own. One would open the enclosure and jump to safety while the other one would capture the animals fleeing their habitats on their cameras. So it went on and on all night. They even returned to some of the habitats after your employees captured some of the animals, returning them to their enclosures. And then these idiots would release them again! A couple of my deputies spotted them in the act. It's all in the memories of their cameras! We'll be booking these morons and confiscating their cameras as evidence. Case solved!" finished Michael with satisfaction.

The female suspect, the only one with a vocal response, said something unintelligibly exclamatory but was ignored.

"Well, that's going to be an immense help!" David spoke up. "The hemorrhaging of new animals being released has now been stopped. Now we must locate and recapture the remaining animals and hope that no loose animals escape the walls of the park during the night. God only knows how many are still out there!"

Hiding behind a half wall, Mia and Andrew were eavesdropping on the meeting. Both twins heard what Sheriff Raphael had to say about apprehending the perpetrators. They stood up and came forward. Moving with exaggerated slowness, Mia circled the suspects with indignation written all over her face. She said nothing as she stood next to her father. Looking up, Mia asked, "Are these the people who deliberately released the animals?"

"It appears so, Princess," confirmed David.

"Good! They should all go to jail!" uttered Mia. "Or better yet, put them on display in one of the zoo enclosures. And put up a sign saying Local Ignoramuses!"

"If I could, I would," answered Sheriff Raphael, laughing. He signaled to the deputies to take the "local ignoramuses" to the precinct for booking.

"I heard what you said about your concern of the loose animals that are still free," spoke up Mia. "And how they might fight with one another or, even worse, escape the fencing around the park. I think we can still help, Dad! What do you think, Andrew?" Mia looked over to her brother. "Should we finish this up tonight? We don't want any animals to escape the walls or get hurt during the night. We wouldn't be able to live with ourselves if that were to happen!"

As Andrew was trying to contact their guardian angels via mental telepathy, both Mia and Andrew saw them appear in the room, nodding in the affirmative.

"Okay! Let's do it," grunted Andrew as he high-fived Mia.

"Mom, Dad, I think we can help even further. Let's go outside, but this time we are going to need to use the large amphitheater. Mom and Dad, could you please follow us? We promise you"— Andrew smiled—"we won't let any of the animals harm you."

"I'm sure that you won't let that happen," David replied very confidently. "I trust you and Mia now more than you can ever imagine."

The group in the room followed the twins to the main amphi-theater and was asked to remain in the amphitheater's fold-down chairs.

"We know the procedure now," replied their mother.

"What procedure?" asked Michael. "What's this all about?"

"Just sit back and enjoy, Michael," was all that David said.

Mia and Andrew walked to the center of the amphitheater and then faced their parents and seemed to be meditating. Nothing was quite what it appeared to be. Nothing could be taken at face value. Both Mia and Andrew turned their eyes skyward, searching for help, searching for answers. Everyone tried to hear every sound, but none could be heard. There was total silence. It took no longer than three or four minutes before animal after animal started to walk into the amphitheater, walking right past the group sitting in the wooden fold-down chairs, ignoring them as they walked to the center of the largest amphitheater. The animals started to encircle the twins, in total respect of them and each other. And yes, standing next to them were their guardian angels, Star and Simon!

"It's okay now," called Andrew, "you can come down and join us now." At first everyone was afraid to respond, where the instinctive reaction precedes rational thought and everyone involved obeys his own spontaneous spark for survival. That was until David was the first to stand up. He was no longer hesitant as he was in the African sanctuary. He was certain that his children had the situation totally under control, and he felt the raw thrill of adventure. David felt unquestionably that Mia and Andrew were mature far beyond their years, capable of a degree of personal commitment and dedication unmatched within their age group or any age group. They showed such incredible strength and perseverance, utterly devoid of artificial restraints or personal reservations toward comfort and convenience.

David and Rachel were the first to reach their children, joining in a group hug. Slowly the others followed suit until the twins were completely smothered.

It took the rest of the night and part of the following morning for all the animals to be safely returned to their enclosures. Finally, everyone gathered at the clinic.

"Dad!" cried Mia. "We forgot all about Noah! He hasn't had his dinner yet! We still have his pizza in the car."

"Okay, let's all go home," suggested David, stifling a yawn. "I guess we can sort this out later. We're all tired and could use a good night's sleep. Maybe all this might make more sense in the morning after a good night's sleep."

Mia started to laugh. "Dad, it's not nighttime anymore. It's seven in the morning! You mean a good daytime sleep, don't you?"

As Mia jumped up and ran to say goodbye to each animal, giving special attention to Rehab, Jennifer, and Kevin, Dr. Steward and David were summarizing the developments of the last twenty-one hours.

"David, if you don't mind, I would like to follow very closely the progress of Mia's and Andrew's special talents. They both have a unique gift that needs to be encouraged and given every opportunity to develop. As I said earlier, I'm more than willing to open every door for them that is available to me. I find them both to be quite remarkable, and God only knows what incredible journeys lie before them. They are going to make history for themselves and earn a legacy that will be matched by no one else."

"Okay, we're ready to go, Dad. A good night's sleep is going to have to wait until after mass, and Frank wants us to meet him at our favorite pancake house for delicious pancakes with lots of fresh strawberries on top!" proclaimed Mia as she and Andrew headed for the employees' parking lot.

For being such a long day, the twins realized that for some reason they weren't so tired after all. Maybe it had something to do with both Star and Simon at their sides. Yes, it was obvious there are going to be many more interesting adventures coming their way soon!

CPSIA information can be obtained
at www.ICGtesting.com
Printed in the USA
FSHW010630080220
66792FS